CONTEMPORARY SOCIAL THEORY
General Editor: ANTHONY GIDDENS

This series aims to create a forum for debate between different theoretical and philosophical traditions in the social sciences. As well as covering broad schools of thought, the series will also concentrate upon the work of particular thinkers whose ideas have had a major impact on social science (these books appear under the sub-series title of 'Theoretical Traditions in the Social Sciences'). The series is not limited to abstract theoretical discussion – it will also include more substantive works on contemporary capitalism, the state, politics and other subject areas.

Published Titles

Martin Albrow, *Max Weber's Construction of Social Theory*
Tony Bilton, Kevin Bonnett, Philip Jones, Ken Sheard, Michelle Stanworth and Andrew Webster, *Introductory Sociology* (2nd edition)
Emile Durkheim, *The Division of Labour in Society* (trans. W.D. Halls)
Emile Durkheim, *The Rules of Sociological Method* (ed. Steven Lukes, trans. W.D. Halls)
Anthony Giddens, *A Contemporary Critique of Historical Materialism*
Anthony Giddens, *Central Problems in Social Theory*
Anthony Giddens, *Profiles and Critiques in Social Theory*
Anthony Giddens and David Held (eds), *Classes, Power and Conflict: Classical and Contemporary Debates*
Geoffrey Ingham, *Capitalism Divided? The City and Industry in British Social Development*
Terry Johnson, Christopher Dandeker and Clive Ashworth, *The Structure of Social Theory*
Douglas Kellner, *Herbert Marcuse and the Crisis of Marxism*
Gerry Rose, *Deciphering Sociological Research*
John Scott, *The Upper Classes: Property and Privilege in Britain*

THEORETICAL TRADITIONS IN THE SOCIAL SCIENCES

General Editor: ANTHONY GIDDENS

This series introduces the work of major figures in social science to students beyond their immediate specialisms.

Published Titles

Barry Barnes, *T.S. Kuhn and Social Science*
Ted Benton, *The Rise and Fall of Structural Marxism: Althusser and his Influence*
David Bloor, *Wittgenstein: A Social Theory of Knowledge*
Christopher G. A. Bryant, *Positivism in Social Theory and Research*
Ira J. Cohen, *Structuration Theory: Anthony Giddens and the Constitution of Social Life*
Mark Cousins and Athar Hussain, *Michel Foucault*
Bob Jessop, *Nicos Poulantzas: Marxist Theory and Political Strategy*
William Outhwaite, *New Philosophies of Social Science: Realism, Hermeneutics and Critical Theory*
Julian Roberts, *Walter Benjamin*
Rick Roderick, *Habermas and the Foundations of Critical Theory*
James Schmidt, *Maurice Merleau-Ponty: Between Phenomenology and Structuralism*
Dennis Smith, *Barrington Moore: Violence, Morality and Political Change*
Dennis Smith, *The Chicago School: A Liberal Critique of Capitalism*
Piotr Sztompka, *Robert K. Merton: An Intellectual Profile*

Series Standing Order

If you would like to receive future titles in this series as they are published, you can make use of our standing order facility. To place a standing order please contact your bookseller or, in case of difficulty, write to us at the address below with your name and address and the name of the series. Please state with which title you wish to begin your standing order.
(If you live outside the United Kingdom we may not have the rights for your area, in which case we will forward your order to the publisher concerned.)

Customer Services Department, Macmillan Distribution Ltd, Houndmills, Basingstoke, Hampshire, RG21 2XS, England.

Max Weber's Construction of Social Theory

Martin Albrow

First published 1990 by
MACMILLAN EDUCATION LTD
Houndmills, Basingstoke, Hampshire RG21 2XS
and London
Companies and representatives
throughout the world

ISBN 0–333–28544–1 (hardcover)
ISBN 0–333–28546–8 (paperback)

A catalogue record for this book is available
from the British Library.

Printed in Malaysia

Reprinted 1992

To the memory of Editha Hirschmann

Contents

vii

Foreword

Thirty years ago, almost to the day, I was sitting in the British Council Library in Cologne, completing my reading of Marianne Weber's biography of her husband. It had been a laborious task, chosen as a way of learning German and understanding Weber at the same time. It also took up the generous spare time allowed by the school which employed me as an English language assistant.

It was a way of developing an interest which had been fired in Cambridge by a course on the History of Historiography given by Brian Wormald, whose lectures tantalisingly stopped short of treating the last items on his book list, which happened to be on Max Weber.

I went to the London School of Economics after Germany to begin work on Max Weber's idea of rationality under Morris Ginsberg's supervision. He took the view that this was too narrow a subject for a PhD and that the idea of rationality *tout court* was more appropriate. That was somewhat discouraging and I left without completing my thesis.

But in some sense Ginsberg was right. Weber cannot be understood except through an appreciation of the idea which became his driving force, his demon, namely rationality. This book represents my acquiescence to that insight after many years of trying to understand its implications, challenge it or simply ignore it.

Had this book been completed earlier I would not now be able to agree with what it would have said. To that extent a decade or two of delay has been beneficial. But in that time my intellectual debts have mounted alarmingly, so that there is no possibility of acknowledging all the useful discussions I have enjoyed. Only the most notable are mentioned here.

Norbert Elias was simultaneously sceptical, challenging and enormously kind in my early lecturing days in Leicester; Stanislav

Andreski gave enthusiastic support in Reading; while Paul Halmos in Cardiff gave great encouragement. Since then I have enjoyed the stimulating friendships of Anton Zijderveld, Horst Helle and Johannes Weiss, each in his own way having a unique insight into Weber and always ready to share it.

In 1973–4, at the Max Weber Institute in Munich, I had the privilege of many discussions with Johannes Winckelmann who had already forgotten more about Weber than I shall ever know. Gert Schmidt was very helpful to me at that time, as was Constance Rottländer who first gave me an insight into Weber's economics. I hope it is also not too late at this stage to thank the Leverhulme Foundation for its support during that year.

As befits those who shared student days, Tony Giddens and I have always found snooker more interesting than Max Weber when we have been together, and I can only express my appreciation that he has given support at times when it was most needed and has assisted greatly in commenting and making suggestions which have proved beneficial in cutting an unwieldy document down to size. Jem Thomas gave the same first draft a thorough Weberian vetting and I am grateful to him for doing that necessary task. Chris Harris has been extraordinarily generous with his time and inspired me to make those unpalatable changes which turn a text written for myself into one which a reader can find useful. Paul Atkinson made helpful comments on Chapter 11. Liz King has, apart from assisting me in editing *International Sociology*, found time to prepare the word-processed text with her usual extraordinary speed and meticulousness. To all these people my particular thanks are due.

Above all I need to express my deep gratitude to my wife Susan Owen (Economic Adviser in HM Treasury), formerly Lecturer in Economics at University College, Cardiff, who shared with me the last throes of that institution before its enforced merger, made sure that my priorities were right and morale high and, at the same time, coped marvellously with demanding changes in her own work. Without her, this book would not have been written.

The dedication fulfils a promise made a good ten years ago to someone who had listened to lectures by Rickert and Jaspers, and took into her life's work the lesson that patients are people.

Cardiff
June 1989

Martin Albrow

Max Weber: a Brief Biography

Max Weber was born on 21 April 1864 in the German town of Erfurt. His father was a lawyer and member of a family of prosperous textile manufacturers. His mother's family placed a high value on education. She was a religious person with an active social conscience.

The Weber family moved to Berlin in 1869 where his father became a member of the German Reichstag as a National Liberal. Max received a classical education and went on to study law at university. He did his military training and practised as a lawyer in Berlin until 1893.

He lived in a period which, with the benefit of hindsight, we can see as leading to the catastrophe of the First World War. The great European powers struggled for world mastery. Their societies were transformed by the emergence of the class of industrial workers. Karl Marx inspired an international working-class movement, while state leaders tried to pacify the demands of the masses with social legislation and to win their allegiance in the international conflict.

It was also a period of value crisis. The Christian world view was challenged by natural science on the one hand and by the glorification of power and freedom for self-expression on the other. Darwin, Nietzsche and Freud became the mentors of the younger generation.

Weber responded to these conflicts and challenges by holding fast to the values of German high culture, to the spirit of Kant and Goethe, at the same time as committing himself to a heroic ideal of intellectual integrity and service to the nation state.

It was the early period of establishing institutionalised social and economic research for policy purposes. He obtained his academic qualifications by studying the history of law and the ancient world. But his social awareness drew him to the Association for Social Policy.

While working as a lawyer he completed in 1892 a major research project on the social and economic conditions of the Prussian peasantry. His academic reputation grew and in 1894 he was called to a Chair of Economics in Freiburg, from where he moved to a similar position in Heidelberg in 1896.

His fame grew as he stated in the starkest possible terms the conflicts which were inherent in the simultaneous pursuit of national security and economic liberalism. He seemed to have glowing possibilities for careers both in politics and in academic life. But following the death of his father in 1897 Weber fell into a depression and nervous illness.

The tensions in Weber's personality have been the subject of prolonged speculation. He wrote a lengthy self-analysis (unfortunately destroyed) and sought the help of his friend, the philosopher and psychiatrist, Karl Jaspers. Those inner conflicts are frequently referred to in the great biography which Weber's wife, Marianne, published after his death.

He had married in 1893. Marianne was a second generation cousin, a formidable intellect who became a prominent leader of German feminism, surviving him until 1953. She idolised her husband, but it was a marriage of the mind and daily companionship and he at least sought sexual fulfilment in other relationships.

Weber recovered gradually from his illness. He gave up his teaching position in 1903. He travelled frequently in Europe and in 1904 spent a stimulating four months in the United States. His intellectual interests shifted. He worked on the religious basis of human rationality and on the development of Western capitalism. He began to write on the philosophical implications of empirical social science. He became well known as a political commentator.

The years from 1903 to 1920 were marked by a stream of writing which continues to be a treasury of ideas for later scholars. He wrote on topics as various as the Russian Revolution and the sociology of music, the religion of China and the development of the city, industrial psychology and bureaucratic structure. They culminated in his conceptual framework for sociology which was linked to his enormous study of the relations between the economy and society.

Although he gave up teaching Weber maintained an intense involvement in academic life. He was in constant contact with the leading scholars of his time and he and Marianne kept open house in Heidelberg for young and old alike.

As a journal editor he turned the *Archive for Social Science and Social Policy* into the major forum for applied social research. He played the leading part in the debates on value-freedom which took place in the Association for Social Policy between 1909 and 1913. He worked strenuously to help found the German Sociological Society in 1910.

When the First World War broke out in 1914 he committed himself fully to the German cause. He served as an officer administering military hospitals but after leaving the service in the latter part of the war he wrote numerous articles criticising its conduct.

At the end of the war and immediately after Weber was prodigiously active in numerous directions. He joined and campaigned for the German Democratic Party. He wrote and spoke against socialist revolution. He was a member of the German peace delegation at Versailles. He wrote and spoke against right-wing violence.

Finally he took another permanent Chair in Munich in 1919. He lectured in overflowing lecture theatres on basic concepts in sociology, on economic history and on political science. He had laboured for years on his great works, the three-volume *Sociology of Religion* and the two-volume *Economy and Society*. He prepared them for publication, dedicating them to his wife and his mother respectively, who had just died. He was never to see them in print. He died of pneumonia on 14 June 1920.

Time Chart

The historical time over which the account in this book spreads and the thematic explorations extend over a much longer span than just Max Weber's lifetime. The chart below may help the reader by locating the events and books referred to here within that period.

Events	Books	Weber's Life and Works
	1781 Kant's *Critique of Pure Reason*, 1st edn	
	1785 Kant's *Foundation of the Metaphysics of Morals*	
	1788 Kant's *Critique of Practical Reason*	
1789 The French Revolution		
	1801 Goethe's *Faust*, Part I	
1814–15 Congress of Vienna	1818 Schopenhauer's *The World as Will and Idea*	
	1821 Hegel's *Philosophy of Right*	
	1835 Strauss' *The Life of Jesus*	
	1837 Hegel's *Philosophy of History*, lectures of the 1820s published	
	1841 W.E. Channing's *Complete Works*	
	1846 Marx and Engels' *The German Ideology*	
	1848 Marx and Engels' *The Communist Manifesto*	
	1859 Darwin's *Origin of Species*	

Weber's life	Cultural and intellectual	Political
1864 Max Weber born in Erfurt		1862 Bismarck becomes Prussian Prime Minister
		1863 General Union of German Workers founded
	1866 F.A. Lange's *History of Materialism*	
	1867 Marx's *Capital*, Vol. 1	
1869 Weber's family moves to Berlin		
		1870 Vatican Council Decree of Papal Infallibility
		1871 The Second German Empire founded
	1872 Nietzsche's *The Birth of Tragedy*	1872 *Kulturkampf* begins
		1872 Verein für Sozialpolitik founded
		1875 Gotha Programme
1882 Study in Heidelberg		
1883– Military service 4	1883 Dilthey's *Einleitung in die Geisteswissenschaften*	
1884– Study in Berlin and 6 Göttingen. Qualifies as junior barrister		
	1887 Nietzsche's *The Genealogy of Morals*	
1889 Doctoral dissertation *On the History of Trading Companies in the Middle Ages*		

Events	Books	Weber's Life and Works
1890 Bismarck dismissed	1891 Windelband's *Geschichte der Philosophie*	
		1892 Lectures in Berlin. Completes report for the Verein für Sozialpolitik (Social Policy Association) *The Situation of Farm Workers in Germany East of the River Elbe*
		1893 Marries Marianne Schnitger
		1894 Chair in Economics at Freiburg
		1895 Inaugural lecture, *The National State and Economic Policy*
	1896 Stammler's *Wirtschaft und Recht nach der materialistischen Wirtschaftsauffassung*	1896 Chair at Heidelberg
		1897 Death of father
		1897– 1903 Suffers nervous illness

		1903 *Roscher and Knies and the Logical Problems of Historical Economics*
1902 William James' *The Varieties of Religious Experience*		
		1904 Weber visits World Exhibition in St Louis. Takes joint editorship of the *Archive for Social Science and Social Policy, Objectivity in Social Science and Social Policy*
H. Rickert's, *Die Grenzen der naturwissenschaftlichen Begriffsbildung*		
1905 First Russian Revolution		1905 *The Protestant Ethic and the Spirit of Capitalism*
1906 Nietzsche's *Will to Power* published		1906 *Critical Studies in the Logic of the Cultural Sciences*
		1907 *Rudolf Stammler's Surmounting of the Materialist Conception of History*
1908 German naval programme	1908 Simmel's *Soziologie*	1908 *On the Psychophysics of Industrial Work*
		1909 Editor of the *Outline of Social Economics*
1910 First Congress of the German Sociological Society	1912 Troeltsch's *Protestantism and Progress*	

Events	Books	Weber's Life and Works
		1913 On Some Categories of Interpretative Sociology
1914 Outbreak of First World War	1913 Jaspers' Allgemeine Psychopathologie	1914–15 Service with the Military Hospitals Commission
		1915–16 Work on the sociology of religion
		1916–19 Newspaper articles on the war
1917 The Russian Revolution		1917 The Meaning of 'Value-freedom' in Sociological and Economic Sciences
1918 End of First World War	1918 Spengler's Decline of the West, vol. I	
1919 Treaty of Versailles		1919 Weber takes part in Versailles peace negotiations. Takes chair in Munich. Science as a Vocation. Politics as a Vocation. Weber elected to executive of German Democratic Party.
		1920 Dies of pneumonia
		1920– Gesammelte Aufsätze zur Religionssoziologie
		1922 Wirtschaft und Gesellschaft, Gesammelte Aufsätze zur Wissenschaftslehre

xxi

Introduction

I

Since his death in 1920, the reputation of Max Weber has grown until he is now recognised as the major social theorist of the twentieth century. He is cited by political leaders, and at least one of his key technical terms, 'charisma', has entered everyday language. Ideas such as 'legitimation' and 'life chances' have become an integral part of the language of politics.

When he died he enjoyed fame in Germany as a political commentator and an independent intellectual who strove for the autonomy of the social scientist. He was first drawn to the attention of the English-speaking world by R. H. Tawney who found inspiration in Weber's study of the influence of Protestant religious ideas on the growth of Western capitalism.

Then three great American sociologists – Talcott Parsons, C. Wright Mills and Edward Shils – worked to introduce his sociology to students in the United States and Britain. At the same time, someone whose intellectual impact in his own country was similar to Weber's in Germany – Raymond Aron – did the same for France.

By the 1960s Weber was being hailed and reviled equally as a prophet for the twentieth century and as an exponent of the technical reason of capitalist society. He was held also to have anticipated the Nazi period and, like the bearer of bad tidings, to have shared in the blame. He was praised by the West German persident Theodor Heuss, and attacked by Herbert Marcuse. In the Marxist takeover bid for Western social science, Weber presented the greatest obstacle, to be circumvented, accommodated or attacked, but impossible to ignore.

1

Weber survived that bid and if the sciences of the social retain an independence in the 1990s, more is owed to him than to any other single figure. The astonishing range of his scholarly work is now universally acknowledged. He is translated into the major languages of the world. The secondary work on him is vast and growing. Conferences on his work have been held in the socialist countries of Eastern Europe, in Latin America and Japan, and one was planned for September 1989 in China until the events in Tianammen Square caused its postponement. The dominant response to his achievement is one of awe.

It cannot be otherwise when he wrote penetratingly in terms which are as fresh today as seventy years ago, about stock markets and socialism, mediaeval trading law and the modern civil service, the philosophy of social science and the sociology of music, ancient Israel and the Russian Revolution, Islam and rationalisation. The list could be extended many times over.

This corpus of writing is a treasury without a cheap stone in it. It consists of substantial monographs and research reports which have provided the spur to several generations of scholars in a wide diversity of disciplines and academic specialisms. But to it we can add political commentary which stands comparison with de Tocqueville and Bagehot. And we can add one of the great personal statements of all time, the confession of faith of the twentieth-century academic, 'Science as a Vocation' (Essays: 129–56).

Yet with all this acclaim and these acknowledged contributions to such a diversity of fields, there is a paradox in the reception of Weber's work. In the last ten years of his life he sought to establish the discipline of sociology as the obvious intellectual base for comparative historical and contemporary social research. He endeavoured to identify the concepts and methods which he derived from his own research experience and thus to provide the principles of an empirical sociology. Here few sociologists have been inclined to follow him.

Indeed, from Parsons onwards, including Jürgen Habermas (1981), W. G. Runciman (1972), Anthony Giddens (1989) and Jeffrey Alexander (1983), no major theorist has been prepared to follow Weber's lead more than very partially. His systematic conceptual framework has remained undeveloped, while his overarching interpretation of the trajectory of modern society, the thesis of all-embracing rationalisation, has been almost completely neglected. Yet these were core features of his work. We might say that a prophet is not without honour save in his own discipline.

Many reasons can be suggested to explain this relative neglect: the fragmentary nature of the published works; the successes of Marxist theory or phenomenology; the changing social reality; or even intellectual advance. My own view is that is is because the roots of Weber's work have been concealed. Its inner logic has not been apparent because the historical origins of his central concern for rationality in the Protestant experience have ceased to be accessible to modern theorists. He therefore appears to the student today as the archetypal *post*–modern writer – the possessor of fragmented insights.

If we can recover those origins we stand some chance of understanding the central concerns from which those insights were generated. We might also have a chance to recover the coherence and direction which sociological work has so often missed in recent years.

II

The purpose of this book is to establish the meaning of Weber's work and to convey this author's understanding of it to a much wider readership than simply to other Weber scholars. This means it makes a contribution towards the task which Ralf Dahrendorf recently stated remained the prime requirement for work in the field: to 'weld his life, his works and times together in the best tradition of *Verstehen*' (1987: 580).

Verstehen, 'understanding', was for Weber the goal for any scientific exploration of social life and we shall examine just what that meant for him. But we will turn that method back on him and his work to try to solve the problem it raises, its worldwide reception but fragmented appreciation.

As a method it is often called 'interpretative sociology' but its scope is much wider than that might imply. It is historical because meanings are generated over time, sometimes over centuries; it is theoretical in that ideas have to be pursued beyond their limits in existing thought. We look back but we also look beyond the present.

The three parts of the book are therefore three phases in the process of understanding, each of which is as important as the other. The first part examines the origins of Weber's ideas and his creativity; the second identifies the way he constructed something new from the old material; and the third explores the implications of that new construction for contemporary social theory. Each part has therefore a definite function in relation to the whole, and it may be useful at this point to give the reader a brief indication of those functions.

The first part is not history or biography in the usual sense. It is a theoretical reconstruction of the forces which impelled Weber's work. Any creative product may be interpreted as the outcome of motives, ideas and capacities set in a context of problems and resources.

The purpose here is to show that in Weber's case he sought to resolve the most long standing and deepest dilemmas within the Protestant Christian world-view, most dramatically expressed in the conflict between Kant and Nietzsche. In common with many of his contemporaries his inspiration to solve that conflict came from Goethe. The result was an attitude to exploring the facts and meaning of the human condition which coincided with the demands of the German state for a science of social facts.

This approach is in accord with Wolfgang Mommsen, who identified the links between Weber's scientific and political opinions (1984: 419), but it seeks to extend the consideration back in time. It is also not inconsistent with Arthur Mitzman's psychoanalytical account (1970) of Weber's bouts of depression, but the emphasis here is on the analysis of much longer periods of creativity.

The second part of the book examines the power of Weber's work which, in the view presented here, originates in his command and understanding of what, following Daniel Bell (1976: 7-12), we can call the axial principle of Western culture, namely rationality. It is the principle which underpins, binds together and generates other principles in the culture.

In this respect Weber can be seen as having a strategic position in the development of that principle. Kant developed the pure philosophy of it. An important transformation was effected by Hegel who historicised it. Marx politicised it. The contribution which Weber made was to sociologise it, to make rationality both method of and topic for empirical social science.

In the course of developing that programme for a science of social reality Weber identified the process of rationalisation as the dominant process of development in world history. In effect, although that was not his purpose, he thus linked himself through his science to that process.

The third part of the book seeks to explore the implications of Weber's approach to a science of society for issues which are in the forefront of debates in social theory today. In doing so it concentrates on the blockages to the understanding of Weber which arise variously from the partial reception of his writing in the English-speaking world, from misleading translation or from ideological commitment.

I do not subscribe to the view that there are two Webers; the one of the insights into how the world works, and the one of the method which doesn't work. On the contrary, it can be asserted that the widespread absorption of Weber's contribution in special fields, such as the study of comparative religion, social stratification, professionalisation, the theory of the state, is testimony to the soundness of his approach.

But his methods do derive from his work rather than the other way round, and since in his work he tried to capture the direction of changes in the society around him, we should also expect that our changed social reality will require his ideas to be explored, expanded and amended. That is how their meaning will best be grasped and we can even approach a better understanding of his own ideas than he might have had himself.

III

Weber's concern always was to depict and explain social reality. Again and again he attends to the problem of bringing intellectual constructions back to some kind of reality test. That is always inherently problematical because intellectuals are always capable of imagining the world to be other than it is. Without understanding that concern Weber's work is not intelligible.

The secret of his method was that he was able with the utmost sophistication and deployment of all the intellectual resources of argument of his time, to dispel obscurity and to hold sociology to several simple principles. They are in brief that:

- society is made up of people acting in certain ways;
- we can explain what people do;
- we understand people through their motives;
- people are in the main responsible for what they do;
- ideas influence people;
- we all accept some things as facts;
- organisation constrains and provides opportunities at the same time.

An empirical sociology which begins with these principles has a firm basis for providing general accounts of social structure which have explanatory power and wide-ranging intelligibility. A social theory which disputes these principles will be doing something else.

Moreover, in so far as those principles we have just outlined are part of a commonsensical view of the world, criticism of them must at least replace them with something as good. Weber was persistently scornful of radical attempts to devalue the ordinary. He took his stand on everyday reality and was equally dismissive of anything which could be called materialism or idealism as an account of reality.

Human beings are for Weber *sui generis* and their actions constitute everyday reality, the commonsense world. For this reason, for him society is not language, nor is it an organism. It is not art, nor is it machine. The closest resemblance it bore to anything it was not was to a game. But there his stress was on the outcome and not the rules. If you wanted to explain the *result* of a game, you would refer first to the abilities of the players and not to the rules by which they played.

A vast amount of social theory has been concerned to pursue analogies with society or to provide alternatives, political or otherwise, to commonsense reality. This may do credit to the intellectual ingenuity of the authors of these ideas, but it does not assist in the task of explaining why the world is as it is. Moreover, almost by definition, and sometimes intentionally, the authors marginalise themselves.

The current malaise of sociology and its vulnerability to political attack are a result of its failure to hold on to such simple principles as starting points for its work. It has instead sought without success to replace them or to pursue an infinitely receding ultimate foundation. It has taken the cue from Weber's questions and ignored the answers. Weber's social theory takes us relentlessly towards an empirical sociology.

The reason for this thrust in his work was ultimately his reservations about the principle which he held to be of paramount importance in providing a direction in human history, namely rationality. There were limits to reason for him, in the natural world, in human emotion, in intuition and faith. Reason itself could not found reason.

In consequence Weber was attuned to history, even the history of rationality, and he could acknowledge the irrationalities of power, of solidarity and of religion. His sociology was not merely grounded in answers to intellectual puzzles. It also registered the historical movements, the forces which moved nations and raised charismatic leaders.

The success of his sociology does not therefore stem from formulae. Rather the importance of his concepts and methods is assured by his sensitivity to the social reality he apprehended. If his work has stood the test of time, it is precisely because he was in tune with the movement of twentieth-century history. A similar point has been made by Alasdair Macintyre: 'The contemporary vision of the world, so I have suggested, is predominantly, although not perhaps always in detail, Weberian' (1985: 108).

In this respect the Marxist response to Weber, that he represents bourgeois consciousness and is a representative of the capitalist world, is warranted. Weber made something of a virtue of that. He understood the power of Western rationality in all its guises. But it had to be understood first in its own terms to appreciate its success in moulding the rest of the world after its own image.

In a whole range of respects, Weber, as an avowed product of the Western mind, has been more successful in conveying an appreciation of the non-Western than that other product, Karl Marx, who sought to overcome his origins and reshape the world. Because Weber saw the limits of Western rationality he was able not only to identify the sources of nationalism and mass movements in the capitalist world, he was also able to accommodate the full range of value positions which provide a basis for the great world religions and for quite different responses to everyday life from those characteristic of the West. In this respect it is Weber

who provides the stimulus today for the development of indige-
nous sociologies which are true to the specific social reality of
different cultures.

At the same time, wherever Weber is assimilated, and wherever
empirical social research is conducted, whether it be Japan or the
Soviet Union, Nigeria or Mexico, a transcendental message is
being transmitted and received, which, if he is right, is at the heart
of a genuinely empirical sociology. The collection of data about
individual people is based on the assumption that they are agents,
capable of making up their minds, and the interpretation of those
data to generalise about society and its direction and its wider
dissemination feed into the decision-making centres of power in
the modern world. As such this is a novel feature of the
rationalisation process which can contribute to humanisation and
democratisation.

IV

This book covers a lot of ground but at the same time seeks to be
accessible to anyone who wishes to acquire an understanding of
Max Weber's work. In consequence, it is not overloaded with
technical argument and bibliographical references.

However, fellow Weber scholars will recognise that the positions taken up in this book are contentious in the light of well-
known controversies in the field and I hope they will enjoy the
discussions.

For instance, the relative influence of Kant and Nietzsche has
been a fraught issue at least since 1964. I disagree with those who
feel that Marx set the agenda for Weber's work. To my knowledge
the influence of Goethe has never been highlighted before to the
extent it is here.

I am at one with Tenbruck (1959) in emphasising the priority of
empirical research in Weber's motivation and his purely secondary
interest in methodology. However, as far as method is concerned,
it will be controversial to accord Dilthey as much importance as
Rickert.

I accept neither the phenomenological nor the neo-Marxist
critiques of Weber, or at least believe that both Schutz and
Habermas may have identified viable alternative directions in

social theory without demonstrating inherent defects in Weber's own vision. Weber's pragmatic theory of understanding in which power, rationality and facticity are all ingredients can grasp historical and social reality in a way which is not supplanted by these later approaches.

Neither Leo Strauss (1950) nor Peter Winch (1958) seem to me to have taken adequate account of the fact that the *experience* of value is central to Weber's depiction of social life, and that life is not grounded in philosophy. In this respect history has priority.

Further, this book makes a big effort to dispel the impression, largely cultivated by Parsons, that Weber was uninterested in structure. The case is made here that, on the contrary, he was, explicitly and consistently, directly concerned with the problems of identifying structure in social action while at the same time seeking to prevent illicit structural interpretations of human action.

Finally, contrary to many, I take the view that the construction of sociology based on social research was regarded by Weber as a prime goal of his work throughout the last decade of his life. What is now called social theory refers to a much wider penumbra of issues on which Weber had strong views but from which he sought to distinguish sociology.

This book seeks to bring sociologists to take Weber seriously, not as a seer to revere because he happened to have done some things well and got some things right, but as the systematic founder of a discipline.

There are special difficulties in appreciating Weber's work in this area which stem from the dispersion of his writing on this theme and from the fragmentary way in which it has been published. What I hope to have done is to reconstruct the core of his argument on the nature of sociology, and thus to encourage the full utilisation of his ideas and their further development in future sociological work.

Weber was the first to acknowledge that scientific achievements were ephemeral. 'Every scientific "fulfilment" raises new "questions"; it *asks* to be "surpassed" and outdated' (Essays: 138). But it has to be understood, we might add, before it can find its place as a mere historical achievement. My contention is that he has not yet been adequately understood and my hope is that this book will assist in that process and allow Weber to have that for which he asked.

PART I

The Formation of Weber's World-View

Hinter der Handlung steht der Mensch

('Behind the action, there stands the human being')

Max Weber, *Wissenschaftslehre*, p. 492.

Preamble

If we wish to understand Weber's work, by his own interpretative methods we need to attend to his motives and beliefs and the structures of meaning in which they were embedded. His concerns were so far-reaching that this has to lead us to the main currents of Protestant thought and, in particular, the crisis which the challenge of Nietzsche posed to the Kantian frame of thought with which he was imbued.

That crisis was expressed in bringing to the surface the deep conflicts between rationality and irrationality, and idealism and the materialism which troubled the conscience and outlook of the German educated classes. Weber sought to transcend these conflicts through a commitment to empirical science which owed much to Goethe as the universally respected voice of those classes.

His world-view accommodated these deep value-conflicts by treating them as facts, as material for knowledge. Scientific activity became his own most cherished value and deepest drive. It was a commitment which matched and responded to the emergence of the 'social' as a contested arena and to the needs of the German state for social research.

Such an interpretation of Weber's creativity needs to be counterposed to those accounts which concentrate on his personal troubles and illness. The reason we attend to Weber today is because he appreciated and responded to the strongest intellectual forces in the making of the modern world. He succeeded in both developing them and identifying their thrust and direction which persist to this day. Above all he understood that rationality had become both the irrational drive and rigid frame of modern life.

1

Religious Faith in An Intellectual's World

As the global recognition of the significance of Weber's contribution to social science grows, there is a danger that the historical roots of his work will be disregarded. When this happens, new circumstances may be forced to fit old and inappropriate ideas and it becomes difficult to sift the essential from the inessential. The contribution becomes a canon, a source of doctrine, rather than something understood as a living structure of thought, to be criticised, refined and developed under new conditions.

Historical analysis is not the same as antiquarianism. The search for the roots of ideas is precisely to reveal their potential for development. It provides an understanding of their dynamic relationship with the real world.

For these reasons it is important to stress an obvious but all too frequently ignored fact: Weber wrote within a Christian tradition. This chapter will propose that his social theory cannot be understood adequately without taking account of this fact.

Note well: I am not saying that Weber was a Christian. He was unable to affirm identifiable religious beliefs. But no one who wrote such an extraordinary series of essays on the world religions as he did can be considered as uninterested in religion. Indeed, his relationship with the Protestant faith of his family was profound and complex. We will see that it defined much of his intellectual agenda.

Weber's quest to understand religion was very much an exercise in self-analysis. For this reason, if we approach his work by this route, we can come much closer to understanding the motive forces behind his intellectual activity.

13

1   Weber's religiosity

Max Weber's wife, Marianne, had no doubt about the personal significance of his work on religion. Of the 'Protestant Ethic' studies she wrote, 'It was the first work to make Weber's star shine again after a serious nervous breakdown' and was 'connected with the deepest roots of his personality and in an undefinable way bears its stamp'. She went on to say, 'Perhaps this tendency of his quest for knowledge – a permanent concern with religion – was the form in which the genuine religiosity of his maternal family lived on in him' (1975: 335).

Marianne's reference to the maternal family is to Weber's mother Helene and to her sister, Ida Baumgarten, who exercised considerable influence on him when he spent a year at Strasbourg as a student. Both his mother and aunt were devout Protestants endeavouring throughout their lives to subject each day to God's moral law, given to studying the writings of Protestant divines and actively engaged in good works for the suffering and needy. They and Weber conversed and wrote to each other on religious topics.

Religion had deep emotional significance for Weber. It shaped his intellectual passion. One of the strongest statements on this comes from a leader of the German feminist movement, Gertrud Bäumer, who wrote: 'The culture of the Protestant confession is the abiding foundation for the shaping of Max Weber's life's work, fate, ideas and development. . . . This not in the philistine sense of a restricted moral life, but rather as something much more powerful because it dominates and shapes the demonics of a personality which is both passionate and under nervous strain' (König and Winckelmann, 1963: 117). She then went on to point to the mother as the source of this formative influence and as representing one of the finest examples of perfected Protestant culture.

In the family Weber came from and in his subsequent life, daily decisions and the directions of activity, social gatherings and political commitments were infused with texts, creeds and intellectual argument. In the letters Weber wrote as a young man we have ample evidence of this rarefied cultural atmosphere. When his younger brother, Alfred, was confirmed, Max wrote to him to explain that a Christian had the right and duty to do something for all mankind, but also that each member of the Christian community had to solve the great riddles of religion in a unique way: 'Like any other Christian, you are now being asked to develop your own views as a member of the Christian community. . . . You will be responsible only to yourself, to your conscience, to your mind, and to your heart for the way in which you perform the task that you are now facing for the first time' (Marianne Weber, 1975: 100).

Inner peace, said Max, would only come from the fulfilment of these duties. When later Alfred suffered religious doubts after reading Strauss' *Life of Jesus*, Max wrote at length to examine the concept of 'myth' and to tell him that the 'incomprehensibility' of religious matters was by no means a settled issue. We have to ask, he wrote, 'What *value* did they have for people in the past and what value do they have for me?' And there could be no instant answer to that (ibid.: 103). It was the question he was to ask on and off in personal and public life until the end of his days.

The majority of his contemporaries who attempted to offer obituaries or appreciations of his life and work found that the Kantian and Protestant ethics were decisive in shaping his personality. His close friend Ernst Troeltsch wrote, 'he was satisfied to find the meaning of life in duty in the simple and strict sense which Kant gave it' (König and Winckelmann, 1963: 46).

Leopold von Wiese regarded the vigour with which Weber rooted out value-judgements from scientific work as being diametrically opposed to his own nature, a true expression of his own asceticism. Injustice prompted him to the ready defence of just causes for the moral imperative was deeply embedded in his person (ibid.: 30).

Helmut Plessner acknowledged that the dogmas of Christianity meant little to him personally and that was one of the reasons he sought to understand them in their effects but, on the other hand, he said, 'No one has yet doubted that he was a Protestant, a Lutheran with a keen eye for Calvinist competition and someone who suffered from the split between the ethics of conscience and of responsibility' (ibid.: 32).

All these comments point in the same direction, namely to a personality which had been shaped profoundly by Christian motives but was unable to accept any other person's definition of true faith. Weber retained a deep interest in theology and debates between rival creeds throughout his life.

Yet he never felt able to give himself up to religion. His responses varied from disdain, to respect for its social function, to awe for its power to render life meaningful, to regret for something he felt he was missing. But he was unable to do what the Protestant faith demanded, to believe. In a letter to the great sociologist Ferdinand Tönnies in 1908, which has often been quoted, Weber wrote that any religion which asserted there were 'supernatural facts' was bound to come into conflict with science. But it was also grievously mistaken to think that the Catholic church in particular would be shaken by scientific results. And in all honesty he would not take part in any anti-clerical 'metaphysical' naturalism. He then went on:

> It is true that in respect of religion I am absolutely unmusical and have neither the need nor the ability to erect some spiritual 'edifice' of a religious character in myself, – that's not on, or I reject it. But on closer inspection I am neither antireligious nor *irreligious*. In this respect I feel myself to be a cripple, an amputee, whose inner fate it is to have to admit this honestly and to come to terms with it so as not to lapse into romantic swindle (Baumgarten, 1964: 670).

The point was that Weber also shared his father's attitude which Marianne described as 'the cosmopolitan coolness of their father who respected religion but had less and less personal use for it as time went on' (ibid.: 99). In this respect Max was a constant disappointment to his mother. In 1885, as a student, he wrote to her saying that in spite of her protests he had to regard Sunday as a day to lie in. He did read some of her favourite Protestant writer, Channing, but was unlucky in the text he chose because Channing rejected war except as an extreme expedient.

Weber rejected any notion that Christian belief was against the use of violence (ibid.: 88–9). It was only later in life that he felt bound to acknowledge that there was a deep rift in this respect between the world and Christian requirements. In any event at this time, having done military training, studying for his father's profession, he was not prepared to give way to his mother's ideals. Later in life Marianne recounts that he retained a 'profound reverence for the Gospels and genuine Christian religiosity. . . . But, since his maturity, he was not under any particular constraint, and thus he was able as a thinker to turn to all religious systems with equal interest' (ibid.: 337).

This contrast between the self-denying piety of his mother and the practical attitude of the man of the world which his father displayed created a tension within Weber's personality which was to be expressed in a variety of ways. The sharp opposition he postulated between an ethic of conscience and an ethic of responsibility was one way. The difficulties he had, both in managing his relations with his parents and in his inner conflicts of duty and desire, were another.

Artur Mitzman's book *The Iron Cage* (1970) has explored the sources and outcomes of these conflicts in depth and there is a very strong case for seeing them as a factor in Weber's emotional illness which dogged him for many years. That story has been told elsewhere. What has been less emphasised is the creative outcome of these tensions. We can also see them as the source of a major intellectual achievement, won admittedly at a considerable personal cost. That is no more than Weber's own account of the Protestant personality would suggest.

2 The Protestant individual

There is a problem in writing about the way Protestantism moulded the personalities of those who had the faith, namely the fact that Weber's own account overshadows the whole discussion. It is a special case of what has been called the 'hermeneutic circle': in order to understand Weber, his person and work, we need to appreciate the influence of Protestantism, but our understanding of Protestantism has been deeply influenced by Weber. We cannot escape this by turning to his critics either, say to R. H. Tawney or Werner Sombart, for however much they disagreed with Weber about the consequences of Puritanism for the capitalist economy, they still shared with Weber a very common estimation of the qualities of the Protestant personality.

Reinhard Bendix has pointed out that Weber drew on a tradition of writing about the Puritans which he took for granted. It was commonplace to think of them as restrained, disciplined, sober, dispassionate, industrious, rejecting pleasure and companionship, devoted single-mindedly to the task in hand (1971: 299).

Werner Sombart thought that Protestantism had restricted capitalistic development because of its concentration on religious feeling, but his characterisation of the Protestant was entirely consistent with Weber's: 'Puritanism re-echoed the old watchwords: Rationalize life; keep the passions under control; let reason dominate the natural inclinations.'

Sombart cited Isaac Barrow's treatise *Of Industry* as a summary of the fundamental teachings of Puritanism: 'We should govern and regulate according to very strict and severe laws all the faculties of our soul, all the members of our body, all internal motions and all external actions proceeding from us; we should check our inclinations, curb our appetites and compose our passions.' In Sombart's view, 'So the habit was formed of fashioning the whole of life on the basis of reason, in accordance with the will of God' (1915: 250–62).

Sombart's view was that these virtues were also preached by the Roman Catholic Church and that the only distinction possessed by the Puritans was that their religious feelings were more intense. But this difference was one which went to the heart of Max Weber's own understanding of Protestantism, for, underlying all these commonplaces about Protestant conduct, Weber felt there was an attitude to the world as a whole which was intimately connected with both the institutional position and the theology of Protestantism. In particular the awesome Calvinist doctrine of predestination gave the religious faith of the ascetic Protestant a special quality of intensity constituting very definite differences from Catholicism: 'In its extreme inhumanity this doctrine must above all have had one consequence for the life of a generation which surrendered to its magnificent consistency. . . . This, the complete elimination of salvation through the Church and the sacraments (which in Lutheranism by no means developed to its final conclusions), was what formed the absolutely decisive difference from Catholicism (PE: 104).

The doctrine of predestination is crucial for understanding Calvinism but other factors were also vital in laying the foundations for the development of the Protestant personality. The ideal of controlling one's conduct, of rational self-control in the service of God, had its origins in Catholic monasticism. But the insistence of the reformers on individual conscience as against the teachings of the Church and the fact of their successful rejection of the authority of the Catholic Church pushed the individual into a position of isolation.

This isolation was felt in everyday interpersonal relations. Weber pointed out that any ethic which rejected feelings was bound to cast suspicion on emotional relationships. These were felt to compete with the exclusive direction of love towards God (ibid.: 224). It meant also that the social organisation of religion for Calvinists was always dependent on individualistic rationalism. The glory of God and salvation were always rational motives and the individual never entered emotionally into social organisation, a factor Weber felt influenced peoples with a Puritan past to this day (ibid.: 223).

The isolation and anxiety induced in the Protestant by his or her direct relationship with God, who remained mysterious and unapproachable, unassisted by a caring Church which could mediate, was assuaged only by a more resolute adherence to Christian conduct in this world. Protestantism, then, left the individual with the lonely task of constructing life for God with little reassurance from outside. However this task was completed, it had to be outside the traditional authority structures associated with the Roman Catholic world order.

It should thus be apparent that the creeds which sprang from the Reformation are not simply to be assessed from the point of view of their stimulus to economic accumulation. That was Weber's specific interest when he wrote *The Protestant Ethic and the Spirit of Capitalism*, but he clearly saw this as embedded in a much wider context and that was reflected in his work in other places, as in the discussion of authority.

We have to recognise the full range of social, political and intellectual revolutions associated with the Reformation to grasp the significance of Protestantism for the individual personality. We can thus understand what has often given rise to puzzlement, namely how it was that Protestantism could generate both the rigours of the disciplined sect and the individualism which rejected limits on economic activity. Tawney pointed out how everywhere Puritanism went through an evolution from regimentation to utilitarian individualism and that its tendencies were differently expressed in different political and economic environments (1938: 226).

We can put a further gloss on this. The tendency common to the sectarian revolutionary, the self-made businessman and the agnostic intellectual alike, was that none of them acknowledged an authority outside the activities in which they were engaged, whether in building a utopian community, developing new markets, or elaborating a theory. All were actively engaged in constructing something new upon which their inner security and self-respect depended.

In Protestantism one can see what amounts to the seeds of the specific character of modernism in a much broader sense than mere economic activity. That was certainly the view of Weber's close friend, Ernst Troeltsch, who, in a series of lectures entitled *Protestantism and Progress* (1912), saw it as 'a religious spirit peculiar to the modern world' (179). According to him it expressed a rationalistic individualism opposing Church civilisation and substituting the rational conviction of the individual conscience. He aligned himself with Weber in designating this 'inner-worldly asceticism' and saw its influence in every sector of modern life, in economic and social organisation, science, art.

Troeltsch extended the *Protestant Ethic* thesis into the intellectual sphere. He went to some lengths to distinguish two major variants in modern religious feeling. Superficially, he argued, the modern world appeared to be Calvinistic and individualistic, fitting an Anglo-Saxon business ethos. But there was a deeper, more spiritual, level of Protestantism in the idealist philosophy and literature as it had developed in Germany. This was a movement which was not confined in origins or influence to Germany but nonetheless had its deepest expression there. 'Kant, Fichte and Hegel could hold that they were only formulating philosophically the fundamental idea of the Reformation' (Troeltsch, 1912: 201). It was a 'religion of personal conviction and conscience . . . homogeneous with and adapted to modern individualistic civilization' (ibid.: 203). Troeltsch expanded on this theme in the following way:

> What is meant is most clearly indicated by the names of Kant, Fichte, Carlyle and Emerson with which we may associated the ripe wisdom of Goethe, which one would fain point to as the expression of modern humanity in general. Here the essentially Protestant basis of this movement is clearly evident, the transformation of the idea of freedom and grace into the ideas of

the self-directing personality and a spiritual fellowship having its roots in history, all on the basis of a theism which has taken up into itself the idea of immanence. Moreover, this modern religious temper, in a thousand various modifications, has been so thoroughly absorbed by large portions of modern Protestantism that the latter can scarcely be distinguished from the former (ibid.: 183).

For us the importance of Troeltsch's interpretation of movements in Protestantism is that he indicates a genealogy of ideas in which Weber can be seen as a late descendant, for although Calvinism was something with which he was thoroughly familiar through family connections, the main influence on him in his formative years was the Pietism of his mother and aunt, the broad movement which bridged Lutheranism and Calvinism and was also the background into which Kant was born.

We can even actually identify a link in this chain of ideas in the preaching of the founder of American Unitarianism, William Channing, for whose influence on the young Weber we have the testimony of Marianne. She recounted how Weber read Channing while in sick quarters during military service and how a letter to his mother was the sole indication of any religious excitement on the part of the young man. Weber wrote that Channing had 'an entirely original and often magnificent view of the nature of religion . . . There can be no doubt that his views are universal and based on real needs of the spiritual life' (Marianne Weber, 1975: 86).

It is of interest to note the qualities in Channing which Marianne felt it worthwhile to single out: he believed in the 'harmony between reason and revelation'; he saw 'religion and morality as identical'; God is grasped not in ecstatic emotionalism, but in the fulfilment of clear and simple duties'; the essence of spiritual freedom he saw in 'mastery over one's senses and over matter, mastery over fate'; he saw the state serving the individual, the human spirit being greater than the state (ibid.: 87).

Marianne went on to point out that Max would have been acquainted with the doctrine of freedom in its strictly logical form from the works of Kant and he made it a basic law for himself all his life. Similarly, he believed that the development of the autonomous personality was the purpose of social and political institutions, a doctrine expressed by Kant and Fichte and also espoused by Channing, whether independently or borrowed from them. It was only Channing's rejection of war which offended him for reasons we saw earlier.

Channing, like Kant, was expressing the authentic spirit of the Reformation: rejecting authority, affirming the individual and a faith based on reason, accepting duty and rejecting feeling where it endangered reason and duty. The autonomous personality developed through Protestant doctrine was as much a product of the Reformation as the establishment of new churches and sects and political upheavals. It was the counterpart of seeking to fulfil God's will on this earth by regulating all in life according to his presumed wishes. No one in Weber's time doubted that the Protestant personality was a special nature. He recognised and understood it well because he possessed it himself.

For us what is important to grasp at this juncture in our exploration of the formation of Weber's world-view is that Channing appealed to him because he intellectualised faith to the point where it could not be distinguished from reason. This non-dogmatic Christianity represented an apotheosis for the intellectual, or the secularisation of Protestantism. Either way, the individual was left facing the world alone.

3   Meaning in the world

For all Weber's lack of religious faith, the fact remains that religion had exercised a formative influence on his character and intellect and we must expect to see that reflected in his work. His academic interest in religion was in part a coming to terms with his own biography, and what he says about religion is an expression of his own beliefs. There are many passages in his writing on religion in which he expresses himself on the conditions of human existence where he is also outlining the parameters of his own life. Indeed, it could not be otherwise. Short of assuming divine status, an author making statements about 'the world' is part of that world. In Weber's case we will find that some of the most central and strategic concepts in his academic work are also at the heart of his world-view.

As an example we can take what he said about the religious

prophet: 'To the prophet, both the life of man and the world, both social and cosmic events, have a certain systematic and coherent meaning. To this meaning, the conduct of mankind must be oriented if it is to bring salvation, for only in relation to this meaning does life obtain a unified and significant pattern' (S of Rel: 58–9).

This looks like a statement confined to the religious sphere, but Weber goes on to generalise it to any intellectual quest for meaning: 'The ultimate question of all metaphysics has always been something like this: if the world as a whole and life in particular were to have a meaning, what might it be, and how would the world have to look in order to correspond to it? The religious problem-complex of prophets and priests is the womb from which non-sacerdotal philosophy emanated, wherever it developed' (ibid.). Now it has to be stressed: this is no mere incidental speculation on the part of the scholar enjoying the luxury of a personal marginal comment. It is offered as a statement aspiring to truth, it applies to the world and the people in it; it applies to the author too. Weber knew from personal experience what that question meant and how it generated the 'strongest tensions in man's inner life' (ibid.).

The terms 'meaning' (*Sinn*) and 'meaningful' (*sinnvoll*) are pivotal concepts in the whole of Weber's work. This passage revolves around them. They are developed right at the beginning of the compendium of fundamental sociological concepts which Weber completed towards the end of his life. There they appear as detached, even arid, sets of definitions and fine distinctions. They are in fact the distillation of both intellectual and personal experience. Weber is renowned for having asserted the separation of science and practical decision, for insisting on the demarcation of fact and value, but his whole endeavours towards justifying that insistence were produced by the most intimate connections between his chosen fields of study and his personal experience.

Weber's account of meaning will be given extended treatment later. The term to which we should give greater attention at this moment is 'world'. This is a term which does not figure in the compendium of sociological concepts, but it should not be thought just for that reason that it has an unimportant place in Weber's thought or is used unreflectingly. Indeed, for someone brought up in the devout Protestant atmosphere which Weber experienced, that would not be possible. 'The world' in the Christian gospels is the everyday life of mundane existence, the world where people marry, are born, die, pay taxes, obey the law, or disobey, fornicate and sin: the everyday experience of ordinary people. Jesus offered escape from this: 'And he said unto them, Ye are from beneath; I am from above: ye are of this world; I am not of this world. I said therefore unto you that ye shall die in your sins: for if ye believe not that I am *he*, ye shall die in your sins' (John 8: 23, 24). The Christian definition of the world as ordinary, terrestrial, mortal, routine, messy existence is counterposed to the Christian message of hope, the replacement of the kingdom of men with the kingdom of God, the chance of life everlasting, the removal of sin. It is a world above which is being offered.

Weber was brought up to take such distinctions for granted. Just before his confirmation he wrote to his mother, 'I really believe that a man who could honestly say that he had absolutely no conviction or hope of a hereafter must be an extremely unhappy creature' (Marianne Weber, 1975: 58) – fateful words for the mature man 'under no constraint'. That Christian definition of mundane existence became a taken-for-granted foundation for Weber's subsequent work and the tension between this world and a conception of another world was generalised to become the frame for his analyses of Protestantism, of religion in general and indeed of ideas and the material world.

This generalisation of Christian, and more specifically Protestant, ideas about the world should not be seen as a simple matter of narrow-mindedness or lack of vision. Weber was after all committed to science and not to Christianity, but the fact was that the scientific outlook of his time had in the first place prospered in the seedbed of intellectualism which arose from religion. If we look at a characteristic Weberian statement about intellectuals we can see how closely their strivings approximate to the Protestant world-view:

It is the intellectual who transforms the concept of the world into the problem of meaning. As intellectualism suppresses belief in magic, the world's processes become disenchanted, lose their magical significance, and henceforth simply 'are' and 'happen' but no longer signify anything. As a consequence, there is a growing demand that the world and the total pattern of life be subject to an order that is significant and meaningful (S of Rel: 125).

Just like the Christians, therefore, the intellectual is faced with a world which is mundane and routine, things just 'happen'. Just like the Protestant, the intellectual attempts to subject life to order. Modern science takes us beyond that stage even: it gives up altogether the task of finding an ethical order, discovering the meaning of life, but it is left still with 'the world' and the various quests to find meaning in it as part of its subject matter.

4 The symmetry of science and religion

Weber generalised the terms in which he analysed the way in which prophets and intellectuals interpreted the world into a basic statement about the methodology of the social sciences. His essay, 'Objectivity in Social Science and Social Policy', has become, with the later account of value-freedom, the seminal argument for most of the discussion in the rest of this century on the topic of fact and value in the social sciences. In it he took it for granted that a social science was bound to see human beings as cultural beings, namely investing their lives with significance:

'Culture' is a finite segment of the meaningless infinity of the world process, a segment on which human beings confer meaning and significance.

The transcendental presupposition of every *cultural science* lies not in our finding a certain culture of any 'culture' in general to be *valuable*, but rather in the fact that we are *cultural beings* endowed with the capacity and the will to take a deliberate attitude towards the world and lend it *significance* (Sinn) (Meth: 81).

What we find here is a symmetry between the terms in which Weber discussed religion and the terms of social science methodology. Just as the Puritan takes hold of life in the world and rationalises it in the direction of another world, fashions it into something which can give salvation, so in general human beings hew a segment out of the meaningless infinity and make it meaningful.

The social scientist, or, as at this time Weber preferred, the cultural scientist, has in no way transformed or overturned the religious view of the world. What the scientist, as scientist, lacks is faith, but he or she too is confronted with a fundamentally meaningless world in which meaning is conferred by human belief:

> The fate of an epoch which has eaten of the tree of knowledge is that it must know that we cannot learn the *meaning* of the world from the results of its analysis, be it ever so perfect; it must rather be in the position to create this meaning itself. It must recognise that general views of life (Weltanschauungen) and the universe can never be the products of increasing empirical knowledge, and that the highest ideals, which move us most forcefully, are always formed only in the struggle with other ideals which are just as sacred to others as ours are to us (ibid.: 57).

About the same time, in another essay on method, Weber was concerned with the principles of historical explanation and he criticised a number of writers for attempting to import ostensibly objective standards of evaluations into historical writing where they were rooted in human values. He was critical, for instance, of attempting to ground 'progress' in necessary laws of historical development when in fact all the historian had done was to consider a particular 'cultural development', namely to see that something had grown as measured against certain values, e.g. growth of knowledge. In this case something was 'lifted out of the meaninglessness of the endless passage of infinite multiplicity' (WL: 61).

It is a repeated theme in Weber's writings on method that the social scientist is faced with an endless multiplicity, a chaos of events and perceptions into which order is injected only by the fact of selection which is guided by cultural values. Indeed, 'Empirical reality becomes "culture" to us because and in so far as we relate it to value ideas' (Meth: 76). 'Order is brought into this chaos only on the condition that in every case only a *part* of concrete reality is interesting and *significant* to us, because only it is related to the *cultural values* with which we approach reality' (ibid: 78).

In the end, Weber concludes his objectivity essay by emphasising the hair-line which separates science from faith. Empirical social science depends on its relationship to evaluative ideas which cannot themselves be validated by science. Infinite reality is subjected to meaningful analysis, but those standpoints are constantly shifting. He repeats a point he makes earlier in the essay, namely that life has an inexhaustible store of possible meanings. There can never be final and conclusive set of problems and answers so long as ossification of cultural life does not take place.

> The belief which we all have in some form or another, in the meta-empirical validity of ultimate and final values, in which the meaning of our existence is rooted, is not incompatible with the incessant changefulness of the concrete viewpoints, from which empirical reality gets its significance. Both these views are on the contrary in harmony with each other. Life with its irrational reality and its store of possible meanings is inexhaustible. The *concrete* form in which value-relevance occurs remains perpetually in flux, ever subject to change in the dimly seen future of human culture. The light which emanates from those highest evaluative ideas always falls on an ever-changing finite segment of the vast chaotic stream of events, which flows away through time (ibid.: 111).

Nothing distinguishes the language as far as eloquence, passion and metaphysical depth are concerned from Weber's writing on religion or his personal correspondence. Nor can it, since the same problem recurs in each context. Life, reality, the world around us, is meaningless without meaning conferred on it from outside. The Christian faced with the irrational reality of this world finds meaning given by God, the intellectual seeks a substitute for that source of meaning, the social scientist is in no different position. In the end, some principles of order and selection have to be made. We all, says Weber, believe in the meta-empirical validity of ultimate values.

One of Weber's last statements on this theme came in the lecture 'Science as a Vocation' which was delivered as part of a series to students in Munich in 1919. He is still working around the same set of ideas. 'Every theology . . . presupposes that the world must have a *meaning*' (Essays: 153). The scientist cannot assume that: to do so means sacrificing his intellect. Indeed, Weber quotes

Tolstoy with approval: 'Science is meaningless because it gives no answer to our question, the only question important for us, "What shall we do and how shall we live?"' (ibid.: 143).

Only by adhering to certain values, that is initially by accepting the rules of logic and scientific method and assuming that the results yielded are worthwhile discovering, is science possible. The worth of science and, in the social sciences particularly, the directions of enquiry, are not given by science itself, but come from values outside. Meaning in the world is not discovered by science: science derives its meaning from those commitments which equally make sense of the world.

2
Reason and the Individual: The Kantian Unity

The Protestant motivation in Weber's work can be established beyond reasonable doubt. it will be manifest in a variety of contexts in later parts of this book. But in itself, of course, it is insufficient to explain the particular intellectual thrust which gave rise to Weber's social theory.

In an important sense the Protestant Reformation was an intellectual movement. It initiated a critical discourse around text and individual conscience which broke the bounds of traditional authority. It was a movement with an inherent potential for development. The single most important stage in that development between the Reformation and Weber's work is represented by the philosophy of Immanuel Kant (1724–1804).

It is sometimes dificult to appreciate in the English-speaking world just how dominating the influence of the eighteenth-century professor from Königsberg was for the German-speaking world for at least 150 years. One of the major commentators on him, writing in Weber's lifetime, said 'he forms the centre of the academic study of philosophy . . . Our students nowadays are referred to Kant on all sides, by measure of lectures, discussions and examination requirements' (Paulsen, 1902: xi–xiv). The major philosophers after Kant, from Hegel to Windelband to Husserl, all took their starting point from Kant and philosophy itself held a pivotal place within the humanities which has no equivalent in anglophone countries. As one commentator on German intellectual life has said, 'Kant's position thus affected almost every aspect of German learning' (Ringer, 1969: 91).

There are three broad aspects of Kant's thinking which we need to appreciate in order to understand Weber's:

- *the rationalisation of Protestantism.* The experience of the reformers, revelation, conscience, the organisation of daily life were intellectualised in the search for the ultimate foundations of thought.
- *the unification of consciousness.* Intellectual activity was directed by the drive to bring disparate ideas together, to synthesise, to create unity and system in thought.
- *the universalisation of experience.* There were no boundaries to thought. It comprehended the 'world', 'reality' outside of which there were no facts or experiences. It became possible to speak of a world-view.

Kant offered the German world a comprehensive vision, and German culture in turn absorbed that to make it the frame for its own development in the nineteenth century. With 'reason' as its core idea, culture itself became an arena for criticism, debate and the embracing of new ideas. The advance of mind became a dynamic factor in German education and the state. The result was the production of generations of academically educated professionals imbued with the Kantian ethos. Weber was one of them.

Weber rarely refers directly to Kant. He was not a philosopher professionally and had no need to cite chapter and verse. In any case, Kant was so much part of his cultural heritage, he could take it for granted that the reader or hearer would understand terminology and pick up allusions. Like other students he read Kant in his last years at school. If he used terms such as 'transcendental' or 'critique', which were given special weight by Kant in his system, the Kantian allusion would be well understood by any educated person – in English that frame of reference is largely missing.

Weber's position within the Kantian tradition thus poses special problems of interpretation for the English-speaking world. For a start there are really two vocabularies to understand. In the foreground, to which nearly all the academic attention has subsequently been directed, is the technical terminology he developed – the language of action, relationships, authority, power and conflict. To this he gave explicit attention and usually formal definitions.

In the background was a rich abstract treasury of terms, including the world, reality, individual, ideas, values, interests, spirit, none of which he needed to define, all part of 'Kant-speak' developed from within the master's framework, often, as with 'values', going beyond it but all constituting the discourse of the educated person.

In that taken-for-granted, everyday philosophical language the key term was 'reason'. Such was the penetrative power of Kantian thought that 'reason' became simply a fact of life, constitutive of all kinds of activity in state, education, business and religion.

When Weber worked with the idea of rationality, he was already acting with a culture which had been transformed by it. No longer simply idea, it had become fact. Kant's view of the 'world' had become a world-view within which it was possible to advance complex scientific argument. Indeed, it sought universality precisely to be able to tolerate and accommodate the diversity of ideas.

Nonetheless, in spite of the aspirations, it remained a product of the Western Protestant tradition. Its limits in the end are arbitrary and historical, and we need to understand their impact on Weber's thought in that light.

1 Knowledge of the world

Kant begins with the naive view of the world – objects or things present themselves to us. We believe we possess direct knowledge of them, or intuition. That term, intuition (*Anschauung*), is one which gives frequent difficulty in English, but Weber also uses it and it renders the sense of a direct and unchallengeable obviousness about the everyday things we see, hear or feel. But like Locke and Hume, Kant asserted that the only evidence for these things in the world came from our senses and our senses only gave us a stream of disconnected impressions.

Objects therefore are phenomena, the sum total of these impressions, but they are not disordered or chaotic. The phenomenon is ordered and unified. That unity is achieved through concepts which belong to the understanding and because the impressions themselves are ordered in time and space. The concepts which organise or synthesise the sense data, which make up the objects of the world we see and hear, are themselves constituted by the categories of understanding, e.g. categories of unity, causality, possibility, which provide a frame for thinking about any object whatsoever.

For Kant, then, the world of phenomena which makes up everyday experience occupies a middle ground between a welter of sense impressions, on the one hand, and a set of concepts with a limited number of features, on the other. The sense data and the concept are brought together in the phenomenon by the understanding. 'Seeing a table' is the outcome of a collection of sense impressions of height, extent, colour, composition, etc. happening at a particular time and place, and the connection of these with a concept already possessed by the observer of the 'table'. But it is only analysis after the event which will give such an account; all the observer had was the intuition: 'that's a table'.

Earlier commentators on Weber have disagreed on the extent to which he can be considered as interested in these issues in the theory of knowledge. Jacob Schaaf, for instance, finds that his theory of science 'is only intelligible as an application of the Kantian basic presupposition of "a chaos of sense-impressions", to the field of history' (1946: 42). Dieter Henrich (1952) regards Weber's epistemological comments as incidental and trivial allusions since he was concerned with the method of social science and not with the theory of knowledge.

The disagreement is in part beside the point. Weber was not concerned with the way sense data are organised to form objects in the imagination. But many commentators have pointed out that, while Kant repeats in innumerable and wearisome ways that the understanding imposes unity upon the elements of sense perception, even he is unable to show convincingly how this is achieved (as he himself admitted). On the other hand, Kant was able to argue convincingly for the importance of concepts and categories in the representation of reality and Weber's activity in demonstrating the relation of social science to historical data was exactly analogous, right the way down to leaving analogous puzzles, e.g. just how are ideal types constructed and applied?

Certainly Weber was extending the Kantian way of thought beyond its original prime field of interest. He was more interested in the multiplicity of historical reality than the manifold of the object, but Kant in any case showed the way in this extension. He applied his own characteristic frame of thought to law, the state, religion and education. Reason was always trying to find unity in multiplicity, for example, as the codifier of law tried to subsume the multiplicity of laws under a general principle (Kant, 1933: 302).

The general point which is important beyond any question of whether Weber can be regarded in a narrow sense as an epistemologist, philosopher of science, or indeed as possessing any particular specialist identity, is that he developed his ideas within a frame which he took largely for granted and which had already been constructed by Kant. he was party to a profound set of assumptions associated with it: the belief that this world was chaotic and disordered at bottom and that order might be introduced by ideas and intellect, that the senses are of this world and that reason is in some sense in, but not of, the world. It was particularly easy for Weber to adopt such ways of thinking, quite aside from common scholarly interest and the educational setting, because he also shared with Kant the Protestant pietist background. It was the way he viewed the world long before it became a part of his world-view.

Kant's is a system of thought which makes order, unity, universality, the world, the central motive and target for the thinker. As such it has been the inspiration for many attempts since to create intellectual order out of a chaotic world. Lucien Goldman says something similar in his account of Kant: 'Kant seems to me to be the first modern thinker to recognize anew the importance of the *totality* as a fundamental category of existence, or at least to recognize its problematic character' (1971: 36).

We can understand now some of the ambivalence Weber had, and therefore the difficulties faced by later commentators in respect of the question of unity in his work. Like Kant, he saw the world he inhabited as derived out of chaos and formed by understanding and reason. But, unlike Kant, he could not assume that form and order were ultimately in tune with the divine; where there could be no faith in religion, the task of construction had to be started all over again.

Max Scheler identified an ultimate attitude in Kant's philosophy which was closely associated with its Protestant background: 'This "attitude" I can only describe as a deep-seated "hostility" or even "mistrust" towards everything which is "given", anxiety and fear of it as "chaos". That is in a word Kant's approach to the world, and "nature" is something to form, organize and "dominate"; it is the "foe", the "chaos" etc. Thus it is the opposite of *love* for the world, of trust, of a gazing, loving devotion to it' (Scheler, 1966: 86). Scheler went on to assert that the outcome was a ceaseless desire for action to dominate the world, so characteristic of the Protestant, and sought to link this with Weber's account of the Protestant Ethic.

If that is the case, one can still say that Kant was successful enough in producing the construction which generated order out of chaos. Moreover, it contained within itself the capacity for self-reflection which in the end allowed for the development of the kind of criticism Scheler advances.

The problem for Weber was that he began with the deep attitudes in the Kantian frame of thought, the thrust to organise was there, the ambition to understand was intense but the religious faith was missing. The multiplicity was all around, the drive for unity was strong, but the faith in the outcome had been lost.

2   Kant and the unity of the 'I'

The bringing to unity, the act of synthesis is the spontaneous product of the human mind. The senses may give us a multiplicity of impressions but the combination of these, so that we can claim to be thinking of objects, is a function of human understanding. The various ways in which that unity in understanding is achieved are summarised in Kant's categories, concepts of quantity, quality, relation and modality which he held to be an exhaustive list of the functions of the understanding. But each of these functions presupposes synthetic unity, which thus in turn must rest on something more fundamental.

This argument, which Kant included within a section of the *Critique of Pure Reason* entitled the 'Transcendental Deduction', is both pivotal in his work and symptomatic of his style. He advances an argument, asserts its validity: he then proceeds to ask and seek to answer the question of how we are in a position to advance the argument in the first place. If we reflect on objects, then our judgements about them, the way their unity is displayed will be in terms of concepts of quantity, quality and so on. But we can only think in these terms because that unity is already presupposed. The employment of the categories, which portray the unity of a complex object, already assumes its unity. To this form of argument, which he termed transcendental, Kant attached one of his most important doctrines. He found the fundamental, the transcendental, source of all unity in the human mind, in the *individual* self-consciousness.

Kant's views on the vital importance of the individual self-consciousness for any possible representation of unity in the world are expressed in a variety of formulations. In bare summary, he held that anything anyone thought of could necessarily be prefaced by 'I think'. For a person to be said to have thoughts at all, they had to be recognised as that particular person's thoughts. No object can be constituted out of my experience unless it is mine. The persistence and identity of myself is presupposed in attributing unity to an object.

This 'abiding and unchanging "I"' Kant also termed the 'original synthetic unity of apperception' or 'the transcendental unity of self-consciousness'. The possibility of unity, of combination, of synthesis does not lie in objects themselves but in the subject. In Kant's own words, 'the thought that the representations given in intuition one and all belong to me, is therefore equivalent to the thought that I unite them in one self-consciousness, or can at least so unite them' (1933: 154). This is a matter of the understanding. As a principle it is 'the highest in the whole sphere of human knowledge'.

Kant's individual could not be more bloodless. It has a pure and formal unity, a logical function in relation to the world of objects, but otherwise no qualities whatsoever. But that logical function is nonetheless of unrivalled importance: it permits the construction of the world of objects and, being the focal point for reason and understanding, the world is accordingly constructed. Grasping the importance of this will go a long way towards understanding what otherwise for so many has appeared mysterious, namely the enormous emphasis Weber placed upon rationality as the central concept in both social science and the development of human society. It is also the case that the bald and dramatic quality of Kant's doctrine is sufficient to draw attention to its contentiousness, indeed its patent one-sidedness.

Kant's philosophy is dominated by the drive to find unity in multiplicity and that unity is to be found ultimately in the transcendental 'I'. Unity is not found in the relations between objects or people, it is not empirical, natural, or social, but logical. C. D. Broad has commented succinctly on this doctrine:

> Kant's theory seems to take no account of the existence of a plurality of intercommunicating persons. He ignores the fact that an essential feature in each person's notion of the external world is that it is perceptible not only by himself but by others, and that each person's knowledge of it is based jointly on what he perceives himself and what other persons report to him that they have perceived. If we take Kant's theory literally, each person has his own private time and space and physical world, which he has constructed for himself (1978: 136–7).

This is not the place to conduct a detailed examination of the doctrine which should not be belittled. Its hold on nineteenth-century thought was tenacious, in large part is may be suggested because the argument went beyond the bounds of ordinary logic and appealed to cardinal features of the faith and motives of the time. It was rooted in Protestantism and expressed a radical individualism. It was a lynch-pin idea both for Kant and his followers and has been vehemently defended.

A vivid illustration of this is provided by Norbert Elias in his reminiscences of his early career. He recounts how an intimate relationship with his highly-respected teacher Richard Hönigswald ended in a violent quarrel when he presented his doctoral thesis to him. Elias had come to the conclusion that everything which Kant considered prior to experience, whether the idea of causality or the moral laws, 'had necessarily to be learnt from other human beings together with the appropriate vocabulary if it was to be present in the consciousness of the individual human being' (1984: 19). Hönigswald insisted that the section had to be deleted: it was simply wrong, although he could give no reasons. Elias complied.

That kind of reaction is only understandable where an idea has strategic significance for a person's beliefs and self-image. The point is that Kant's whole philosophy, not only his theory of knowledge but also his ethical theory, hinged upon a pure concept of the individual as the bearer of reason. Pervaded as it was by Protestant attitudes coming to dominate the teaching of philosophy in universities and schools, it came to serve as almost an official philosophy, associated with all the conventions and proprieties of what was held to be the behaviour and ideas of the good citizen. To refer to 'the social' rather than to 'the individual' or to 'reason' was to challenge the sacred legitimating notions of the society in which one lived.

We are now nearer to appreciating the force of that paradox that individuals for Kant are in the world but not of it. The individual is at the core not even human, for its ultimate quality is unity, the fount of reason. In this way the individual is close to the divine, to the other-wordly, rather than this world. This made it possible for Kant to operate on the assumption of a fundamental similarity in the experience of the natural and moral spheres. Reason could be identified in the sphere of morality too and the same transcendental starting point established: 'But since moral laws should hold for every rational being as such, the principles must be derived from the universal concept of a rational being generally' (Kant, 1949: 71).

The complementarity of Kant's ideas of the world and the individual should now be apparent. They belong on either side of a dichotomous system of ideas. The 'world' is associated with chaos, the senses, the variable, the material; the 'individual' is associated with mind, reason, unity, the eternal. Ideas which operated in the everyday consciousness of the Protestant Christian have been pushed to the highest level of philosophical abstraction. But the original connotations of the world as a field of irrational forces where the individual struggles for salvation are never lost.

3   Reason and the moral agent

It is impossible to appreciate the direction of Kant's argument unless one bears in mind the Christian belief in two worlds, the material and terrestrial, on the one hand, and the spiritual and heavenly, on the other. Kant's individual drew its meaning from the latter and lived in the former: 'the idea of a pure intelligible world as a whole of all intelligences to which we ourselves belong as rational beings (though on the other side we are at the same time members of the world of sense) is always a useful and permissible idea for the purpose of a rational faith. This is so even though all knowledge terminates at its boundary . . .' (Kant, 1949: 116).

For Kant reason terminated ultimately in mystery, just as equally for the Christian the knowledge of God goes beyond what is possible for human reason to achieve. Looked at from this standpoint it is difficult to see how the essentially Christian, and more narrowly Protestant, roots of Kant's world-view can ever have been doubted. One commentator does protest at the attempted imprisonment of his thought 'in the sectarian squabbles which he detested above all else in matters of religion' (Wood, 1970: 198). But to assert rightly that Kant's thought is characterised by his claims to rationality and universal communicability is actually to identify the thrust behind the many attempts to transcend sectarianism which are indeed rooted in it.

The biographer of Kant, Friedrich Paulsen, identified the fundamental dimension upon which Kant may be classified as a Protestant thinker: 'Indeed one may in a certain sense regard Kant as the finisher of what Luther had begun. The original purpose of the Reformation was to make faith independent of knowledge, and conscience free from external authority' (1902: 7). Kant allowed a person both to have the commitment to reason which characterised the Enlightenment and to have a faith based on the individual conscience in line with the sincerity and earnestness of the German Pietists.

The general thrust of the Kantian system was towards a resolution of the problems involved in the Christian world-view once the institutionalised Church of Rome had been rejected. These were the problems posed in the sharpest form by the predestination doctrine and its attempt to combine the requirements of a God with infinite power and wisdom inhabiting another world with the human being inhabiting a sinful, sensuous world, with the capacity to reason and the ability to choose. Just as it is badly mistaken to see Kant as a doctrinaire Protestant, so it is equally impossible to understand him without recognising that the frame of thought within which he worked was the ascetic individualism of the Reformation.

Kant's ethical philosophy was largely contained in the *Foundations of the Metaphysics of Morals* and in the *Critique of Practical Reason*. In these he developed his theory of the universal principle of morality, a practical law which was presupposed by any particular moral imperative. Reason alone could determine that the source of morality was a law, universal for all human beings.

The supreme imperative, the categorical, was one must act in such a way that the principle of one's own action was at the same time a law for all human beings. Now closely associated with this doctrine was a nexus of ideas about freedom, the will, causality, duty and personality. Weber's idea of the individual is pervaded by these and it is important to understand the peculiar and definite connections which existed between them in the Kantian system.

How does one combine the idea that everything is caused with the belief that the human will is free? If no one else can tell me how to act, how should I act? If I am free, why should I not do entirely as the whim takes me? If I am part of an ephemeral world of pain and pleasure, how can I also be part of an eternal world of the spirit?

Perhaps for the ordinary person in Christian countries in the late twentieth century these are no longer obvious question. Outside the Christian tradition they have rarely surfaced and never in this precise combination. But from the sixteenth to the nineteenth centuries in Europe and North America they preoccupied a large section of the population. Kant's philosophy was only the most powerful single system of answers to these questions. Unnumbered preachers, theologians and philosophers hazarded answers to them in the Protestant countries. But it was Kant who, through the scope and grandeur of his enormous enterprise, captured the syllabuses of the German universities and laid the foundations of German idealism.

Like the other philosophers of the Enlightenment Kant centred his system of philosophy around the idea of reason. Reason was the highest achievement of human intelligence. In the most obvious and everyday form it was exhibited in the identification of and search for reasons. In that way it underpinned the human understanding in its organisation of human experience and went beyond experience because it was dependent on ideas which transcended it altogether.

The categories of understanding which shaped our experience were themselves dependent on concepts of pure reason, in particular the idea of the unity of the thinking subject and the idea of the unity of appearances in the object (Kant, 1933: A334, B391). In utilising reason the human being exhibited both the ultimate powers and the limits of the human mind. It was not possible to think except in terms of subject and object and there was therefore no way in which experience could modify those ideas.

It was the necessary unconditioned nature of the idea of the subject which Kant linked to the doctrine of human freedom. The subject could not help but think of itself as free. Anchored securely in reason the subject transcended experience. But that freedom was not revealed in capricious or unpredictable acts. Reason was able to identify the laws of nature; it was also capable of identifying the principles or laws to which the subject could submit itself. The freedom of the subject was found in self-determination, in exerting the will in practical action in accord with freely chosen principles.

If in physics the human reason discovered the laws of nature, in ethics reason identified the laws of freedom. In human action law and freedom were not opposed to each other: indeed, freedom meant precisely the capacity to act by the light of the principles of human reason. 'Reason must regard itself as the author of its principles' (Kant, 1949: 103). The human will could make reason the cause of an action. In this way, the human world was the sphere of 'causality through freedom' (ibid.: 157).

But what were the principles of freedom? Kant was in no doubt that they were identical with the idea of morality. Just as in his account of natural philosophy he combined a respect for and acceptance of the everyday sense of what was true with a belief in the transcendental nature of human reason, so in his moral philosophy he took for granted the everyday moral experience of good and bad, of measuring action against standards, and insisted on the necessary and transcendental nature of this experience.

For Kant the moral law was given as a certain fact of pure reason, of which we are a priori conscious (ibid.). For both nature and morality the idea of a law was fundamental. But in accordance with the importance of human freedom, law in relation to morality had a different function from law in nature. Reason identified laws governing nature, but in the case of practical affairs it was the *idea of law* which regulated action. The idea of conforming to a law was in fact the principle of morality.

Now laws became important for practical action in the form of imperatives. Any science exhibiting laws required human beings to observe them in shaping their actions. Thus the laws of nature became imperatives of skill, hypothetical in the sense that human beings were bound to observe them *if* their objectives implicated them. But in morality action was subjected to the idea of law in general, the imperative which emerged was thus categorical.

The supreme moral principle was to act in such a way that the maxim underlying the action could hold universally for all human beings. If the human being were perfectly rational, action would always follow this path, but the intrusion of sensual inclinations meant that pure rationality was never fully attained. For Kant this gap between ideal and reality was expressed by the human experience of obligation, the reference to 'ought'. Obligation was itself purely a feature of reason. It excluded any reference to wants, or needs, or sensuality. What was done from duty emerged from the reason and will, not from feeling.

Kant accepted as incontrovertible that it was duty which embodied the law of morality. Duty was done out of respect for law, every motive had to give way to it, and it was the very principle of moral knowledge. Indeed, any motive which led one to perform a duty for reasons other than simply the fulfilment of the duty could only detract from the moral worth of the action. The source of the moral act had to be reason working in accord with law. The law, however, was not one imposed by an external agency, it was the law of the self-determining human person who, in each and every case, was entitled to be accorded the respect which was due to an autonomous site of reason.

Such ideas were not incompatible with the idea of a divine being. Indeed, Kant regarded the belief in God as being as necessary as the conviction in moral obligation. But our knowledge of God was derived from reason: 'We shall not look upon actions as obligatory because they are the commands of God, but shall regard them as divine commands because we have an inward obligation to them'.

In the same breath Kant went on to say that the use of moral theology was to enable us 'to fulfil our vocation in this present world by showing us how to adapt ourselves to the system of all ends, and by warning us against the fanaticism, and indeed the impiety, of abandoning the guidance of a morally legislative reason in the right conduct of our lives, in order to derive guidance directly from the idea of the Supreme Being' (1933: A819, B847).

There could be no better expression of the Protestant Ethic as Weber himself perceived it, namely a system of morality which discovered in this world what behaviour God willed by the pure light of human reason and which thus permitted us to 'fulfil our vocation'.

4 Weber's individualism

Weber did not have to search far to infer profound consequences for the personality of the individual from the pursuit of this moral code. Kant saw an intimate logical connection between it and the very idea of a personality. Since the subject, or self, was transcendent and both the basis of and founded on reason, since self-determination was the moral law and this was realised in the pursuit of duty, it followed that the human being, pursuing duty, was the perfect personality. In one of the most eloquent sections of the *Critique of Practical Reason* Kant sang the praises of the special connections between duty, reason and personality:

> Duty! Thou sublime and mighty name that does embrace nothing charming or insinuating but requirest submission and yet seekest not to move the will by threatening . . . what origin is there worthy of thee . . . ? It cannot be less than something which elevates man above himself as part of the world of sense. . . . It is nothing else than personality, i.e. the freedom and independence from the mechanism of nature regarded as a capacity of a being which is subject to special laws (pure practical laws given by its own reason) (1949: 193).

Kant went on to argue that the idea of personality aroused respect and gave a person dignity in the eyes of self and others. The comfort this aroused in the bearer of respect was something quite different from happiness. Indeed, the pursuit of happiness only destroyed the purity of the moral disposition. 'The majesty of duty has nothing to do with the enjoyment of life' (ibid.: 195).

The point about a person's own happiness for Kant, which made it subordinate to duty, was that it stemmed necessarily and naturally from the satisfaction of the senses. It was not a matter of reason, but of nature and could never share the sublime character of duty. Happiness was merely the satisfaction of the animal side of the human being. It might be a proper and moral thing to pursue for others but never for oneself.

We can understand therefore the force and conviction which lay behind Weber's rejection of his predecessor Karl Knies' view that the events of the social world were unpredictable because of the possession of free will by human beings. With Kant the freedom of the individual was expressed in the autonomous pursuit of the moral law, and since this was apprehended through reason and applied to all human beings, it provided a firm and predictable basis for human social life.

Weber clinched a long and tortuous account in an essay on Knies with a conclusion which was entirely Kantian in its spirit. Human action which was unconstrained by outside force or by emotion and was entirely motivated by the best choice of means to ends was entirely open to rational analysis and in respect of means could be seen as completely 'determined' or predictable. But one could go further than that:

In the sense which is being employed here 'free action', namely action which does not bear the marks of 'natural events', is precisely that which brings the concept of 'personality' into play, which finds its essence in the constancy of its inner relations to certain ultimate 'values' and 'meanings in life'. The more these are realised as purposes and converted into teleological-rational action, the more the romantic-naturalistic idea of the 'personality' . . . which seeks the sacredness of the personal in what the 'person' shares with the animal, disappears (WL: 132).

The romantic idea of the personality in Weber's view simply pushed any historical or social scientific analysis into a quest for unfathomable roots of individual behaviour when for the historian it was the case that the interpretation of the personality was most intelligible when it was most rational. 'Above all linking "freedom of the will" with "irrationality" was to be avoided' (ibid.: 133). Just as Kant did, Weber finds that the only usable concept of free will was to be linked with rationality and this applied to social science too: 'Even the "laws" of theoretical economics necessarily presuppose the prevalence of "freedom of the will" in the only possible meaning of the word as far as the empirical world is concerned. And this is naturally exactly the same with any purely rational interpretation of a particular historical event' (ibid.: 133).

The Kantian notion of free will then provided Weber with his methodological justification for a rational and individualistic method in social science. It equally sustained his resistance to any cult of personality, to the romantic quest for 'experience' and the search for identity in the emotional life. It was the inspiration for the heroic stoicism of his account of academic life in 'Science as a Vocation'.

Only the person devoted to the specialised task could become a 'personality'. This was not a matter of experience but of 'inner devotion to the task'. 'Personality' and 'personal experience' were the idols of a cult for youth which was profoundly mistaken. In talking about Stefan George, whose advocacy did so much at the time to popularise such notions, Weber is reported by Paul Honigsheim to have said, 'The whole of individualism is a swindle for sure – Stefan George may be a personality, but not every policeman and cab-driver' (König and Winckelmann, 1963: 184).

Weber's theory of the individual was one which operated simultaneously as a methodological principle, a source of personal inspiration and a canon for historical interpretation. The theory he put forward in the essay on Knies echoed in very similar terms the view of the individual which he imputed to Puritanism. In the *Protestant Ethic* he wrote:

> The Puritan, like every rational type of asceticism, tried to enable a man to maintain and act upon his constant motives, especially those which it taught him itself, against the emotions. In this formal psychological sense of the term it tried to make him into a personality. Contrary to many popular ideas, the end of this asceticism was to be able to lead an alert, intelligent life: the most urgent task the destruction of spontaneous, impulsive enjoyment, the most important means was to bring order into the conduct of its adherents (PE: 119).

We may recall in this context Channing's insistence that 'duty restrains the passions, only that the nobler faculties and affections may have freer play' (1884: 62). In the same way, Kant affirmed the concept of a personality which 'proudly rejects all kinship with the inclinations' (1949: 193).

Protestantism, German idealism, Luther, Calvin, Kant, Channing: this was the heavy atmosphere which the fire of Weber's ambition and the cold precision of his intellect distilled into the basic concepts of sociology. The famous types of action sharply distinguishing the rational from the emotional, the insistence on individualistic method, the rejection of psychological argument in sociological context have their origin in the Protestant world-view.

Several generations of sociology students, both mystified and fascinated by the most tightly framework of concepts in the discipline, have in fact unwittingly been confronted with the secularised answers to the problems posed by the Protestant reformers: If everything is determined, how are people free? How does reason guide creatures of flesh and blood? In a world of sin and chaos what is the source of certainty?

If Weber's framework of sociological concepts has been compelling, it is not so much because their scientific quality is obvious. The sharpness of the distinction between the rational and emotional becomes ragged under closer scrutiny. The fact is that Weber captured in his formulations so much of the routines of a modern life which had been indelibly marked by Protestantism. They were the concepts of the rationalised world of politics, business and administration as it had developed by his time. The individual in a vocation, following the impersonal rationality of markets or bureaucracies, was already the characteristic personality of the age.

Yet for all its rationality, its transcendental unity, its personality forged in the pursuit of duty, Weber's individual was not untroubled. Still it was necessary to live in the world. Weber's own life's work was the product of toil and torment. The pursuit of duty in a chaotic world required effort, all the more so because human beings had a dual nature, endowed with reason but sharing qualities with animals. The formal opposition between reason and feeling was only an outward expression of conflicts which were deeply embedded in the Weberian world-view and to which we must turn before we can complete our picture of it.

3
The Nietzschean Challenge

The Protestant and Kantian definitions of reality provided Weber both with the cognitive framework for his view of life and with a motivational structure. The world was mastered by reason, but intellect was accompanied by duty and the need for salvation. The sharpness of the conflict between rationality and irrationality was not a mere intellectual problem, it was a dilemma he felt deeply.

A world-view which depended on the suppression of emotion set the terms on which opposition to it could be grounded. Wherever the requirements of the Kantian ethic proved too demanding, there was always the lure of a world-affirming irrationalism, the promise of free expression and emancipation from unnatural restraint.

With the growth of the natural sciences, acceptance of the world of physical reality could be extended to an acceptance of the physical individual. Given the clashes between religious and scientific views of nature, it was not incongruous to find a clash between religious and scientific views of human behaviour too.

The resolution of these dilemmas became a vital part of Weber's personal and intellectual life and the most important contributor to intensifying and highlighting the conflicts between reason and feeling was Friedrich Nietzsche (1844–1900). In this chapter we can identify the extent to which Weber's world-view and morality were challenged by Nietzsche and the way in which he accommodated the forces which that subverter of established order sought to release.

As we shall see in the next chapter, Weber felt impelled to re-establish a world-view which transcended Nietzsche by associating science with the deepest drives of the individual. The scientist as hero was to emerge from the encounter between Kant and Nietzsche in Weber's struggle to define his own identity.

1 The assault on Christianity

An indication of the strength of the forces threatening the Christian-Kantian world-view is suggested by the judgement of Max Weber's brother, Alfred, who considered Nietzsche to be the final confirmation that the old ideas of European culture had burnt themselves out. Himself a major sociologist of culture in his own right, Alfred Weber attempted a broad brush interpretation of the rise and trajectory of modern civilisation. He saw the First World War resulting from the collapse of European optimism which had been born in the eighteenth century and which had been carried through the generations by a humanistically educated stratum believing in progress. After 1880 the forces released by imperialism and capitalism engendered a blatant struggle between nations and a realism which rendered the old ideals useless.

Nietzsche was the genius of this change, the one who set himself the task of dispelling the veil of illusion spun by Christian humanitarianism. According to Alfred Weber everything associated with any attempt to construct a new attitude to life was under his shadow. 'The emergence of Nietzsche was the decisive factor: the honest confession that the fire in the old ideals in Europe had burnt out' (1950: 396).

Of course, nothing in history is completely new and Nietzsche had his forebears. Schopenhauer was one of his earliest influences. In the *The World as Will and Idea* (1883), first published in 1818, he made knowledge dependent on the will. Incorporating Hindu and Buddhist ideas he advocated the suspension of will as the way to overcome suffering and obtain the peace of nothingness. Schopenhauer rejected Christian doctrine while embracing the pacific morality of Christianity.

On the other hand, David Strauss' *Life of Jesus* (1846) and *The Old Faith and the New* (1873) rejected both much of traditional doctrine and advocated a more muscular and assertive ideal for daily life. It was Strauss' emphasis on the mythical character of Christian belief against which Max warned Alfred in a letter of 1886 acknowledging that it had originally made an 'extraordinary impression' (Marianne Weber, 1975: 101).

Strauss' views had a widespread impact compounded with the perturbation caused by the publication of Darwin's *Origin of the Species* (1859). This simultaneous contradiction of the biblical account of the Creation and the emphasis on the 'Struggle for

Existence' and natural selection served to reinforce opposition to the Christian emphasis on values of love and altruism. Indeed, opposition to conventional Christian belief and practice was a major and developing current of thought throughout the nineteenth century, most obviously elaborated as part of a wider system of thought in Marxism, but very widely simply associated with rationalism and a belief in the natural sciences as the only true source of knowledge.

Nietzsche's materialism was taken from the ideas of Friedrich Lange, whose *History of Materialism* had impressed him at the age of 20 and who had confined knowledge to Kant's phenomenal world leaving other worlds absolutely removed from human examination. Nietzsche then treated beliefs in other worlds as facts of life with corresponding effects, though whether those effects were good or bad was a question to which he never found a firm' answer. Asceticism and Puritanism might variously be necessary to school and discipline the individual for great deeds or, alternatively, they might involve the negation of the very joy of living. In fact Nietzsche embraced such contradictions because he could not believe in a world which corresponded to human ideas. The real world was full of contradiction, deception, pain and malice. Any other view was wishful thinking.

Nietzsche sought both to reject Christian belief and to transcend the arguments of its critics. He rejected all that went before him but climbed on their shoulders to see further. His early devotion to Schopenhauer was later replaced by a strenuous rejection of his nihilism, substituting for it the 'will to power'. He found David Strauss to be a narrow nationalist and rationalist. As for Darwin, 'I incline to the belief that Darwin's school is everywhere at fault. That will to power in which I perceive the ultimate reason and character of all change, explains why it is that selection is never in favour of the exceptions' (1910b: no. 429).

It was Nietzsche's purpose, as expressed in the sub-title to *The Will to Power*, to attempt the 'transvaluation of all values'. That attempt contained its own problems. For a start, Christian morality in its Kantian form had become an intellectualised doctrine, an extension of transcendental argument set out in philosophical treatises and proclaimed in lecture theatres. It was a literary form and medium of communication which Nietzsche rejected. Regarded as a genius by his early teachers, Nietzsche's first book, *The Birth of Tragedy*, published in 1872, was regarded as a monstrous breach of scholarly convention by some and thereafter he shunned the normal methods of presenting argument and scholarly authority. Where Kant had chosen cool reason, Nietzsche employed invective. He became the anti-intellectuals' intellectual.

He chose to emphasise his own individuality by aligning himself with everything which ran counter to the idealistic framework of morality. In writing about his first book fourteen years later Nietzsche said he 'laboured to express in Kantian and Schopenhauerian formulae strange and new valuations which ran fundamentally counter to [their] spirit' and he regretted he had been unable at that time to find the 'individual language for such individual contemplations' ('An Attempt at Self-Criticism', 1909b: 11). On his own account he had not yet been able to treat Christianity with more than a guarded and hostile silence but its intention was deeply anti-Christian and inimical to morality which he held to be a 'will to disown life'.

It was in that spirit that he lauded the Dionysian, the source of vitality, excitement, frenzy, the creative generative joy of existence, unshaped and unconstrained. That response to life he contrasted with the Apollonian, the quest for perfection, for the finished shape which constrains life within timeless forms, the reality of the dream as opposed to the reality of the drunken Dionysian.

No one was more aware than Nietzsche that the very framing of the opposition between the Dionysian and Apollonian was a mythical and metaphorical expression of the form/matter distinction which was fundamental to Kantian thinking and where Kant himself could clearly be identified with the Apollonian. In order to attack Kant, Nietzsche availed himself of the master's basic assumptions.

Hans Vaihinger, the great Kant scholar and author of the widely influential theory of fictions in human culture in *The Philosophy of 'As if'*, remarked that, although Nietzsche 'repeatedly and ferociously attacked Kant whom he quite misunderstood', yet the origin of his thought was to be found in the real spirit of the great idealist (1935: 342). Indeed, one might almost say that the frequency and ferocity of the attacks was an index of the enormity of the task to which Nietzsche felt himself to be committed, to oppose the greatest exponent of rationality in human knowledge and life and in that opposition not to succumb to the temptation of using the weapons which Kant had forged.

2 The sensual philosophy

It is easy to be misled by the sustained invective of Nietzsche into dismissing or simply not recognising the intellectual force of argument which provided the real penetrative power to enter the culture of his time. In spite of Vaihinger's view that he did not really understand Kant, one can say that Nietzsche was supremely capable of exposing those sensitive and unexamined presuppositions of Kantian doctrine, even if he was uninterested in engaging directly with his chosen antagonist in technical philosophical argument. To have done that would indeed to have been to concede the contest at the outset. He was not prepared to accept that truth could only be achieved by the methods of what had become both a professional discipline and a covert takeover of morality. At the same time Vaihinger and his successors were unwise to dismiss the potential challenge to the Kantian position and genuine possibilities for an alternative philosophical development contained in Nietzsche's diatribes.

Kant's doctrines represented for him the apotheosis of wishful thinking, a preposterous exaggeration of the importance of morality, a rejection of the senses, in which the philosopher had no confidence, in favour of concepts which were mere distortions, but to which he was attracted because he lacked the confidence in anything except the ability to think. Truth indeed was not something which could be achieved by philosophy, it depended on belief, faith that such and such was the case. There was no such thing as a unitary 'truth'. There was, however, the confidence gained from the strength and security of the senses. That was the foundation of what was called true. In fact truth lay in the feeling of power. We will find traces of these ideas in Weber's occasional reflections on the methods of a science of social reality.

Nietzsche located truth in the senses, not in formulae arrived at by pure reason. At the same time he acknowledged the necessity for logic and mathematics, originating in the human need to find identity, to classify and to be able to organise the world. That also was a will to power, rather than any will to truth. For in the real world identical cases did not exist. They were merely the artefacts of the need to impose regularity upon the chaos.

Similarly artefactual was that lynch-pin of Kantian epistemology, the idea of the subject. The belief that the unity and identity of the 'I' was a necessary presupposition for rational thought merely reflected the grammatical custom of providing a personal agent for every action. Any analysis of the human being had to begin with the body, and as far as the subject was concerned it was just as plausible to imagine a plurality of subjects struggling in the body as to imagine the single subject.

The doctrine of free will itself was based upon the fiction of the responsible subject, consciously intending a result, whereas all genuine action stemmed from the darkest depths of the body. But that doctrine also provided the point of anchorage for moral thought, for the imposition of conscience on the human being, which was nothing more than the requirements of the undifferentiated mass, the herd interested only in uniformity and collective safety rather than in the merits of the exceptional.

Kantian universality, the imposition of equal rights and duties was only a short step away from socialism, a particularly ridiculous creed absurdly optimistic about the perfectibility of man and blithely ignoring the facts of violence. Morality itself originated in violence, depended on restraint and was only to be justified if that restraint generated a self-discipline capable of great deeds.

Nietzsche's opposition to Kant spanned the whole breadth of his doctrines because he began by rejecting the premise from which Kant began, namely that there were mundane and spiritual worlds: 'To divide the world into a "real" and an "apparent" world, whether in the manner of Christianity or in the manner of Kant (which is after all that of the *cunning* Christian), is only a suggestion of *decadence* – a symptom of *declining* life' (1968a: 39).

Throughout his writing Nietzsche sought to deny any kind of independent existence to 'mind' or 'reason', 'thought', 'consciousness', 'soul', 'will' or 'truth'. These ideas were fictions, not references to another world and he regarded the speculations of idealist philosophers and the imagery of the Christian as being on a par with each other as sources of error. It was always the case that the other world was conceived as a criticism of this world and hence was a symptom of a failure to come to terms with living. Nietzsche sought to overcome the dualism of this world-view and replace it with a vision of a unified, life-affirming, powerful man. For him only one man fully measured up to these requirements:

> What he aspired to was *totality*; he strove against the separation of reason, sensuality, feeling, will (– preached in the most horrible scholasticism by Kant, the antipodes of Goethe); he disciplined himself to a whole, he *created* himself. . . . Goethe conceived of a strong, highly cultured human being, skilled in all physical accomplishments, who, keeping himself in check and having reverence for himself, dares to allow himself the whole compass and wealth of naturalness, who is strong enough for this freedom; a man of tolerance, not out of weakness, but out of strength, because he knows how to employ to his advantage what would destroy an average nature; a man to whom nothing is forbidden, except it be *weakness*, whether that weakness be called vice or virtue (1968a: 102–3).

To his image of this man, Nietzsche was prepared to give the name which he regarded as sacred – Dionysus – and he regarded the two giant figures as utter antitheses and sought to represent the greatest figure of German literature as wholly on his side.

As a personification of the contrasts Nietzsche was trying to draw and the conflicts he sought to stimulate, the Kant-Goethe dichotomy was a highly effective rhetorical device. It did violence to the actual relations of the two men since Goethe respected the power of Kant's thought, even if temperamentally, as the poet, he sought to join together what the philosopher's distinctions severed.

Nietzsche, however, wished to associate the poet with a unitary vision of the world, which did not merely reconcile spirit and nature, but refused to recognise the duality at all. But what he was effectively doing was to shift the balance of attention in the German cultural tradition of the nineteenth century over in favour of romantic, as opposed to ascetic, individualism (cf. Gerber, 1954: 104–12).

As we shall see in the next chapter, Weber too drew inspiration from Goethe, but in order to legitimate his own peculiar brand of heroic intellectualism, pursuing science in a demystified world.

3 The influence of Nietzsche on German culture

Although his chosen antagonist was Kant, it was not on academic philosophy that Nietzsche's influence was primarily felt. The phenomenological philosopher of value, Max Scheler, writing about the state of German philosophy in 1922, asserted that the only professional philosopher on whom Nietzsche had exercised specific influence was Hans Vaihinger, with his doctrine of the necessary place of fictions in human thought and action (1973: 297). Scheler went on to say that he considered Vaihinger's work to be the biggest blunder in German philosophy for decades. He aligned himself with the views of the neo-Kantian, Wilhelm Windelband, in this respect.

This reaction was not surprising in that Kant's philosophy dominated university teaching and the careers of academics were made out of expounding and developing his ideas. The neo-Kantian school, whose other main representative was the close friend of Weber, Heinrich Rickert, was preoccupied with establishing the inner logic and vital significance for social reality of the timeless values implicated in Kant's account of practical reason. In the context of the unrest of the time, of the challenges to belief and authority, the neo-Kantians sought to anchor belief in painstaking elaboration of the necessity for a permanent order of values.

Nietzsche would not have been discouraged by the professional response. His theory predicted it and he would have been dismayed had it been otherwise. His purpose was to destroy the very preparedness to listen to philosophical argument. It was not what happened in the lecture theatre, but what was agitating the coffee rooms outside, which inspired his concern. In that respect there was no denying his influence.

The eminent professor of philosophy at Berlin, Friedrich Paulsen, wrote a monumental account of *The German Universities and University Study* in which he included a large section on the morals of students. They constituted to his mind a privileged group. 'Whoever devotes himself to university study expects to enter the ruling class of society' (1906: 265). However, that privilege involved duties, which were themselves only learned through the assumption of freedom. But the correlate of freedom was responsibility. Paulsen's account represented the straightforward application of Kantian doctrine to the moral education of the student, a theory of the development of personality through the devotion of the individual to duty, freely chosen self-control. But there were siren voices against which he warned these aspirants to the ruling class:

> Who will not think of Nietzsche, the *Unzeitgemässe* ['out of season'], who felt the call to brush away the mould of German educational Philistinism and the rubbish of academic life . . . ? And following in his wake we see the whole swarm of false geniuses, who, without a spark of the master's genius, imitate his unrestraint, hoping to enter with him into the temple of immortality' (Paulsen, 1906: 269–70).

Paulsen lamented the fact that a 'mania for peculiar and extravagant ideas is manifest in many quarters' (ibid.: 414) and that there was widespread distrust of professional philosophy.

A few years after Paulsen's account, Windelband gave a series of lectures on the place of philosophy in nineteenth-century German culture and felt bound to give Nietzsche his due, albeit as a poet, as the very embodiment of the struggle of the individual against the forces of mass living in the modern world. It was not for nothing that his vaunted 'transvaluation of all values' (*Umwertung aller Werte*) had become the slogan of the age. It was the expression of a desperate cry for help on the part of the individual in a world in which all the old values had gone into flux (1909: 116–20).

In his widely used textbook on the history of philosophy, Windelband also concluded that the beginning and end of the road along which nineteenth-century philosophy had journeyed was marked by Kant's 'autonomy of reason' and Nietzsche's 'free-will of the superman'. The latter direction involved the rejection of philosophy altogether and for Windelband the situation could only be saved by turning to the theory of values, derived through reason and universally valid (1907: 564). But Nietzsche represented the most formidable possible opponent, a poet with the objective of killing philosophy and thus infusing German culture with an irrationality of mass appeal.

The result of the breadth of Nietzsche's appeal was that virtually no major literary contributor to the culture of the time was uninfluenced by him. A spate of writing about the decadence of

European civilisation and its impending doom took its inspiration from Nietzsche. Oswald Spengler's *Der Untergang des Abendlandes* (*Decline of the West*, 1926), published in two volumes in 1918, 1923, was the most prominent of these with its account of the relativity of cultures and the necessary decay to which they were all subject.

So comprehensive was the scope of Nietzsche's critique of his time that scarcely any new creative moment could occur without it either being inspired by, depicting, or reacting against the Nietzschean influence. It was expressed in themes such as decadence and vitality, mass culture and elitism, power and impotence, romanticism, individualism. Writers of immense stature like Thomas Mann, Hermann Hesse and Franz Kafka, consciously addressed Nietzschean themes. Richard Strauss and Gustav Mahler wrote music to Nietzschean texts. Nietzsche's project was to change the character of the age. The magnitude of such a project was matched only by the achievement of becoming the trademark of the time.

4 The Weber–Nietzsche controversy of 1964

It was not necessary for Weber to engage directly with Nietzsche, for his thought, like Kant's, was part of the organising framework of ideas of the time, the medium, however defective, through which Weber sought to find the solutions for the specific problems he set himself. The direct reference to Nietzsche is therefore rarer than the unacknowledged use of an idea and this makes any assessment of dependence a complex matter. That is one barrier to coming to an estimation of the Nietzschean influence on Weber.

Another and more serious barrier has been the use of Nietzsche by a cultural movement which expressed the breakdown of one world order and culminated in the most inhuman product of Western civilisation in the form of Nazism. Not surprisingly, this has produced at least an embarrassment in acknowledging his influence at all.

Most serious of all as an obstacle to recognising the importance of Nietzsche in the formation of Weber's thought was the fact that in the period when the Federal Republic was established after 1945 and when the connecting links with classical sociology and political science were forged afresh, Max Weber was regarded in some sense as the major representative of the abiding German commitment to democratic values. The widespread propagation of his sociological thought in the English-speaking world already made him an acceptable representative of the new de-nazified Germany and there was the additional advantage that he was systematically hostile to Marxism.

It is fair to say that the incisive introduction the German President Theodor Heuss wrote for the new edition of Weber's political writings in 1958 made very clear allusion to the Nietzschean thrust: 'He understood early on that it was his unpleasant task to tear down the "veil of illusions" behind which the Germans in his view had begun to feel all too comfortable, in the way perhaps the late bourgeoisie had forgotten 1848 and 1862 and cultivated a casual "will to impotence"' (PS: xxx).

But it was not until 1964 that the storm broke, as recognition spread outside the German-speaking world that power and domination rather than democracy were the pivotal ideas in Weber's account of social structure. The Heidelberg German Sociological Congress devoted its proceedings to a commemoration of Max Weber's centenary. Raymond Aron gave an address on 'Max Weber and Power-Politics' which stated clearly that Weber's commitments were to the power of the nation-state and that 'the Darwinian–Nietzschean view of the world constitutes a framework within which Weber's conception of *Machtpolitik* is integrated' (Stammer, 1971: 94). Aron saw Weber slipping into a nihilism which made it impossible to apply any kind of moral judgement to whatever means a nation sought to employ in the struggle for power.

Aron was backed up by Wolfgang Mommsen, while other contributors raised the temperature of discussion in other ways. Jürgen Habermas remarked incidentally that it was not possible to ignore the fact that Weber's militant liberalism was the forerunner of the ideas of Carl Schmitt, the leading Nazi political theorist (ibid.: 66). Herbert Marcuse offered a critique of Weber's conception of rationality, where science was liberated from moral judgement and value-free economics was subordinated to imperial power-politics (ibid.: 133–51).

The Congress at Heidelberg was a turning-point in the estimation of Max Weber and ever since arguments about his work have needed to take account of the fact that it has acquired symbolic value in some of the major ideological cleavages of our time. This makes it all the more necessary to separate reality from stereotype; to be able, for instance, to recognise the possibility that Nietzsche was both extraordinarily brilliant and at the same time more than a little pernicious, that Weber could have been influenced by Nietzsche in vital respects without becoming his follower, and that Weber might have been a fervent nationalist without subscribing to, or indeed contributing in any way, to the holocaust which was to come.

Once Weber was recognised rightly as bearing a vital relationship to the ideological conflicts of the nineteenth and twentieth centuries, it became all too tempting to apply ideological tags to his work rather than to probe further into the foundations of his thought. In the same year as the Heidelberg Congress (1964) the first substantial estimation of the relation of Weber and Nietzsche was written by Eugène Fleischmann. He found the influence of Nietzsche on Weber to be overwhelming.

Fleischmann argued that Marianne had been very successful in propagating a piously distorted view of her late husband and that the internal evidence of Weber's writing gave quite another picture. He listed a number of basic features in Weber's thought which were part of the Nietzschean framework; the multiplicity of values, the impossibility of making a rational choice between them, the emphasis on power and structures of domination, the rejection of happiness as an appropriate goal for the human being and relentless intellectual integrity and asceticism.

So emphatic was Fleischmann that Weber was completely under the spell of his iconoclastic predecessor that Wolfgang Mommsen, whose still unsurpassed study of Max Weber's political outlook and involvement had given full weight to Weber's German nationalism and commitment to power politics, felt bound to enter a cautionary note. He pointed out that Weber's leader was not the embodiment of the idea of the superman ruling for the sake of his own aristocratic qualities and Weber's charismatic leader was filled with a sense of responsibility for the people he led rather than with contempt for the herd (Mommsen, 1974: 130 ff.).

The point was that Fleischmann exaggerated Weber's leanings to Nietzsche by setting up an artificial choice between Nietzsche and Marx and overstating Weber's hostility to Marx. These points are subtle but important. In fact the qualities of Weber's relations with Marx and Nietzsche were quite different in kind. The struggle in Weber's soul was not betwen socialism and capitalism, but between two kinds of individualism. 'I am a member of the bourgeois class, and feel myself to be so and have been brought up in its views and ideals' (PS: 20). That was the way Weber expressed his own outlook in the inaugural lecture he gave in 1895. He could do battle with Marx with an easy conscience. Far more troublesome were the inner conflicts engendered by strife within the bourgeoisie.

5   Nietzschean themes and attitudes in Weber

As soon as one recognises the roots of the conflict of ideas in Weber's own outlook, then one can recognise that some of the themes attributed to Nietzsche's influence by Fleischmann are more properly identified with Kantian individualism. Try as he might self-consciously to negate Kant, Nietzsche was locked in a battle for the bourgeois conscience of Germany. Like Kant he placed all his faith in the individual and like him he advocated a rigour and a discipline for higher things which made the quest for happiness something menial. Max Scheler has pointed out that while Kant and Nietzsche differed on the question of the worth of the individual (for Kant there could be no question of persons being of intrinsically different worths) yet they both saw individuals as the source of values and as solely and separately responsible for their own actions (1966: 506).

When, therefore, in his inaugural lecture Weber spoke of the solemn duty to undertake the political education of the nation and of the fact that we were not on this earth to create human happiness, he was evoking both Kantian and Nietzschean echoes in the bourgeois soul. On one thing the three men agreed: there were stern tasks which a man (always male) could not shirk. Whether rooted in transcendental reason or in the struggle for life of the human organism, whether in idealism or materialism, Weber's lecture could take for granted that the individual was the source of action in the world.

Leaving that aside, there is no doubt that the inaugural lecture was a blatant piece of Nietzschean rhetoric. Economic policy for the German state had to be a national policy designed to secure national greatness in the everlasting conflict with other nations. For that reason, 'we are not going to endow our descendants with peace and human happiness, but with the eternal struggle for the maintenance and upgrading of our national stock' (PS: 14).

The rhetorical tone and the emphatic affirmation of the relationship between national power and self-assertion were thoroughly Nietzschean, but Weber distanced himself from the glorification of the superman as hero and leader. Both here and in subsequent political writing he regarded this as irrational dreaming, ill-adapted to the needs of the time. Leadership would come from a class as a whole and modern economic conditions made it essential for the bourgeoisie to take over this role. The danger for the German nation lay not in a threat from the masses but in the political ignorance and lack of responsibility of the bourgeoisie.

Nietzsche attracted attention and dictated modes of thought much more than he provided doctrine. When Weber rejected any idea that a closed system of concepts could possibly contain within it the multiplicity of problems which were raised within human culture, one is instantly reminded of Nietzsche's maxim: 'I reject all systematizers and avoid them. The will to system is a lack of integrity' (1968a: 26). The association of ideas is made even stronger by the fact that in the same breath Weber spurned 'a Chinese ossification of intellectual life' (Meth: 84), and for Nietzsche China represented the dead hand of all-embracing moral regulation. Not for nothing did he call Kant the Chinaman of Königsberg.

Weber's explicit rejection of Nietzsche at crucial points is of great importance, but equally important is his acceptance of the thematics of Nietzsche's work. Just as he rejected the idea of the superman but acknowledged the importance of power and struggle, so he explicitly rejected Nietzsche's theory of resentment as the source of religious ethics (Essays: 270). At the same time he paid it the unusual compliment for him of a lengthy consideration, but he did this by treating substantially the same set of topics as Nietzsche had made central to his critique of Christianity as definitive for the problem of religion in society. In singling out Nietzsche for critical attention, he showed how he was dependent on him for identifying the three major variables in his treatment of religion: meaning, salvation, and ascetic rationalism.

But there was something more than thematics which Weber imbibed from Nietzsche. Alongside power and ascetic rationalism as central themes, accompanying the rhetorical style which Weber assumed in his inaugural lecture and later when he addressed the Munich students at the end of his life, there was also an attitude, a rigorous detachment, a willingness to call a plague on all your houses, a refusal to acknowledge any authority save his own, and a commitment to an ultimate value, truth, which he acknowledged at the same time to be irrational. It was an attitude expressed in his doctrine of value-freedom (more precisely freedom from value judgements) and his account of the demystification of the world.

Weber spurned all the self-styled prophets for reasons we shall consider shortly, but he did not hesitate to use much of the language and many of the rhetorical tricks of the master of them all. In his writing on the German state system, in which Weber advocated a democratic electoral system under strong and responsible political leadership, he had no scruples about using the Nietzschean term *Herrenvolk*, master race, although he did it in the service of political ideals quite opposed to the mass irrationalism of the false prophets: 'Only a politically mature race is a 'master race', and that means one which keeps control of the administration of its affairs and has the decisive say in the selection of its leaders through elected representatives. Only master races have the vocation of putting a spoke in the wheel of world history' (PS: 430–1).

In a recent study of Weber and Nietzsche's approach to the problems of political leadership, Robert Eden has drawn attention to the risk that Weber ran in employing Nietzschean terminology in the service of democratic argument. He might thereby become an effective populariser for the most vehement anti-democrat (1983: 201). But it ought to be added that there was no risk of this for the German readership Weber was addressing in his own time. For them Nietzsche was already entirely known and Weber's intervention was all the more powerful because of the very explicit limits he placed upon Nietzschean irrationalism. At the end he was still committed to a Kantian ethic of duty and intellectual integrity, and it was on that basis that his notion of responsible leadership was erected.

The problem has been caused by the dissemination of Weber's work in the English-speaking world, which he was not addressing, and which, on discovering his affinities with Nietzsche, has found profound difficulty in recognising that Weber's relations with him were ones of intimate knowledge and profound detachment. Two World Wars have resulted in Nietzsche being ignored or suppressed, sometimes bowdlerised, but very rarely addressed in the way that Weber did. Our understanding of Weber has been jeopardised as a result.

4
The Scientist in Search of Salvation

This chapter completes an account of the origins of Weber's world-view and thus the premises of his social theory. It will depict Weber's resolution of the conflicts which were contained within the Protestant Kantian ideal framework and which Nietzsche had sought to magnify to the point of destroying traditional morality.

I contend that Weber achieved an active and on-going resolution of conflicts by adapting ideas of personality from an exemplary figure for Germans, Goethe, who had long represented the ideal of a perfect blend of culture and experience.

To do this Weber had to treat rationality as a matter of experience, a fact of life, and a ruling passion simultaneously. Kant's transcendental reason was brought to earth as Nietzsche demanded, but became the creative drive of the intellectual seeking to make sense of the world.

Treating rationality as a fact of life meant the wholesale importation of the Kantian conceptual framework into accounts of human actions and at the same time as irrational commitment to rationality as the hallmark of the intellectual personality.

In this way, a cognitive frame of reference and a motivational structure were established which were appropriate for a scientist of social facts. Weber's social theory was thus to become an authentic expression of the rationalisation process he depicted and sought to understand. It was equally an exercise in self-understanding.

We can go further than this, and seek to identify the secret of the success of Weber's work. It was because of the reflexive use of the idea of rationality, at one moment property of the subject, at another the object of scrutiny, the switch between Kantian and Nietzschean modes of analysis, that he was able to capture the dynamics of Western culture.

The switching process, from construction of concepts to empirical assessment of their realisation, corresponds to the ceaseless transformation of social life which has characterised Western culture and of which Weber as a social scientist was so much a representative.

Rather than allow himself to be caught in a sterile destructive conflict between Kant and Nietzsche, between reason and life forces, Weber drew on the creative synthesis of Goethe. But such was the process of rationalisation that the heroic personality to which Weber aspired was no longer the poet but the scientist.

It was a tragic twist in human development, for the scientist was impelled to search for the basis of meaning in life and yet was bound to find no final resting point. The quest for meaning became an endless task, compulsive activity without an ultimate end.

The contention of this chapter is that we can identify the creative moments in Weber's beliefs and motivational structure and that we can see how these are imported into his intellectual output. It is more usual to identify the sources of failure than of success. This has already been done by others for Weber. It makes it more important now to understand the achievement.

1 Understanding Weber's creativity

We are fortunate in having numerous memoirs and reminiscences of Weber, many of which have now been published, although until the voluminous papers and letters by him have been fully evaluated we still have to rely on Marianne as the main biographical account. There have also been attempts to provide a deeper analysis of Weber's personality, the most well-known being those of a Freudian kind by Gerth and Mills (Essays: 28–31) and by Mitzman (1970).

The burden of these accounts has largely been to seek an explanation for the period of collapse and exhaustion which afflicted Weber especially between 1897 and 1903. Both place great emphasis on the contrasting natures and demands of Weber's parents and on the oedipal situation in 1897 when he ordered his father out of his house in order to give his mother peace and quiet and how in quick succession there followed his father's death and his own collapse. For much of his life thereafter he was to suffer from episodes of depression followed often by intense activity.

There can be little doubt that Weber's condition has a Freudian textbook quality about it, but concentration on the illness does tend to draw attention away from the persistent traits of character and the abiding beliefs which provided the impetus for all that Weber achieved when he was active. If his illness was attributable to the strain imposed on him by his relations with his parents and their contradictory demands, it was equally the case that his driving ambition, intense desire for autonomy and integrity, and his concern for great causes were also greatly influenced by them. For us, evaluating his work, the sources of activity must be of prime interest even if they carried with them dangers which were not confined in their impact to Weber.

Weber's contemporaries were in no doubt that his personality as a whole was formed out of major cultural movements of his time. One of them, the feminist Gertrud Bäumer, identified three essential traits constituting the basis of Weber's personality. They were: first, the membership of a specific German cultural stratum, namely the educated Protestant bourgeoisie; second, the idea of national power as a right-thinking man of the 1870s would have conceived it; third, philosophical idealism on the basis of Kant's theory of knowledge (König and Winckelmann, 1963: 116).

Bäumer's evaluation of the significance of Protestantism for Weber's personality is important, for she identified something more than simply a restrictive morality. It was far more a question of structuring and directing the 'demonics' of a passionate and nervous disposition. At bottom a deeply serious sense of moral obligation provided the foundation for Weber's personality. We have seen how significant the idea of duty was in the thought of Kant and Channing. It was certainly never far from his thoughts either.

For Weber, work was demanding to the extent that meeting its requirements was often a matter of heroic determination. Marianne recounts the following example: 'One day when Weber was asked what his scholarship meant to him, he replied: "I want to see how much I can stand"' (1975: 678). The same kind of heroics were expressed in his lecture 'Science as a Vocation'; 'Ladies and gentlemen. In the field of science only he who is devoted *solely* to the work at hand has "personality". And this holds not only for the field of science; we know of no great artist who has ever done anything but serve his work and only his work' (Essays: 137).

The deep relations between the man, the work and the message were on one occasion vividly exemplified in a letter Weber wrote to Rickert saying, 'I am working – amidst horrible torments, to be sure', and then promising to send him an essay about 'Protestant asceticism as the foundation of modern vocational civilisation' (Marianne Weber, 1975: 356). The sacred call of duty for Weber had been anchored for modern man in the notion of a vocation, of a consuming commitment to work, and he felt himself to be as much bound by its requirements as any follower of a Puritanical sect.

Weber exemplified in the purest form the logic of the ascetic personality believing in the supernatural God. He was unwilling to trust any of those feelings which brought him close to the faith of other people and could only seek God in the closed-off fastnesses of his own conscience. The strictest requirements of integrity and autonomy cut him off from any overt religious observance or adherence to sect or church. His asceticism, rooted in his Christian background, cut him off from religious feeling, left him religiously 'unmusical', but at the same time, as with Kant, the voice of duty and the power of God could not be dissociated from each other.

Honigsheim recounted one occasion when he felt that Weber let slip some part of the veil covering his deepest motivation when they were discussing the philosopher and biologist Hans Driesch and his proof for the existence of God. Weber appeared to mock Driesch's proof but immediately looked seriously at his younger companion and said: 'In all truth that doesn't mean that it is not very vital to me to seek to stand in the proper relation with the Lord' (König and Winckelmann, 1963: 270). Honigsheim felt that one could detect here the key to the understanding of the innermost parts of the man: 'the Kantian imperative has taken on a singular form of religiously based autonomism in this case' (ibid.). In his view there was no other person apart from Martin Luther himself, for whom these famous words were a more apt expression of his basic attitude: 'Here I stand, I can do no other, so help me God.'

Yet Weber was renowned for the passion with which he took up causes, the force with which he argued his case, and the vigour with which he engaged in contests. That may appear paradoxical from the point of view of logic, but emotionally there is an evident relationship between self-denial and duty, on the one hand, and passionate self-assertion, on the other. As much as his stern and ascetic sense of duty, the power and assertiveness of his personality impressed themselves on his contemporaries. More than one saw the qualities of political leadership there.

Ernst Troeltsch considered him at heart to be a politician with a store of leadership qualities which his nation did not know how to use (ibid.: 46). Theodor Heuss, who himself became President of the Republic of Germany, was of the same opinion, and considered Weber to have a nature which was born to rule, but which was avoided and feared by people of mediocrity (ibid.: 72). Heuss, in referring to Weber's personality, also spoke of the 'demonics of his soul' (ibid.), and in so doing evoked a theme in Weber's own writing.

2   Goethe's demon

The idea of the demon has a strategic place in Weber's thoughts. But it has a peculiar resonance in German culture, only adequately understood by reference to Goethe. To the Anglo-Saxon it might appear a random literary reference, aligning Weber with Nietzschean forces. That would be a profound misapprehension. Weber was alluding to a whole theory with vital relations to education and to the attempt in German culture to synthesise rationality and experience in the rounded personality.

Georg Simmel dedicated to Marianne Weber a study of Goethe, which was first published in 1913, in which he gave a particularly pointed description of the polarity involved in the individualism of the nineteenth century. On the one hand, there was that way of thinking which viewed individuals as equal units, formally separate and free in principle. On the other, there was the view that each unit possessed unique qualities, identifying and unrepeatable characteristics (1923: 142–6).

The two types of individualism Simmel called the formal and the qualitative, and whereas in the eighteenth century the former had been predominant, in the latter part of the century the qualitative, or romantic, version gathered strength. On Simmel's account Goethe combined an emphasis on the living creativity of each individual with a recognition of the universality of the metaphysical structures through which people were bonded with each other.

However much Nietzsche called on Goethe's name, it was not to advocate such a synthesis, but to seek to enlist him in support of radical opposition to any metaphysical ordering of human life. Weber on the contrary called on Goethe's demon in order to bridge the polarity of the two kinds of personality theory. He was distancing himself from Nietzsche by reasserting the synthetic nature of Goethe's personality theory and by making rationality itself a matter of fact and experience. The nature of the bridge Weber was attempting to build may be understood better if we turn to Goethe's idea of the demon. It received its most brilliant formulation in a set of poems, the Primeval Orphic Sayings, one of which was called simply *Dämon*.

In the same year as the poem was first published, 1820, Goethe wrote a short commentary on it to bring its meaning out more explicitly. The very title needed some explanation, he said: '"Demon" refers here to that necessary and limited individuality of the person which is directly expressed at birth, the characteristic features which distinguish one from another however great the similarities might be' (1978: 403).

If one pursues Goethe's references to the demonic and follows their contexts it becomes clear that he is attempting to evoke a range of human experience which is both outside and prior to consciousness. The sources of creativity, the roots of personal power, the elements of attraction between people, are emphasised again and again by Goethe as primitive, the forces which are held in bound by reason, but without which reason has no content or strength.

Goethe summoned up the demonic and it served to fire generations of aspiring geniuses, including Nietzsche who tried above all to assume the mantle of his great idol. But that could only be done by neglecting the emphatic way in which Goethe insisted that the demonic was a force which required channelling and which, unchecked by reason, could be destructive. Unconscious strivings had to be converted into clear purposes, reason had to negotiate between the inner necessities and chance events.

In fact, says Stefan Zweig, in a book dedicated to Sigmund Freud, the contrast between Goethe and Nietzsche permits an almost mathematically precise specification of the polarity between two types of response to the demon, which penetrates every aspect of their life and work. They are at opposite poles in respect of personal and family relations, in secure respect in the community, in living habits, in the ability to learn through experience and to shape life in the round. 'Goethe's method is in that respect completely capitalistic: every year he saves a measured portion of experience as spiritual; profit, which he records at the end of the year systematically in his diaries and annals like a meticulous merchant. His life bears interest as the field bears fruit' (1925: 17).

Goethe summoned up the demonic only to demonstrate his mastery in controlling the unconscious forces. Surrounded by family and friends, honoured by the state, enjoying the fruits of fame, he also inspired generations to believe that the poetic imagination could be combined with the bourgeois existence, that power could be combined with rationality, that the nation could draw on the deep recesses of the personality. He revelled in pinpointing the polarities of the human condition and at the same time bridging them.

> I'd like to unify myself,
> But I seem to be always two;
> In everything I live to do
> One of me's here, one there,
> The first one praying hard for rest,
> The other all astrain!
> Yet there's good council for a truce
> Between the warring twain'
> After the joy of knowledge
> To the joy of deeds amain!'
>
> *Gentle Reminders* (1933: 100)

3   Libido and rationality: bridging the dualism

Weber would have been entirely familiar with the nuances of the idea of the demon both with Goethe's multifaceted view of individuality and with the Nietzschean emphasis on vitality and lifeforce. He also engaged directly with its interpretation in the cultural unrest of his time. When Marianne used the term 'demonic', it was frequently a reference to sexuality and the problems Weber had in acknowledging and containing it.

It was the connection between the demon and sexuality which excited Weber's contemporaries to the extent that one of them, Otto Gross, a preacher of sexual liberation influenced by Nietzsche and Freud, planned a magazine to be called *Daimon* for the psychoanalytic interpretation of culture (Green, 1974: 70). Both the Webers took a keen interest in problems of the relations between the sexes and were much involved in the arguments about the morality of marriage and the liberation of women which were in part associated with the early impact of Freud's theories. They both supported the political and domestic emancipation of women, but regarded the association of this with any kind of sexual liberalism as superficial and misguided.

It is particularly revealing that Marianne Weber, writing about the controversies about sexual morality in which she and her husband were involved, made the most explicit references to notions of duty and responsibility. 'Absolute' ideals had to be defended constantly in the sphere of sexual morality, 'for it was in this area that "law" and "duty" demanded the most perceptible sacrifices' (1975: 370–1).

Max Weber was also clear that the discussion of Freud's theories of sexual hygiene had to take place within the context of ethical theory. A so-called Freudian ethic could only offer shabby calculations about 'costs' to health, which are not really ethical considerations at all.

But self-discipline was not without cost. Marianne attributed to Max's mother the responsibility for having 'implanted in him indestructible inhibitions against a surrender to his drives' (ibid.: 91). By intellect and will-power, according to his wife, Max 'restrained a demonic passionateness which now and then burst out with a destructive blaze' (ibid.: 170).

According to Arthur Mitzman, the costs of adherence to Christian and Kantian ethics were even greater than Max was prepared to admit to Marianne. He reports the testimony of Eduard Baumgarten, relative and friend of the Webers, that their marriage was never consummated and that Weber himself was terrified by an inability to control sexual impulses. In spite of this, for a period of several years, he did form a sexual relationship outside marriage of which Marianne knew nothing and in the course of this softened some of his deep-rooted hostility to things sensual (Mitzman, 1970: Ch. 9).

Mitzman is of the view that in the later period of his life, after 1910, Weber's new experiences 'threw increasingly into question that ethic of transcendence, self-renunciation, and mastery which had for over a century served Europe as the moral backbone of bourgeois society and which had earlier been the core of his personality and work' (ibid.: 296).

That judgement does, however, require some qualification. Even if the Kantian *ethic* was challenged, the broader *ethos* of intellectual asceticism was unimpaired. There is no indication after 1910 of any decline in Weber's creativity, although there are indications of a shift in themes which do take account of new experience. The point with Goethe's demon was precisely that it expressed the possibility to develop an *intellectual passion* through experience. That self-discipline on which Weber set so much emphasis was not confined to the sexual sphere, and there is a strong case for saying that sexuality is marginal to explaining Weber's creative work. Goethe's demon gave equal possibility to a variety of drives and capacities to become the dominating passion in a person's life. In Weber's case it was the intellect as such.

One of the most famous of all Weber's utterances involves a reference to the demon in the context of defining the tasks of the scientist. At the very end of 'Science as a Vocation', he offers a stark choice to the budding academic: either return to the arms of the old churches or face up to the duty of intellectual integrity. There was no room for the prophet in the lecture theatre and nothing was gained by yearning for one to come. He concluded: 'We shall set to work and meet the "demands of the day", in human relations as well as in our vocation. This, however, is plain and simple, if each finds and obeys the demon who holds the fibres of his very life' (Essays: 156).

Weber's evocation of Goethe's idea of the demon is the most vivid illustration of the magnitude of his own task. Goethe took almost divine proportions for generations of Germans, revered from all sides, for he in particular had combined the opposites in the religious and secular sides of German culture and transformed them into a continuous creative production. We have seen how around those opposing sides not only debates, but whole styles of life were crystallised and how they generated the stock of concepts within which Weber formed his *Weltanschauung*. The Protestant/ Kantian frame was one in which the intellectual and the moral merged with each other to make a highly charged set of presuppositions. This is obvious from just listing the most obvious pairs of ideas:

this world	other world
human	divine
sensual	ideal
chaos	order
individual	universal
meaningless	meaningful
unconscious	conscious
emotional	intellectual
mortal	immortal
sinful	moral
condemned	saved
irrational	rational

Nietzsche sought to remove the moral moment altogether and Weber was unwilling to follow him that far. Instead, like Nietzsche but with more authenticity and justification, he evoked the spirit of Goethe and sought to maintain each side of the polarities, not by way of some feeble juxtaposition, but through creative activity which could result in the one intensifying the value of the other: the rational could serve the irrational, the unconscious could activate the conscious, the individual could become universal. The 'joy of deeds' which Weber experienced was the creation of new products of knowledge.

4 The search for salvation

The resolution of the dualisms of the human condition which inner-worldly asceticism encouraged was the harnessing of the deeper needs and urges of the human being for higher purposes, and ultimately for those purposes to be regarded themselves as the deepest needs. The result was an intellectualisation of the idea of need, on the one hand, and, on the other, the demonisation of intellect.

On one occasion (a letter of 15 July 1909), Weber wrote, 'My decisive inner requirement is "intellectual honesty": I say what is'

(Mommsen, 1984: 43). When Weber speaks of human need, then the spiritual is often associated with it. Weber speaks of 'ideal needs', a formula close to another famous effort by him to bridge the material and ideal divide when in 1915 he wrote about the idea of salvation, 'Not ideas, but material and ideal interests, directly govern men's conduct' (Essays: 280).

The reason intellectuals sought to develop ideas of salvation in the context of a general world picture was their interest in finding a moral meaning to human suffering on the basis of an inner need to understand the world. 'The intellectual seeks in various ways, the casuistry of which extends into infinity, to endow his life with a pervasive meaning, and thus to find unity with himself, with his fellow men and with the cosmos. It is the intellectual who conceives of the "world" as a problem of meaning' (E&S I: 506). This quest of the intellectual was, said Weber, the core of genuine religious rationalism, although the results of this 'metaphysical need for a meaningful cosmos' varied widely (Essays: 281).

It is impossible to exaggerate the significance of the association for Weber between the needs of intellectuals, the search for meaning in life and the nature of religion. It is profoundly important for the development of a conception of sociology seen as a discipline which has as a central aim the interpretation of the meaning of social action. The idea of meaning, which Weber elaborates for his sociology, was generated by his wrestling with the problem of the relations between rationality and irrationality in the formation of methods and concepts and by his concern to develop a notion of meaning which was compatible with scientific requirements.

Weber's resolution of these intellectual problems paralleled and in large part represented the highly sublimated outcome of his own engagement with the cultural, religious and sexual conflicts of his own and his contemporaries' lives. His general account of religion, in particular, must be seen as a middle ground between personal experience and scientific ratiocination in which we can identify his own personal resolution of those conflicts. Relating the quest for meaning to the deepest needs of the intellectual was in fact a far more complex solution to the conflict between Nietzsche and Kant than might at first seem to be the case.

We have now reached the point of being able to address the fundamental positions which underlay both Weber's response to living and the foundation of his social theory. For him 'meaning in life' and 'meaning' as a sociological and methodological concept were ultimately analogous. It is worth stating this in the simplest possible terms at this stage before any more precise analysis.

We understand human beings when we can identify the feelings and purposes which underlie their actions, that is the same as grasping the meaning of action and in doing so we both explain and understand. Those feelings and purposes might need to be pursued in far-reaching ramifications, taking in frameworks of meaning which underpinned whole economic and religious systems, but the only ultimate bearers of meaning were human individuals. Ideal meaning, the ideas which human beings produced, even in their purest form as logic and mathematics, only operated in and through the individual. The greatest intellectual systems, the achievements of a Calvin or a Kant, at the end of the day are only made real through the experience and suffering of countless individuals.

The quest for meaning was itself a basic human need, involved in trying to relate the world to human purpose and in trying to understand other people. But in that sense it was not specifically an intellectual's quest. At several points Weber alludes to the position of the simple peasant, intimately tied to natural processes, as far as engaging the very muscles of the body in an immediate relation with the forces of nature through work. He contrasts this with the position of the urban tradesmen who, torn from their ties with nature, working in a rationalised environment, are led to speculate on the 'meaning' of existence because it has indeed become a problem. This is a rationalistic question which always tends to religious speculation (E&S II: 1178–9).

In this context Weber uses the term *Entfremdung*, 'alienation', to designate the position of those urban groups to mean precisely the separation of daily life from a unity with nature. Peasants have a form of religiosity which corresponds to their bonds with nature, a reliance on spirits who rule over the natural forces and can be summoned through magic to assist with their lives. Agricultural strata consequently do not understand 'sin', nor do they seek salvation for they do not see what they should be saved from.

For Weber the salvation belief had meaning and a psychological quality which was structured by a place within a system of ideas about the world as a whole. These could vary widely and provided a résumé of the wide variety of possibilities of salvation – from impurity, from passion, from evil, from punishment. In every case something was seen as 'senseless' and salvation was required from it. But the character of the quest for salvation varied very much according to the character of the social strata which were the bearers of the religion, while its compelling nature depended very much on the extent to which it had been rationalised by intellectuals.

For the moment the briefest way in which one might characterise Weber's theory is that it is a developmental theory of human need in which the needs of a person are met, conditioned, created by specific social and cultural circumstances. Needs and interests (not identical, but often used almost interchangeably by Weber) are compelling forces in society which have to be satisfied one way or another. Both historically and at any moment of time they are organised hierarchically. At one point Weber says, 'In keeping with the law of marginal utility, a certain concern for one's destiny after death would generally arise when the most essential earthly needs have been met, and thus this concern is limited primarily to the circles of the noble and well-to-do' (E&S I: 520).

In this respect we can see that intellectuals have a derived and secondary position. They rationalise other people's needs for salvation and that intellectual activity in turn becomes a deep requirement for themselves. The meaning of meaning becomes the intellectual's problem and by its very asking opens up the infinite regress from which there can be no salvation.

5   The philosophy of the scientist's life

We are now in a position to understand the strength which the idea of a vocation took on in Weber's life and thought. In the modern world activity had become specialised to the extent that the ideals of life were largely associated with particular occupations. Georg Simmel said at one point: 'If you were to ask educated people today by what ideals they live, most would give a specialized answer derived from their occupational experience' (1968: 15).

Addressing his student audience in his lecture 'Science as a Vocation', Weber said 'for nothing is worthy of a man as a man unless he can pursue it with passionate devotion' (Essays: 135).

This was a hymn of praise to specialisation in science as the only way to achieve the deepest experience. It was a 'strange intoxication', a 'passion', 'enthusiasm', 'inspiration', all terms which Weber used extensively in discussing religious ecstasy, which were all necessary to bring to the cold calculation of science.

Weber, like the Protestant ascetics about whom he wrote, could only cope with the problem of meaning in life by harnessing his full emotional energy to his chosen occupation, in this case science. It had to involve the kind of total commitment which equated the aim of his sociology with the very quest for the meaning of human action, the self-same search which he attributed to the intellectual satisfying a metaphysical need in the elaboration of the meaning of life, in the quest for salvation.

Simmel also argued that at the end of the nineteenth century a new idea arose to dominate the *Weltanschauung* of the period, and that was *life*. It had been ushered in by Schopenhauer asking for the first time 'what is the meaning of life, purely as life?', and by Nietzsche finding that meaning in life itself, not in anything outside it. It was this feeling, said Simmel, which dominated all those thinkers who resisted closed systems.

For Weber life and work were equated. Work could become an end in itself where all the energies of the person were employed and engaged in it. Indeed in the modern irreligious world this was what had happened. The case of the intellectual was special in that the very quest for meaning, which characterised intellectual work, could not receive an intellectual answer. In this sense Weber accepted the Nietzschean position that the meaning of life could ultimately only be found in life. It was therefore not in the answers to its questions that intellectual activity gained meaning, but only in being recognised and acknowledged as a basic need at least for some people. One of the most rarefied and advanced activities of modern culture, that of the scientist, both generated and arose out of the need to know and understand.

It was a fundamental tenet of Weber's view of the world that those who maintained an intimate relation with the organically prescribed cycle of natural life experienced meaningfulness at the level of the unconscious, prior to even conceiving meaning to be a problem at all. Human culture was always a roundabout way of leaving the self-evident nature of life only to return at a later stage. Culture, which by definition was the sphere of meaning, could only make sense as a whole in relation to natural existence. Reflections of this kind underlay one of the most deeply pessimistic passages in Weber's writing in the essay he published in 1915 linking his reflections on the religion of India to those on China. 'Viewed in this way, all "culture" appears as man's emancipation from an organically prescribed cycle of natural life. For this reason culture's every step forward seems condemned to lead to an ever more devastating senselessness' (Essays: 356–7).

Judged by its own standards, then, culture was senseless. Culture was tied to the need to strive for infinite perfectibility, but the segment of culture to which any one person could be dedicated was only a finite and miniature portion of all that was possible. It could not possibly give sense to life as a whole and the pursuit of science in particular created an aristocracy of intellect, without personal ethical qualities and unrelated to their fellow human beings.

It is a deep pessimism which contrasts with the dedicated vocationalism of 'Science as a Vocation'. It was a pessimism, which could only be lifted by acknowledging that the need for meaning on the part of the intellectual was indeed satisfied by the intellectual quest for meaning. In this way it corresponded with the fate or destiny of the individual, was *in fact* the demon in the soul.

For Weber the answer to the problem of the meaning of life was to be found in life itself and not in meaning. The problem of meaning was not one which could be answered intellectually within a particular structure of meaning. It is for this reason that Weber does not make ideal structures of meaning logically prior in his basic principles of sociology. The criticism has been made, by von Schelting (1934) and Parsons (1937 and 1947) in particular, that Weber neglected structures of meaning (*Sinnzusammenhänge*) in favour of an atomised or individualistic approach.

That criticism is in large part beside the point. Weber paid considerable attention to what he termed the dogmatic disciplines, which were for him the most rationalised forms in which such structures of meaning existed, as for instance law, aesthetics, theology or ethics. They were disembodied ideal systems of meaning and Weber held that they had their autonomy and logic. But an empirical science of meaning was one which examined the way those structures were borne by people in their real lives. It examined what people found to be meaningful rather than any ideal or theoretical statement of particular kinds of meaning.

For this reason Weber was bound to recognise the emotional as being equally generative of action as rational considerations. It was via the personality that the vital forces of human beings were channelled into social life and the processes by which cultures arose were generated. Weber acknowledged that his method was individualistic, but argued that his was the only procedure which was genuinely sociological, namely took account of the social processes by which the motives of individuals contributed to the real workings of collectivities. That said, Weber by no means implied the advocacy of an individualistic value system (E&S I: 18).

But it has to be said that neither Weber's sociological method, nor his personal philosophy of life, can be understood except as his own personal resolution of the intellectual and moral problems which were posed by the challenge to inner-worldly asceticism of the emergent life philosophies of the later nineteenth century.

Weber's life represented the living of an answer to the conflict between Kant and Nietzsche, between Christianity and atheism. The minimal points of agreement between those antagonistic doctrines were on the importance of the individual, of strength, courage and heroism; those were taken for granted by Weber. The way he transcended the points of conflict between them was to turn the intellectualism of Kantian idealism into a Nietzschean primary life force.

As for his life, one may understand why he said he wanted to see just how much he could stand. The outcome was intellectual work of prodigious scope and stature which receives wider acknowledgement with every year that passes.

5

Towards a Science of Social Reality

The first four chapters examined the deeper historical roots of Weber's world-view. This chapter seeks to show how that world-view engaged with the issues of his own time when the demand arose to solve problems defined as 'social' and there was a general requirement for social facts. I shall advance the view that Weber's creative use of his own cultural heritage made him particularly fitted and ready to take up those issues.

1 Cultural heritage

We have seen how the concepts in Weber's world-view were deeply embedded within the Christian, and especially, Protestant experience. The world (*Welt*) and mind or spirit (*Geist*) are not in the first instance scientific ideas but part of the religious frame of experience which, in the Christian tradition, take on connotations of material and ideal, sinful and perfect, everyday and extraordinary.

In the Kantian world-view these primary distinctions take on a special function within a world of thought. The individual's quest for salvation in the sinful world is converted into the discovery of a transcendental home for the individual in pure thought, where the idea of the idea, untrammelled by the real world, becomes the eternal light of rationality, capable of taming the animal forces in the human body. Duty becomes the moral law to which the passions must submit.

It was a frame of thought which carried within it the potential for rigorous self-control and explosive struggle. As Weber saw, the

78

Protestant introduced the heroic asceticism of the monastery and of the saints into the everyday world. Extraordinary demands were made of people by themselves and by others. The foundations for the discipline of the businessman and the bureaucrat equally were laid, as also for the intellectual and the professional.

There was a personal cost in passion frustrated. The Nietzschean challenge to the established order of Christian values drew upon all which was rejected, on power, passion, pride, and elevated them to transcendent appetites to be fed and honoured. The quest for experience was to replace the rational spirit. It was all possible because ultimately the Christian and Kantian view of the world did depend on faith. Rationality itself came up against the boundaries of understanding and that faith was shaken intellectually in any case by the advance of an empirically-based science.

We recapitulate these points in order to recall that the foundations for Weber's social theory were based in the Christian Kantian world-view and in the Nietzschean challenge to it. We will find in the second part of this book that the types of action, the conceptualisation of rationality, the relation of values and faith, the conception of individual responsibility, are the units of Weber's social theory derived from those religious antinomies.

We noted too and accepted Mitzman's argument that Weber's emotional illness, his periods of depression, arose out of the unresolved conflicts between his mother's pietism and his father's patriarchal power, and that here too the cultural contradictions of the period were precipitated in interpersonal conflict and inner distress. At the same time Weber was strong enought to rise above these conflicts, which must equally be seen as the spur for his creativity.

The assumptions in Weber's world-view and the contradictions he sought to resolve were the cultural capital of his period, or more particularly of the educated bourgeois German of the late nineteenth century. They were resources not seriously questioned by Weber. The Nietzschean challenge welled up from within that thought world, an endemic tension erupted, pent-up forces were released. If the Kantian-Nietzschean divide could be bridged, the direct challenge from a Marx could be deflected.

If we may adopt a Kantian expression here, we can say that the elements of the world-view we have attributed to Weber operated as his *categories of experience*. The world was actually experienced as an arena of law, duty, calculation, discipline, faith, emotion, power and responsibility. Weber felt himself to be an individual human being choosing his own fate, following his own demon.

That is a culturally specific experience, not shared by, say, a Hindu, a Muslim or a Chinese socialist. Hence, in an important sense, Weber did not choose to think this way. It was his heritage. But if we accept these propositions a number of difficult questions arise. In particular we have to ask how could it be possible for social theory, and especially sociology with claims to universal applicability, to arise out of this clearly limited cultural experience. And where does Weber's own contribution begin?

For the moment, let us remember that I have only spoken of the categories of experience, not its content in the historical period in which Weber was active. Still further I have not yet discussed his mode of intellectual response, in which we ought to expect his own choices to make a difference. Or, to put it another way, using the cultural capital analogy, it does not produce anything unless it is harnessed to objectives within a market. In this case the period, or the market, expressed a demand for a 'social' product and Weber's intellectual response was to organise the production of 'sociology'. Over time all kinds of tests can be applied to see whether the Kant–Nietzsche capital was adequate for the purpose.

2   Political and religious value commitments

Weber's world-view was created in a particular historical period and it bears the marks of the time. The political life of Weber's time was dominated by the creation of empires both in Europe through the unification of Germany in 1871, and overseas with the partition of Africa between the powers: and also by their dissolution, with the collapse of the second German Empire and the Austro-Hungarian Empire as a result of the First World War and with the overthrow of the Tsar of Russia in 1917. He was himself a keen political commentator both on the events in his own country and also especially in Russia. The struggles between nations and cultures he considered to be part of a universal historical process and provide a frame for all his work.

The same period was one of intellectual ferment which included a major confrontation between religious faith and a scientific outlook which was tending more and more to challenge basic religious beliefs. The publication of Darwin's *Origin of Species* in 1859 and the declaration of papal infallibility at the Vatican Council in 1870 were benchmarks in a process of polarisation between two kinds of faith, in the old Gods and in the power of science. But the old and the new faiths were themselves divided, especially in relation to the state. Roman Catholics in Germany strove to retain independence from the state, while Protestants were more inclined to support Bismarck.

There was also a huge difference between the a-religious rationalism which characterised much of the anti-Prussian socialism of the time and the vehement overturn of all old values and glorification of power in the writing of Friedrich Nietzsche. Weber was subject to these influences in his own life. His mother was a devout Protestant, his father had no time for religion. Weber became a non-believer with a deep sense of the anguish of that state and a commitment and sense of duty which carried the same degree of emotion.

Weber's sense of duty and his intense energy received their ultimate unification in his personality through his commitment to the German nation. It has been a commonplace of observations on nationalism that it appears to offer a means of identification with power which reassures the weak and isolated. In that sense Weber's own devotion to the idea of Germany and its culture can easily be seen as the corollary of his intense sense of autonomy. But additionally it an be seen as the most important way in which he identified with his father, who as a National Liberal member of the Reichstag was a firm supporter of Bismarck and the unification of the German Reich.

Whether interpreted as part of his cultural inheritance or as psychological reassurance (or both), Weber's nationalism was of a transcendent kind, that is, his commitment was to cultural ideals which the power of the state was to serve. In a society deeply divided by class, status and religion, commitment to the 'nation' just as easily could indicate detachment from particular interest groups. In Weber's case it was expressed in his 'prophet of doom' role, addressing a nation which would not hear him from a position of utter isolation. The burden of an abstract collectivity was taken on to the shoulders of the heroic individual. The nation was the vehicle of the great ideals, and they became the measure of the fulfilment of personal duty.

Throughout his later political career, in writing and activity after the Great War, Weber strove to give content to the idea that the nation was not the sum of the people's well-being, but that it was the set of values which those people were under an obligation to cherish and develop. He argued for institutions which would maximise the involvement of people in national values, and at the end of his life reached what was to be the summit of his political influence when he was one of the small body of men who helped to draft the Weimar constitution. Through his influence it contained the provision of the direct popular election of the President of the Reich, a device to ensure the same personal involvement and identification with the nation of each person as Weber felt he had himself. As an individual he could thus contribute to the collectivity as a whole, and not merely to the factional interests which political parties represented in parliament.

Weber's personality was activated by large ideas and images of the most universal and monumental kind. Nothing less than an interpretation of the world and his place in it could satisfy his longings. Only the fashioning of this world and all its contents by the light of the eternal truths was adequate to bring salvation for the isolated soul he possessed. His own life pressed close to the ultimate boundaries of ascetic Protestantism.

Weber had very close relations with the theologians at the University in Heidelberg, especially Ernst Troeltsch. He sympathised with liberal Protestant theologians and, although he could in no way share their optimism and belief in historical progress, he was a frequent attender of the Evangelical-Social Congresses in the 1890s where Protestants and socialists came together. He formed a close relationship with Friedrich Naumann (1860–1919) which was to last throughout their lives. Naumann was a chaplain in Frankfurt-am-Main and a leader of the Christian-Social movement which sought to improve the lot of working people through unifying the classes on Christian lines. Weber became closely involved with the movement, writing for its journals and attending its meetings.

The association with Naumann did much to clarify Weber's own position on issues of religion, social reform and political standpoint. The attraction Naumann had for him was of a person who from religious motivation could appeal to a population as a whole. But Weber could neither share Naumann's concern for working people nor his belief in Christianity as the basis of a viable political party. 'We are not engaging in social politics in order to create human happiness', he said at the 5th Evangelical-Social Congress in 1894, rejecting Naumann's own moving address, 'We want to cultivate and support what appears to us *valuable* in man: his personal responsibility, his basic drive toward higher things, toward the intellectual and moral values of mankind, even where this drive confronts us in the most primitive form' (Marianne Weber, 1976: 136). Those qualities had to be preserved not for the people's well-being, but to maintain the nation.

In fact Weber's relationship with Naumann is very revealing for what it demonstrated about his own unwillingness ever to sink himself wholly into a cause defined by someone else, however noble he felt the motivation might be. He recognised Naumann's qualities and sought to direct them towards his own ideals. Writing to his uncle (a letter of 15 October 1896), who had urged him to drop his connection with the Christian-Social group, he declared that his task was to rid Naumann of his socialist whimsies, not to denounce him: 'I am not a "Christian-Socialist" in the least but a pretty pure bourgeois' (Mommsen, 1984: 136). But like others in the bourgeoisie he was concerned at the threat a discontented working class could pose for the social order.

3 The 'social problem'

It was in the nineteenth century that the 'social' became a 'problem', something to be attended to and solved. Of course, the bonds which held people together and the causes of dissension had been a favourite topic for speculation before that time. Montesquieu, Adam Smith, Ferguson and Rousseau had all contributed to a rich variety of social theory stimulated from three main sources: the experience of other cultures; the growth of markets; and the demand for rights. The French Revolution, however, demonstrated that social order itself could be overturned, that neither principles of cooperation nor of self-interest might be sufficient to ensure a stable society. Sociology was then born out of the idea that social order might have to be managed on the basis of scientific principles.

In the beginning that idea existed on the fringes of popular enthusiasm for the achievements of the natural sciences and, in the country which showed the greatest demand for education for self-improvement, the United States. It was in this way that it entered the college curriculum at the end of the nineteenth century.

In Germany the situation was different. *Die Sozialfrage*, the social question or problem, became the favourite code term for referring to the industrial proletariat and the threat to existing authority posed by the growth of socialism. To Bismarck it was 'the socialist problem', which he sought to solve by a combination of repression and state legislation, which became the model for the twentieth-century welfare state.

Germany was undergoing a process of intense industrialisation in Weber's lifetime. Between 1870 and 1914 German output of coal increased tenfold, output of iron increased sevenfold. Urbanisation proceeded at such a rate that the one third of the population which lived in German towns in the 1860s had become two thirds by 1910. These processes saw the concomitant growth of factory production, great industrial cartels, the growth of trade unions and the increasing appeal of socialism.

Ferdinand Lasselle inspired the German Social Democratic movement and the year before Weber was born saw the foundation of the General Union of German Workers. In 1875 it merged with the Marxist Social Democratic Workers Party on the basis of the Gotha programme. By 1890 the renamed Social Democratic Party had become the strongest party in the country in spite of anti-Socialist laws, and offered a programme which envisaged the complete restructuring of society. The German state met these developments by a strongly centralised set of social legislation measures, by codifying the legal system and allowing no more than the appearance of popular participation in the Reichstag.

Weber's reflections on these processes were a constant companion to and influence on his academic work. Underlying his scholarly analysis of political life is the problem which Bismarck set himself to solve in practice: How were the conflicts in modern societies to be managed so that a population might serve the purposes of a great state and culture?

The nation-state and not democracy has pride of place in this formulation and in this respect Weber's whole work stands in the tradition of the mirror for princes, the provision of techniques for governing, rather than as the expression of a quest for true democracy. In this way he truly stands at the beginning of the vast expansion of managerial and administrative sciences which have grown in this century to meet the requirements of those in authority.

Weber came to maturity in a setting where professors of economics had already combined for 'a discussion of the social problem' and formed an Association for Social Policy (*Verein für Sozialpolitik*) to deal with it in 1872. In the highly bureaucratised society of Imperial Germany, with stratification closely linked with professional and educational status, the explosive growth of an urban working class was considered as a problem for state management but also as a threat to traditional patterns of deference.

The roots of German sociology were really quite distinct from those in the United States, although they were intertwined through cultural contacts at an early stage. They do not arise out of a mass educational movement, nor out of the prestige of the natural sciences. In a state which drew the majority of its officials from the ranks of trained lawyers, where the state and cultural prestige were closely linked through universities and patronage of literature, history and the arts, the acquisition of systematic knowledge was not in any way thought of as the preserve of the natural scientist.

If the state could be seen as rationally administering the economy and culture as well as monopolising the means of violence, then it could equally be seen as capable of attending to the new problem area – 'the social'. While there were obviously enthusiasts in Germany for the new-fangled ideas of Comte and Spencer, they were quite marginal to the main thrust towards a science of the social. In a culture where one could speak as easily of legal science as of natural science, the idea that a social science would have its own principles was obvious once the sphere of the social had been identified as a distinct focus of attention.

The attempt by the socialists to claim the understanding of the social as their own achievement, which reinforced their prediction and demand that the working class should take charge of society, presented a challenge to both professional competence and security for German academics.

The identification of the 'social' as a distinct sphere suitable for academic study was thus itself an oblique way of denying the comprehensive claims of the socialists. Far from being the idea which contained universal humanity and the unity of society, it became a technical supplement to economics and law. In a professionally segmented society welded into a single state by Prussian military power, where the common language itself had been a state creation, the space for what took on the name of sociology could only be within the professional division of labour.

The principles of this new academic specialism therefore had to be meticulously defined if they were to carry conviction with the established faculties and disciplines. The legalistic style and tone of so much of Weber's conceptual work has to be understood in relation to this requirement. If he had pandered to a rising popular demand for nationalist preaching in the lecture theatre, he could have got away with less, but that offended every principle of scientific integrity, at least after his early flirtation with this style in his Freiburg inaugural in 1894. It was all very well for Albion Small in the United States to deride Simmel and Tönnies for their 'can of preserves' obsession in founding a special science (1909). But it was far too dangerous for the professional autonomy of the academic in Germany to ride the kind of popular movement which the early American sociologists were able to do.

The social problem would have been a staple element of the conversation in the intensely political Weber household which Max was born into and which Marianne Weber recalled in her biography. As a member of the Prussian parliament his father received frequent visits from leaders of the National Liberal Party, the party of the bourgeoisie and professionals, property and education, freedom and unity. From a quite different direction, his mother responded to the social problem by organising community aid, founding youth and welfare centres. The social problem could easily function as an integrative focus for a bourgeois family of the time, however much political power and religion could symbolise patriarchy and the conflict of masculine and feminine values. To that extent there was a common message conveyed to Weber by his parents. Whether approached from the standpoint of national power or as an expression of a religion of common humanity, the social problem constituted a proper focus for activity. He chose a professional and academic approach.

4 Historical and social research

Weber came to social science from a training in law, from historical research, from practical experience of social research and the study of economics in that order. The problems he was later to address in his essays on method were treated from the standpoint of the practising social scientist dispelling common misconceptions and not as puzzles which had to be solved before work could being. He sought to derive principles from the practice of social science and not from some general canon for science, and certainly not from the natural sciences. As we shall see, this is of critical importance when we come to assess his contributions to social theory.

His very first published work demonstrates from the first page that problems of theory and method arise out of the concrete problems of interpreting and explaining the course of historical events. In this case Weber examined the history of trading societies in the Middle Ages in order to establish whether the daily practical requirements of merchants were sufficient to generate new legal ideas of whether older legal provisions could be used. The social was the focus of his investigation. He speaks without self-consciousness of 'the fundamental difference between the *societas* of Roman law and the most important groups of modern social forms, the lawfully trading, in particular the open trading society' (GHM: 1).

That early doctorate contained a range of themes which stayed with Weber until the end of his career. Marianne said that he used its results even in his last sociological work (1975: 113). The issue of legal forms and their influence on economic activity, the appropriate institutions for capitalist development, the growth of credit, the separation of the activity and property of the group from the individual members, the household as an economic unit, and the appropriateness of differing cultural assumptions for different kinds of social action are all issues embedded in a close analysis of mediaeval Italian and Latin legal documents.

In the course of that work it was entirely in keeping with his concern for the social sphere that Weber should have joined the Association for Social Policy, and, as soon as the thesis was finished, should have begun a research project to investigate the social conditions of farm workers. He designed the questionnaire which was sent to landowners and wrote a 900-page report on the research which established him as an authority on rural conditions. Marianne quotes Weber as saying at this time: 'When we look back someday we hope to be able to say: at this point the Prussian state recognized its social mission in good time' (1975:130).

This early juxtaposition of historical and contemporary social research became a regular feature of Weber's scholarly life until at least 1911. At the same time as working on the social conditions of farm workers, he was completing his higher doctorate on Roman agrarian history. Later, while working on the social organisation of the stock exchange, he was publishing on the social basis for the decline of ancient culture. While working on the social psychology of industrial workers he was preparing an encyclopaedia article of book length on the economic history of the ancient world. He strove to make the German Sociological Society a collective sponsor and organiser of empirical social research and, even as those attempts were running up against resistance, he was preparing his historical and comparative studies of the world religions.

From the beginning, Weber's historical work had the social as a main focus and in that sense there is no distinction between his historical and social research. His sociology was to be informed by both. In each case concrete reality, in its particulars, was investigated from a point of view, an interest in a value of some kind, but at the same time the 'facts' were already preformed by the culture of the time. The moving dividing line between present and past was consequently of no significance to Weber in his approach to empirical data.

Common to both his historical and contemporary researches was an insistence that in the documenting of facts and the tracing of causes, culture, that is meanings to individuals and as structures, was the guiding light of investigation. Natural events, physiological states could figure as stimuli or boundaries for culture, but the centre had to be culturally shaped.

The reason for this was the presupposition common to both historical and social research, given theoretical expression by

Kant, that the human being as agent was central to any explanation of the course of events. But that agency was expressed in and through meanings which had accumulated over time, and those in turn shaped the qualities of the human being.

Grasping the kind of relationship Weber was talking about has been a prime preoccupation for social theorists ever since the historical dimension of human existence has been recognised. Events or outcomes are doubly determined. The interplay of agent and structure generates novelty. The idea of the dialectic developed to grasp this process of qualitative change in which equally agent and structure are transformed in the course of cultural production.

These are not abstract considerations for Weber. Nor did he seek to develop them into a general theory of the dialectic or of agency and structure. They were an intrinsic and necessary consideration in any research designed to get at social facts. This is how he began his methodological introduction to the survey the Association for Social Policy was to conduct on the vocational choice and fate of workers in large-scale industry and which was to result in seven volumes of results published between 1910 and 1915:

> The present investigation is attempting to ascertain, on the one hand, which effect established large industry has on the personal characteristics, vocational destiny and extra-vocational lifestyle of the workforce, which physical and psychical qualities it develops in them and how these qualities are expressed in the entire way of life of the workforce. And, on the other hand, to what extent large industry in its developmental capacity and direction is bound to certain qualities; qualities which are generated by ethnic, social and cultural provenance, and by the tradition and living conditions of the workforce. Thus two different questions are coupled together, which the theoretician can and must separate, but which appear almost everywhere combined in the praxis of the investigation, in such a way that in the last analysis at least, the one cannot be answered without the other (quoted by Käsler, 1988: 68).

The human being is then both agent and cultural product, and in the course of cultural development has been transformed. Weber concluded his introduction to the survey on an apocalyptical note. He spoke of the monstrous cage which private profit-oriented industry had created but said that it was beyond the scope of their investigation to consider any common ownership alternative. The fact remained, however, that 'the "apparatus", as it presently exists, and the effects which it brings about which this inquiry is going to get to grips with, has altered the spiritual countenance of the human race almost beyond recognition and will continue to do so' (SSP: 60). And this Weber called a 'fact'.

5   A world of facts

Weber was in no doubt that there was a sphere of life which one could call 'social' and that it was possible to establish facts about it. Of course, it had been transformed in historical time and only recently had its nature become so contentious and subject to special consideration. A scientist was obliged to render account of the social which were clear, factual and objective, and could provide satisfying explanations.

So much was part of a wider 'common understanding' in his time. (Here we use his idea of *Einverständnis*, because it is so apt.) And yet there was a great degree of latitude in this 'common understanding'. It was not quite an agreement to differ, but it was not much more than a common view that there were issues to be put on an agenda. The disputed nature of the social was paralleled by the efforts of the state and professionals to obtain information about people and groups in their midst who were strange to them. Those people who had been 'beyond recognition' could be approached by the scientific survey even if they could not become part of one's own community.

The extension of social research in Germany as in other countries was a true expression of the change which had taken place in society. As a form of information gathering it bore to the state the same function as face-to-face relations bore in the traditional community. The facts of everyday life were replaced by the systematically collected data. Occasionally the professional conscience would seek to acquire knowledge of other ways of life on its own initiative, just as the gentleman traveller might follow in the wake of imperial armies and trading companies. But in the first instance it was the interests of state which required social knowledge.

State requirements were matched by growth in autonomous intellectual curiosity. Weber gave us an intimate insight into the professionalisation of law and the development of what he termed the lawyer's 'ideal interest' in defining the autonomous logic of legal reasoning. In the nineteenth century the same process occurred with historians. They asserted their professional independence with one of the most banal, but, at the same time, most repeated catchphrases of the century when Ranke proclaimed their task as discovering 'how it really was'. Finding the true facts was elevated to a specialist task. New opportunities opened up for intellectual employment.

In the twenty years between 1890 and 1910, the number of students in German universities and technical high schools almost doubled from 33 000 to 62 000 (Ringer 1969: 58). The number of teaching posts did not increase proportionately but there was still an expansion of academic activity combined with major progress in applied science and the establishment of the social sciences. Institutionalised science was put at the service of industry and the state.

Weber participated fully in the institutionalisation of social science being active in the Association for Social Policy. Under its auspices he carried out major surveys in 1892 into the conditions of agricultural workers and in 1908 into the motivation of industrial workers. He was a founder editor of what became the major social science journal of the time, the *Archiv für Sozialwissenschaft und Sozialpolitik* (the Archive for Social Science and Social Policy) and he helped to found the German Sociological Association in 1910 (Oberschall, 1965).

The kind of science Weber was concerned to develop was based in facts, real world facts. He spoke repeatedly of a science based on experience, of empirical science, or a science of reality. He sought to retain the nuances of all three expressions, for they do not convey exactly the same meaning. 'Experience' is gained in immediate contact with other people, 'empirical' injects a note of intellectual distance and objectivity, 'reality' is opposed to a world of ideas.

Very many sciences were not of this kind. Theology certainly not, but also philosophy, mathematics, law, or even economics, when concerned to develop pure concepts, had no direct interest in causal relationships in the real world. That did not diminish their intellectual stature, but equally it did not mean that they could take on the functions Weber had in mind for his own science.

The hallmark of this approach to science is a distrust of axioms or what purport to be foundations for knowledge. For all Weber's debt to his cultural heritage, his easy thinking in terms of the unity of the human being, of action in accord with values or for definite goals, the divide between rationality and feeling, in other words, the Kantian conceptual framework, he did not seek to derive propositions about the real world from them. Just how far people were motivated by rationality or feeling, the extent to which they held to values or fulfilled their duty, or even became full personalities, were for Weber always empirical issues, an attitude which extended to framing questionnaires for industrial workers in those terms. To do anything else was to fall into Hegel's error, or more recently Stammler's.

Weber showed quite as much scepticism about general principles for science as the English empiricists, and indeed he cited John Stuart Mill on various occasions, although in his disdain for principles, John Locke was closer in spirit in speaking of what he called general maxims: 'they are of no use to prove or confirm less general self-evident propositions. It is plain that they are not, nor have been, the foundations whereon any science hath been built' (1961, Vol. 2: 199).

Where Weber differed from the Anglo-Saxon empirical tradition was in his emphasis on the theoretical construction of facts. A cultural fact has to be interpreted, it has to be understood in terms of meanings current in a society, before it can even be represented as a fact. But aside from that Weber built into his understanding of social facts a sophisticated variant of a statistical theory of probability and hypothesis formation. The facts of social relationships were always probabilities that certain actions would take place: as such theoretically constructed in everyday life. The 'fact' of an organisation existing was itself a construction of the participants and they and any outside observer were dependent on a vast number of hypotheses about how people would continue to act.

The arguments which have taken place in more recent social theory about the relative and constructed nature of facts go over ground which Weber traversed thoroughly in his analysis of historical method. For him every page of a historical work contained statements of possible causal connections and descriptions of outcomes which were highly abridged imaginative constructions of courses of events, obtained by the isolation of elements drawn from the ceaseless flow of reality. As he put it, 'With this very first step the given "reality" is transformed, in order to make a historical "fact", into a structure of *thought*: or in Goethe's terms, "theory" is actually sitting in the "fact"' (Goethe's maxim was 'The most exalted of all would be: to comprehend that everything factual is already theory' (*Maximen and Reflexionen*, 1907, N. 575).

Such an emphasis on theory residing in facts might appear to clash with that primitive vision of a chaotic world which, it will be recalled, we identified as a basis for Weber's world-view. Undoubtedly we are close to the boundaries of clarity in his thinking and near to the irreconcilable conflicts, which he so often asserted, would result from pursuing ideas to their logical conclusion. It *is* resolved by Weber, but again, as he recognised, pragmatically. Interpreting and accounting for facts will find the deposits of human culture, of meaning, purpose and ideas located there.

But in the end the fact is irrational from the viewpoint of both actor and observer. From the actor's point of view no amount of reasoning will produce the deed. It arises from an irrational base. From the observer's point of view understanding just has to accept some things as given, obvious, or not further explicable. The facticity of understanding places tight constraints on the extent to which theory can extend its scope.

It is only the enormous prestige and hold on the intellectual imagination which the natural sciences have won which has obscured the significance of facts for the social sciences. As we have stressed, Weber, unlike a Comte or a Spencer, did not begin from the standpoint of the natural sciences. They did not have that prestige for him and he was not even motivated by a reaction against them.

The very idea of a fact originates in the human deed rather than the natural event. With its Latin root *factum* (thing done) it came into the English language in the sixteenth century to refer to deeds and as far as the law was concerned a fact was a vile deed. As a root it only finds its way into German through *faktisch*, actual or real, because the exact equivalent in meaning in that language is held by *Tatsache*, the 'deed thing' in a literal translation. So, when Weber is talking about facts, this has just as strong an emphasis on their roots in action as exists in the English language.

It is only a highly foreshortened view of history which sees the social sciences as parasitical upon the natural, or as having to emancipate themselves from a natural scientific parentage. The order is rather the other way round. Natural science had to escape the anthropomorphic vision of the world in which natural events were seen as the outcomes of purpose. More accurately, talking about facts and deeming the natural world to be a different order of things developed *pari passu* as part of a wider recognition that human beings made their own world. But to pursue that idea would take us back to Vico, Newton and beyond.

Seeing the world around as an immense array of facts is not a necessary and universal feature of human experience. The accumulation of dates, names of events, records of past deeds, recollections of heroes, memories of sayings, statistics of births and deaths, presupposes requirements for knowledge which outstrip the daily needs of the self-sufficient peasant community. They are the requirements of communities of people not personally known to each other and a concern for their maintenance comes to be regarded as a necessary function of the state.

As such it was not an original invention by Max Weber. The state-regulated universities became the homes for an army of salaried intellectuals exploring the world as it was and had been. Others sought to define how it ought to be or might be. Weber was able to draw on the work of this army and he did so enthusiastically.

The requirements for empirical social science arose out of the emergence of the modern state, not in its functions as monopoly of force, but in its capacity as rational frame for the representation of and arbitration between conflicting interest groups. In that context social facts were necessary for the decision-making process.

Weber's personal ethic had the maximum elective affinity with that state requirement. His own resolution of the conflicts within the German bourgeois mind, between faith and science, rationality and irrationality, was to make rationality his own life experience and to commit himself to science with passionate devotion. In this way he sought in facts and their explanation the potential bonds of common understanding between people who were otherwise divided by irreconcilable conflicts of value.

PART II

Constructing an Empirical Social Science

Consider well the first line that your pen be not over hasty. Is it the Sense that influences and produces everything? It should stand thus: 'In the beginning was the Power'. Yet even as I am writing this down, something warns me not to keep to it. The spirit comes to my aid! At once I see my way, and write confidently: 'In the beginning was the Deed'.

(Goethe [trans. Hayward] Faust, p. 50.)

Preamble

The scope of Weber's concerns was such that he was able to absorb the diversity of the fast-developing social sciences in the German-speaking world of his day and to fashion an approach which had the comprehensiveness of that of a Hegel or Marx, while insisting on a rigorously empirical method.

He achieves this through the idea of rationality both by accepting it as the source of his concepts and identifying it as the distinguishing and dynamic force in the transformation of the modern world. In this way the Kantian/Nietzschean problematic in which he shaped his own world-view was also the source of his complex analysis of the boundaries between rationality and irrationality in social science and in the real world.

He developed a programme for an empirical science of society in which the individual is the transcendental premise, but also the bearer of meanings in real structures. Contrary to much received opinion the purpose of Weber's work was precisely to establish just in what way social structures of meaning existed and the way they have developed over time.

6

The Scholarly and Polemical Context

1 Weber's contemporaries

The location of Weber's cultural experience at the very centre of
the German intellectual tradition was evidenced by the breadth of
his interest in the work of his own contemporaries. He maintained
a vigilant watch on developments in philosophy, history and across
the range of social sciences. His list of correspondents reads like a
roll-call of the good and the great of his time.

Most frequently Weber sought to distinguish his own position
from that of others, while at the same time absorbing much of their
contribution into his own frame of reference. This has been noted
many times. Hennis, for instance, has shown how Weber both
borrowed from and travestied the arguments of his predecessor
Karl Knies in the Chair of Economics in Heidelberg, when he
wrote on the methods of social science and in his inaugural lecture
on economic policy (1987). Frederick Tenbruck has pointed to the
clear similarity of opinions on historical method Weber shared
with Eduard Meyer even while criticising him (1987: 234–68). I
indicated the clear similarity between Weber's account of bureaucracy and Gustav Schmoller's (1970).

Weber was a person of broad understanding and fine distinctions. He extended his scope over a vast range of topics, at the
same time as always insisting on his own special vantage point.
Very rarely did he give unqualified recognition of the work of
others. Given, however, his central location in German culture
and his receptiveness to the ideas of his contemporaries, his
insistence on asserting his own position resulted in an extraordinarily synoptic overview of the intellectual debates of the time.

97

It is comprehensiveness of his considerations which gives his work that dominating character rather than any special discovery or originality.

It is because Weber operated on a broad front and in the mainstream of a powerful cultural tradition that his work over the years has come to dominate our present characterisation of the period in which he worked. In consequence, figures who were regarded as equal or even more important in his own time have increasingly been overshadowed by the man who has come to be identified with the foundation of modern sociology.

In fact, at the time, Georg Simmel undoubtedly had more international influence on the founding of sociology than did Weber whose work was not widely acknowledged abroad until the 1930s. Simmel's work, on the other hand, had immediate impact in the USA and France particularly. Weber acknowledged Simmel's work, and in many respects comes to formulations similar to those of Simmel, on conflict for instance, or even in defining society at one point as the 'general structural forms of human communities' (WG I: 212). But for Weber sociology had also to concern itself with the content, the direction and motives of human action and not just formal qualities which were so often confused with ideal definitions. Law as form and law as fact of life were two different things for him.

These considerations led him to distance himself also from the philosopher of natural law, Rudolf Stammler, who argued for a concept of social life which was constituted by law as opposed to Marxist materialist views. Here Weber inclined much more to the view that the pure idea of law was one thing, something existing in people's minds another, and actual practice yet something else again.

It was his insistence on the difference between the empirical study of ideas and the logical implications of ideas which caused him to distinguish his own position from his friend, the philosopher Rickert. However much the logic of ideas might exercise an attraction and even a compelling character for individual people, their influence on the course of events was still an empirical, not a philosophical issue.

At the same time the power of ideas in the sense of their logical coherence could not be discounted as an influence on people and in consequence excessive claims for the developing natural scientific approach in experimental pschology or in opinion research as represented by Wilhelm Wundt or Hugo Munsterberg had also to be resisted. An interpretative psychology as developed by his friend and confidant Karl Jaspers was, however, an added tool in the empirical social scientist's armoury (1913).

Jaspers received unqualified praise for his work since it represented an antidote to the exaggerated emphasis placed on the unconscious drives and in particular on sexuality by Freud and his followers. Weber followed the reception of Freud's ideas with great interest and was entirely prepared to allow for the importance of irrational factors and unconscious drives in his historical interpretations, while refusing to modify his own Kantian ethical position on the separation of fact from value.

It was this moral rigour and insistence on the integrity of science which led Weber to resist the nationalist theoretical historical work of Karl Lamprecht. Whimster has recounted how he defended what was indeed the traditional professional historian's affirmation of a concern for the particularity of facts against (1987) attempts to produce laws of history and against the importation of moral judgements. At the same time, while criticising Eduard Meyer, Weber also adopted his broad anthropological and universal historical concerns in his own comparative studies.

Weber made no secret of his political commitments, above all to the idea of the modern nation-state as a vehicle for German national culture in the competition between world powers, and to the need for responsible political leadership. In these respects, as Beetham has pointed out, he was recasting liberalism in elitist terms in the same general spirit as his Italian contemporaries Pareto and Mosca without referring to them (1987). Much of Weber's theorising about democracy and bureaucracy emerged out of his relationship with his younger Austrian friend, Robert Michels, but he could not share the latter's faith in radical solutions. The result is a political theory which has become a guide for the representatives of the modern capitalist state.

In general Weber confined his interactions with living scholars to the German-speaking world. It was the German experience of culture and politics of his time which for him defined the field in which he chose his intellectual tasks. He was not ignorant of what happened elsewhere: he was familiar with American pragmatism and the thought of William James in particular; he cited John

Stuart Mill and gave high regard to his writing on empirical method even if it fell short of complete acceptability. We know he was familiar with French and Italian social and political theory. But it was the unique German situation which commanded his attention, and it was his command of the breadth of German culture which led Jaspers to know him as supremely and essentially German (1932).

2 Controversies on methods

It has long been conventional to see Weber as concerned above all to resolve problems of method for the social sciences. The fact that controversies over methods raged in Germany, and that he took a position on them in trenchant terms, appear to give support to this. Certainly those who are primarily interested in methods have found ample substance in his views.

But to see Weber as a methodologist can only arise out of a concentration on a narrow range of his work and out of the specialist interests of commentators who are themselves mainly interested in methods. Tenbruck has shown convincingly that Weber's essays on methods arise out of concrete problems he addressed or from a desire to remove misleading attempts to legislate for the social sciences (1959).

As others, such as Oberschall, have depicted in detail, the social sciences were already flourishing in Germany (1965). They were a fact, institutionalised in departments of national economy especially and in the flourishing schools of history and law. Debates about method arose out of on-going concerns and Weber's own intellectual biography demonstrates convincingly the huge amount of historical and empirical social research he undertook before reflecting on it in essay form.

To this should be added the ethos of Weber's own work orientation. Above all he was concerned to depict and explain social reality. That is not an empty formula, although its weight has been lost over this century. Such an interest is not shared by all people, nor is it prominent at all times. It is a product of a special period and circumstances.

The explorations in the first part of this book were concerned to find a key to the understanding of this ethos. It begins with the distinction between this world and ideas, material and spiritual reality, which underpins the distinction between natural and moral worlds which is central to Kant's thought. But that is not in itself sufficient to generate an interest in social facts; indeed almost the reverse, because the spiritual world is seen as occupying another sphere. It is when the spiritual world is challenged, when its necessity is questioned, that its hold on people is seen as a contingent fact. The Nietzschean challenge was the precursor to a science of morality because it made mundane the most exalted motives.

Such a challenge assisted in the relativisation of values in that it made the supremacy of one set of values rather than another a matter ultimately of power. Faith was irrationalised, stemming not from reason but from the drive to assert, the will to power. Rationality itself became a cunning device by intellectuals to gain the influence they were unable to gain in any other way.

It was not just the state which required facts in an increasingly managed and problematical social order. People in their everyday lives found it difficult to impute motives to each other, to come to a common understanding, to agree on the facts, even to establish the meaning of their own behaviour.

This was the historical crisis out of which the demands for a science of the social arose. In this respect the importance of and background to the drive to a science of social facts was the same for Weber as for Durkheim. As with any scientist, the only way to work was to get on with the task. Reflections on method were *ex post facto*. It was this which distinguished the founding of sociology at the time of the nineteenth/twentieth century from the pre-history of the subject. For Comte and Spencer sociology had been a programme; for Weber and Durkheim it was a professional practice arising out of reality.

There are phases to debates about methods for the social sciences in the German-speaking world. Thus periods of *Methodenstreit* are often separated from each other but in fact they merge into a continuous background to the practical work. An early phase involved a debate which, like the others, continues to this day. It is associated with the economists Schmoller and Menger who disagreed on the relative importance of historical and analytical approaches to economic phenomena. Later the same issues were raised by the Austrian school of economists who criticised Marxist attempts to discover historical laws and argued for the development of abstract models.

Weber was completely familiar with these debates, and as so often steered a middle course, applauding the development of abstract economic theory, while at the same time denying that it was an account of economic reality.

Another *Methodenstreit* surrounded the distinction between natural and cultural sciences and the extent to which the historical world, the sphere of the practical actions of human beings, could be studied by the methods of the natural sciences, understood as the generation of laws by experimental procedures. It was here that J. S. Mill's work had been influential in shaping the conception of sciences of the mind. Windelband and Rickert debated about the interest of the scientist in generalising or particularising events, while Rickert (1902) insisted that values entered into the very constitution of the objects the historian or social scientist studied (see Burger, 1976).

Again Weber drew from and distanced himself equally from anyone else's position. Value orientations did for him indeed constitute human culture but he was unable to subscribe to any attempt to derive reality from the logic of values. Hence there was no essential and timeless value structure to human society, only a story of striving to realise ideas and that story was capable of being told through generalisation as well as by reference to unique constellations of facts.

It was the emphasis on human striving which aligned Weber as much with Dilthey on these issues as with his friend Rickert whom he acknowledges more. Dilthey emphasised the necessity to view history as the outcome of the human need for self-expression and in this sense placed more emphasis on irrational roots and psychological explanations than on value structures. Dilthey's position involved also a critique of natural scientific approaches to human psychology and emphasis on the immediate data of consciousness (1973).

In this emphasis on history as a human product and facts as constructed and reconstructed by human beings, Weber did not disagree with the thrust of the emerging phenomenological school which Husserl was leading at the time. Weber's methodological essays are replete with comments on the inexhaustibility of possible considerations of principle and fact in the minutiae of human conduct. Where his interest differed from the phenomeno-logical movement was in his insistence that, for practical purposes, accounts of the real world had to be written, motives imputed and causes hypothesised.

That these practical requirements involved commitments was the most fraught question of all for Weber, an issue on which he was prepared to alienate the majority of sociologists at the First German Sociological Congress, by the stridency with which he insisted on the separation of value judgements from empirical statements. This *Methodenstreit* has become the longest and most vigorous of them all, precisely because it is a separation which is intellectually the most difficult to sustain, because it is practically that which is required most of all from intellectual work by the rest of the world, and because its maintenance is the legitimation of a science of the social. Of all the disputes about methods it was the one which reflected most the deep personal involvement Weber's personality had in the cultural conflicts of his time. To this day it remains a deep contradiction within Western culture.

3 Weber's achievement

Protestantism shaped the motive. Kant, Goethe, Nietzsche sup-plied the assumptions, language and frame of thought. His contemporaries gave him stimuli and material to fashion. His own capacities to respond, absorb and create generated the astonishing corpus of writing which over a short timespan set a whole agenda for generations of social scientists and historians. A bare outline can convey the scope and seminal nature of Weber's contribution.

His life was short. He died aged 56 in 1920, and his academic career was curtailed by illness and the First World War. His full participation in academic life was confined to the period 1894-8 when he held chairs in economics at Freiburg and Heidelberg. Briefly after the First World War he lectured in Vienna and Munich, but even that was much interrupted by political involve-ment. His periods of writing were remarkably short given the astonishing output. His early period of writing between 1888 and 1897 saw the production of his dissertation on trading associations in the Middle Ages and on law and the agrarian history of the Roman Empire, as well as a major enquiry into the social conditions of agricultural workers and papers on the operation of financial markets. The latter period of his writing from 1903 to 1920 comprised the whole of what is recognised as his major work on religion, industrial work, law, politics, the city and methodology. If we attempt a review of the significance of that work as a whole we gain the following picture:

1.   In the papers he wrote in 1904 and 1905, *The Protestant Ethic and the Spirit of Capitalism*, Weber made the single most important intervention in the on going argument about ideas in history which arose out of Marx and Engels' development of the materialist conception of history. With his subsequent studies of religion in ancient China, India and Israel, he established the main foci for research on religion and society to this day.

2.   At several points in his work there are accounts of bureaucracy which became the starting point for the major part of modern research on administration and organisation, and the basis for the discussion of any general theory of bureaucracy.

3.   His analysis of the idea of authority and the way he located the notion of legitimacy at the centre of the problems of social order, social control and the state have increasingly begun to dominate both Marxist and non-Marxist accounts of modern political systems. As time goes on it becomes apparent that Weber's classification of authority as traditional, charismatic and legal-rational has the same significance within modern theory as the Aristotelian classification of states as monarchic, aristocratic and democratic had for classical theory.

4.   In examining the phenomena of social stratification he separated class position, as defined by relation to markets, from status, as defined by style of life, and separated these in turn from legal privilege, ethnic identity and political party formation. This amounts to the most important alternative approach to the study of the class structure of modern society to that of Marx and again has set the terms for all modern debate on the subject.

5.   In the course of his examination of the development of modern law, he identified factors of technique and logic, and of group formation, which in combination provided the ingredients for the development of the legal profession. It is an analysis which

has proved influential in the sociology of the professions generally and not just in respect of law.

6. His comparative studies of East and West in respect of political, military, legal, religious, urban and economic structure, much of which was only published posthumously in 1921 as the massive *Wirtschaft und Gesellschaft* (*Economy and Society*), contain what is perhaps the most important statement in this century of the self-understanding of the West, namely that its culture is the agent of a comprehensive process of rationalisation. In so doing he drew on a long history of occidental-oriental comparisons, updated and recast them.

7. Both in empirical research and argument he brought together traditions of thought on the science and humanities from both Anglo-Saxon empiricism (Hume and Mill particularly) and German idealism (Kant, Dilthey and Rickert) and in his fusion of these he anticipated Wittgenstein's analysis of rules and both anticipated and influenced Popper's methodological individualism.

8. His analysis of fact and value took the distinctions forged by Hume and Kant in the eighteenth century and wove them into an account of the relations between science and social and political action in such a way that his doctrine of 'value-freedom' or freedom from value-judgements has become (albeit often in vulgarised form) the major legitimation for the application of science to human affairs in the twentieth century. It has also again set the terms of argument about commitment to values among social scientists until this day.

9. His framework of concepts based on the idea of understanding and action provides what is still to this day the most elaborated and refined exposition of the sociological approach to human behaviour. It is used worldwide in a variety of contexts in an eclectic manner by social scientists who otherwise adhere to competing broad perspectives such as Marxism, functionalism or phenomenology.

10. At a wide variety of points in his work Weber was explicitly or implicitly providing counter-arguments to those of Marx, and in his own political engagement and commentaries his commitment to the notion of responsible bourgeois rule in the interest of the nation and its culture provided a practical

alternative to Marx's own version of uniting theory and practice in support of the international proletariat.

In fact the range and scope of his work can be compared directly with Marx. While the differences in social, economic and ideological structure between modern Marxist states, on the one hand, and Western states, on the other, rule out an exact equivalence, it can be argued that the nearest to a functional equivalent to Marx for the socialist societies is, in the case of the liberal democracies, Max Weber. While his work has to share the shelves with many others, it has perhaps become the most important single guide to the West's understanding of itself.

4 Deflecting Marx

Weber once remarked that Nietzsche and Marx had framed the thought of his time (Bendix and Roth, 1971: 22). That in itself would suggest that he was directly influenced by Marx as much as by Nietzsche. The contention in this book is different. Nietzsche was the discomfort within the German bourgeois psyche; the challenge to the moral order arising out of the very dichotomies between the world and the mind which Kant had codified. Marx was a challenge from outside, and is no way so formative for Weber's world-view.

The post-1945 interpretation of Weber as the bourgeois answer to Karl Marx is ultimately a Cold War interpretation. Weber's work sprang from the dilemmas inherent *within* capitalist culture, and by this I mean the culture of those who managed the state and industry in the late nineteenth and early twentieth century. It is therefore part of the cultural contradictions within capitalism and to that extent a pure expression of that system. From that point of view Marx was not regarded at the time as a major *intellectual* threat to the system.

Some of the misunderstandings of Weber's relations to Marx arises out of his comments on materialism itself. In his own time Nietzsche was regarded as quite as important a materialist as Marx, whose own work was categorised as historical materialism. Only when Weber addresses historical materialism directly should he be interpreted as thinking particularly of Marx. When Weber therefore identifies materialist elements in his own thinking, it is a mistake to conclude that he is compromising with Marx. He is handling an ideal/material dichotomy which had much longer roots in time and culture.

Weber had no difficulty in identifying the thrust of Marx's work, the attempt to generalise and intellectualise the experience of the proletariat and identify the reasons for its ultimate triumph in the necessities of capitalist production. He found fruitful hypotheses there, but it was a world-view he could not share and the science it generated was defective in a variety of ways:

1. Weber regarded the search for ultimate causes as bound to fail, as also was any insistence on the primary importance of any one type of cause. In that sense a general theory of history was doomed to failure.

2. Since for Weber the tension between the ideal and the material was intrinsic to the human condition, any social science was bound to treat each as separate and complementary to the other.

3. Weber distrusted the use of collective concepts in scientific discourse and regarded capital and labour as no more than abstractions useful for analysis but not historical agents.

4. He regarded socialist theories of cooperative production as naive and utopian, while sympathising with their moral concerns. He predicted that economies run on socialist lines would be bureaucratic and give opportunities for privilege and power rather than meet needs.

On all these grounds Weber felt so sure of his position that he never found it necessary to engage in a detailed dissection of Marxist premises. He was never strident in his opposition to Marxism and in some ways, as his essay on Stammler showed, he considered himself to occupy a kind of middle position between materialists and idealists (Stammler). This is not to say he was uninterested in the socialist movement. He kept in close touch with developments through its contacts with people like Naumann and Michels. His social concern did express itself in comments about the domestication and exploitation of the proletariat, although that was outweighed by considerations of national power in his own mind.

As far as his intellectual output is concerned in the broadest sense, the themes which he addressed are often ones which Marxists, or more often socialists, addressed too. To that extent he showed that there are alternative modes of analysis of, say, the rise of capitalism or the decline of the Roman Empire. The economic history of his time was dominated by those with socialist leanings. To that he did not object. His insistence was on rigorous intellectual procedures and too often he found their analyses coloured by wishful thinking. As far as he was concerned, a scholar's socialism should not stand in the way of his or her intellectual integrity, neither on the part of the scholar nor on the part of others in their evaluation of the scientific worth of the work. For this reason he vigorously supported Michels' academic claims.

The major borrowing from Marxist sources one can detect in Weber is his amplificaton of the alienation concept to cover all forms of administrative and intellectual production in the modern world. He quite explicitly generalises the case of the worker alienated from production to the case of the intellectual and the bureaucrat. But, of course, the inferences he draws from this process are quite different from Marx.

Weber took the question of revolution seriously enough to study the Russian events of 1905 in great depth. Like his bourgeois contemporaries he was concerned that the existing order might disappear in turmoil. But the intellectual shape of his work is far less dictated by that threat than was Comte's, or come to that, Durkheim's. The real threat to the social system came not from Marx intellectually but from the disaffected masses, while the intellectual dynamic was relatively insulated from those pressures.

Weber's work was not a bourgeois answer to Marx, even less a technical means to control the masses. It was a pure expression of the intellectual resolution of the personal problems and practical conduct of the educated classes in pre-1914 Germany. It was swept aside by the Nazis for just that reason.

If Weber's work is now unprecedentedly received worldwide, it is because the science of social facts which he practised responds to needs which mirror those of the German class for which he was the greatest representative. That meant seeing the world as a product of the tension between rationality and irrationality rather than a struggle between classes or even between nations.

The universal conflicts which Weber detected were ultimately lodged in the individual soul, in dilemmas and choices to be made in daily conduct, which, aggregated, amounted to forces which could sweep social order away but which, organised, contributed to a process of rationalisation with gathering momentum.

If there was to be a social science, it had to be one which treated the facts of social life as the outcome of human action where the grouping of motives around the poles of rational and irrational was the master categorisation of all categories of daily life. That Protestant conviction was carried through into Weber's social science. It has equally become the ideology of the world social order, the basis of economic and administrative decision-making.

That is a fact; historically specific, of utmost generality, the outcome of theory and theoretically of wide significance. It is the sort of fact Weber's social science served to address.

5 Transcending Hegel

Passionate devotion to rationality was the principle of Weber's personality. Rationality was also the idea upon which the whole edifice of his life's work was erected. The standards against which he measured his own daily activities also became measuring rods for assessing social development and the axioms for models of social behaviour. Continuity between life and work, between biography and theory, may be regarded as the defining characteristic of the intellectual as a type of social character. In Weber's case, we are as close as we can be to an empirical example of the pure type.

No one who turns for the first time to Weber can fail to be astonished by the way references to rationality appear on almost every page of his work. One recent commentator has listed no fewer than sixteen apparent meanings of rationality in Weber's characterisation of capitalism and Protestantism (Brubaker, 1984: 2; see also Kalberg, 1980). Yet at no point does Weber address the idea of rationality directly as a topic for systematic enquiry. It occurs always as the source of axioms, a point of comparative reference or a critical standard. This has often been a source of puzzlement for his readers. If the idea is so fundamental, how is it that it can be used in so uninhibited a manner?

The first explanation is that Weber was drawing directly upon the tradition of thought which identified rationality or reason with the essence of what it was to be human. The idea of reason is the thread which binds together the history of European philosophy from the Greeks through mediaeval Catholicism, Renaissance, Reformation, Enlightenment, German idealism up to the scientific rationalism of the nineteenth and twentieth centuries. The examination of the scope and significance of the idea is synonymous with the study of the history of Western philosophy.

German idealist philosophy in the nineteenth century gave rationality a sublime and central place in the interpretation of the human condition and German university education accorded philosophy the pre-eminent place in the approved curriculum. Weber could draw on philosophical ideas as a taken-for-granted resource, as a frame for enquiry, and a starting point for analysis.

We have seen how Kantian ideas informed Weber's personal attitudes to life and work. Duty, integrity, single-mindedness, self-control as personal standards in themselves could have occasioned some concern for such attributes in the world around. But a more explicit model for the application of philosophy to understanding social life was the deliberate creation of Hegel (1770–1831). He sought to develop philosophical ideas so that they might be equally salient in the interpretation of politics, religion and art; might penetrate alien cultures and the roots of revolution; might guide the civil servant's activities as much as the private citizen.

Hegel did not risk leaving the success of such an enormous enterprise to luck. It was guaranteed at the outset by an act of faith, namely the assumption that the world already embodied the ideas which philosophers sought to expound. They explored what was already there. The world was a realm of ideas. This is the second explanation for Weber's easy use of rationality. He too saw ideas realised in the world, just as generations of students at Berlin before him.

Hegel occupied the chair of philosophy at the most important educational institution of the Prussian state in the 1820s, the University of Berlin, and in that position he exercised dominance over a generation of students. In the words of a distinguished successor of his in the same subject at the same university.

Hegel exerted an important influence upon the entire Prussian educational system. Indeed, his philosophy might be described as the philosophy of the Prussian state during the second and third decades of the century, and that in a double sense; on the one hand, it was the officially recognized philosophy of the government, at least of the Altenstein ministry; on the other, Hegel was the philosophical interpreter of the state as objectified reason (Paulsen, 1906: 56).

We can amplify Paulsen's account of Hegel's significance by taking an even broader context. Set against the eighteenth century when faith in reason set in motion the claims for liberty, equality, the rights of man, in which critical reason was employed to legitimise the overthrow of the existing order and to justify revolution, Hegel's discovery of reason in the state, as it was then constituted, established an alliance between state power and intellectual occupations which has been an abiding feature of the modern state ever since. In German-speaking countries it had its most obvious expression in the training in law which administrators of the state all received, and which Weber himself underwent.

But additionally, Hegel's direction to seek for rationality as embodied in the practices of the world and not in pure reason detached from reality harmonised with the quest to render the activities of men of affairs, politics, business and the military intelligible to themselves and others. It gave an impetus to theorising lives and institutions, to trying to grasp the significance of foreign customs and manners and to rationalising social reform.

Charles Taylor has emphasised that it would be quite wrong to interpret Hegel as simply the conservative reaction to radical ideas (1975). He was much more than that. He gave the fullest expression to the idea that human society and history were the outcome of rationality in practice. Even after his own formulations had long fallen into disrepute, that basic insight corresponded so well with the cherished beliefs of the educated classes of the European states that it underpinned nineteenth-century ideas of progress and underpins twentieth-century ideas of modernity to this day.

Every student knows that Marx turned Hegel on his head – and about Hegel all but very few know any more, while Marx's historical materialism is explored in depth as the most important challenge to capitalist society. But then the reason Marx devoted so much thought and time to overturning Hegel tends to be forgotten, namely that Hegel was such an extraordinary expression of the premises and directions of the society for which he wrote. Long after his particular formulations had been supplanted or forgotten, the spirit of his intellectual programme remained the property of the German state and the academically educated classes who benefited from it and gave it so much support.

Only for his own followers did Marx vanquish Hegel: the bourgeois state and its spirit lived on and flourished. In the sense that his philosophical enterprise was a self-avowed contribution to that state, Hegel was 'conservative'. But his work was so adequate an expression of the forces and tendencies which animated the modern state that Hegel can equally be seen as a representative of those transformative processes which incited Marx to recognise the revolutionary character of the bourgeoisie.

Hegel's achievement was to link a philosophical idea of rationality, couched in the broadest possible terms to comprehend mind, consciousness, the following of rules, the essence of what it was to be human, with the everyday understanding of people about their practical business of learning skills, trading goods, getting married or engaging in state activities.

If one adds to this the fact that for Hegel the state was the supreme embodiment of rationality, and that world history culminated with the European experience, it is possible at this distance in time to understand how he was able to invest his system with world historical significance by drawing on the deepest assumptions and motive forces behind the expansion of the European states into the era of dominant world capitalism.

None of this is to be taken as saying that Weber was a follower of Hegel. The references he made to him were normally dismissive and for him it was a sufficient criticism of an author to say that he was a covert Hegelian to be able to identify fatal flaws. 'Panlogism' was the error Weber detected in those authors like Knies whom he criticised so sharply in his early methodological essays. Indeed, Weber saw himself as the representative of a more enlightened age, one where scientific progress had resulted in the demystification (*Entzauberung*) which expunged religious faith and talk of the divine spirit from serious academic inquiry of an empirical kind.

Yet there were elements of the Hegelian programme which persisted because, as I have suggested, they corresponded so well to the requirements of modern society. They do in fact provide some of the most important deep assumptions of Weber's academic work. There are three of particular importance.

1.   The autonomy of culture. The idea that human beings inhabit a sphere of meaning, a realm which one may call spiritual or ideal as opposed to material, where they determine their own existence, where self-consciousness or reflective thought distinguishes them from the animal world in particular and nature in general.

2.   The universality of human science. There was no facet of human existence, temporally, spatially, of whatever type of specificity, which did not come within the potential scope of Hegel's philosophical method. 'Universal History' displayed the work of the Spirit and it was actualised or made real in the daily lives of any ordinary person anywhere in the world (Hegel, 1956).

3.   Rationality as the principle of modernity. For Hegel both everyday commonsense and philosophical enquiry made reason or rationality the central principle of human activity. Moreover, common to each was the observation that rationality had accumulated, increased in power and scope in historical time so that the present always represented the culmination of developed rationality (Hegel, 1942).

The interweaving of those three fundamental assumptions: the autonomy of culture, the universality of human science, and rationality as the principle of modernity, was a characteristic which Hegel's and Weber's intellectual production had in common. Weber did not have to refer to Hegel for that purpose. Those assumptions of the Hegelian enterprise had become part of the collective consciousness of the German academic classes.

But Weber also rejected Hegel and this was no less fateful for the shape of his scientific activity. The mystical core of Hegel's faith in rationality was for Weber destroyed by the very progress of rationality. There was no way in which Weber could share a belief in the divine nature of the Idea.

In a world where Darwin had rewritten the story of creation, when the life of Jesus could be written as a human story, where Nietzsche had pronounced the death of God and the overthrow of Christian values, and where science had produced technical achievements beyond Hegel's wildest dreams, rationality, far from being divine, appeared more the machinery of a secularised world, deprived of spirit and animated by technique.

Weber faced the fate of his time, not as a philosopher of a benign, freedom-conferring state as Hegel had done, but as a scientist committed by his gifts and a heavy sense of duty to pointing out the unwelcome consequences and the necessary evils which accompanied the rationalisation of every sphere of human life.

7

The Meaning of Rationality

In this chapter I shall consider the scope of the idea which was the frame, burden and resource for the whole of Weber's thought. I will do this by drawing upon those references to it which are incidental and non-technical in his writing, where he is drawing upon the long tradition of Western rationalism in a quite unproblematical manner. The next chapter will turn to his specific technical usage of rationality in the context of the formation of social scientific concepts.

Weber's development of his own theoretical framework lies entirely within the broader tradition on which he drew comprehensively and with little reservation. He never sought to delimit the idea of rationality except in special contexts, but for our purposes some specification of its overall scope and content is an essential preliminary clarification. This has to be done in the broadest possible outline because otherwise so often the result is a failure to grasp the full weight and direction of the intellectual animation of his work. Although they are intertwined intimately with each other, nine major facets of the idea of rationality will be distinguished.

1   Rationality as idea

In the first place rationality is not a natural object, nor a material thing, is neither artefact nor deed, it is not a feeling, a biological process or an event. It is an *idea*. But, at this point we come up against language difficulties. For, of course, we can have an idea of a natural object, both in general and in particular, or an idea of a thing, deed, feeling, etc. But in talking and writing about things, objects, or feelings, etc. we refer to these as points of reference for our ideas, rather than as ideas. To think about ideas is not just to think about something, it means having an idea of an idea. Reason, as the idea of an idea, raises the prospects of an ever receding process of reflection

It is with just this feature of human reason that Kant confronts his reader at the beginning of the *Critique of Pure Reason*. It is the inability of reason to call upon any source other than that which it contains already. Human thought is its own foundation, and in this respect it is not just the idea of the idea, it is also the continuous process of relating ideas to ideas, of finding contradictions and restoring unities, an endless process of creating and ordering the products of the mind.

Applied to nature, reason generates science and technology; in the social life of human beings it generates law, morality and economics. The human being lives by the rational principle, said Aristotle, and is unique in having this gift (*Politics*, 1332b).

In the broadest sense Weber's idea of rationality belongs to this most comprehensive idea of all. We can say this simply because he uses 'rational' and its related forms so profusely. Action and contemplation, magic and art, science and religion, authority and ethics, economics and law, could all at one time or another merit the label 'rational' without Weber ever feeling the need to elaborate the general idea of rationality.

Once or twice he did observe that 'rational' could be used for very different things. He contrasted the 'rationalism' of Confucianism with Western utilitarianism and then in turn considered Yoga to be rational in its very methodical nature (Essays: 293). As he said in *The Protestant Ethic and the Spirit of Capitalism*: 'In fact one may – this simple proposition, which is often forgotten, should be placed at the beginning of every study which essays to deal with rationalism – rationalize life from fundamentally different points of view and in very different directions. Rationalism is an historical concept which covers a whole world of different things' (PE: 77–8).

It could not be otherwise, we may comment. For thought touches on everything, and different forms of thinking still share in the rational idea. At another point where Weber allows himself a rare reflection on rationality as idea, he pointed out that rationalisation might mean the development of increasingly precise and abstract concepts, or it might mean the methodical attainment of given ends with precisely claculated means. But, he added, 'These types of rationalism are very different in spite of the fact that ultimately they belong inseparably together' (Essays: 293).

The ultimate 'belonging together' was not Weber's concern. Reflection upon the idea of rationality belonged to philosophy. It was the multifarious and often contradictory development of the idea in human history which absorbed the attention of Weber as empirical scientist. But as a scientist he also felt himself to be the main beneficiary of the development of rationality in so far as logic and scientific knowledge were outcomes of that development. Here too he was able to avail himself without self-conscious difficulty of the Western taken-for-granted assumption of the rationality of logic and scientifically-obtained knowledge.

2 Rationality as logic

If reason gave shape to the world of ideas, logic was the tool which enabled the shape to be formed. Weber took it for granted that logic belonged without doubt or remainder to the sphere of reason or rationality. Again, as an empirical scientist it was not his task to advance the science of logic, but he did not hesitate to appeal to logic as his authority in discussing the foundations of social science. In his methodological essays, the *Wissenschaftslehre*, references to 'logic' or 'logical' alone exceed references to the rational.

He had ample grounds for feeling secure with logic as part of his intellectual armoury. Kant had provided a forceful statement of the orthodox view that, apart from a few refinements, logic presented a closed and complete doctrine since the time of Aristotle. Its clarity and certainty derived from the fact that it was removed from the real world, it was reason dealing with reason alone. 'The sphere of logic is quite precisely delimited; its sole concern is to give an exhaustive exposition and a strict proof of the formal rules of all thought' (Kant, 1933: 18).

Clarity, consistency, certainty, coherence and system were all attributes which logic brought to reason, providing the form for thought, generated by thought alone. They were the guarantees of what Weber preferred to call 'formal rationality'. They could be employed in the development of any idea whatsoever. Law was in some ways Weber's favourite example because he had personal experience of its practice and it had been his main specialism as a student. Modern law had become increasingly formal, characterised by 'logical rationality and systematisation' taking on 'an increasingly logical sublimation and deductive rigor' (E&S II: 882).

But there are other, ostensibly less likely, candidates for subjection to the canons of logic. Mention has been made of Yoga – it was subject to rationality in the sense of 'systematic arrangement' – but mastery of reality through precise and abstract concepts was demonstrated in such diverse fields as physics, theology and art. Religious belief could be subject to very varying degrees of logical systematisation, and was particularly subject to the need for systematisation in the construction of theodicies, or justifications of the ways of God to human beings.

Formal conceptual schemata could then be applied to any realm of thought, but at the same time Weber posited an 'inner' logic for certain ideas which appeared to have its own direction. The autonomy of ideas or value-spheres (*Eigengesetzlichkeit*) occupied a strategic place within Weber's thinking about rationality, and I shall have occasion to return to it in the last section of this chapter and also in Chapter 12.

Above all, of course, logic shaped science, the supreme product of Western rationality, and it was distinctions found within logic which Weber found most useful in Rickert's classification of the sciences.

In this earliest essay on the historian Roscher (1817–94), Weber distinguished sciences which sought to order the infinite manifold reality of nature through universally valid concepts and laws, from sciences which sought to identify the essential nature of individual concepts, to identify the concrete circumstances, causes and effects of their appearance and to reveal the universal significance of their unique individuality (WL: 1–42). In fact, said Weber, only pure mechanics, in the first case, and some kinds of historiography, in the second, corresponded completely with these models and sciences were often distinguished from each other by other characteristics. But this was still the fundamental distinction to recognise.

In other words, and here we can comment on Weber, it was the regulative idea of logic, much as Kant understood it, which enabled us to understand the twin thrusts of any science whatsoever.

3 Rationality as calculation

One of the directions in which logic led was precision and in this neo-Kantian division of the sciences, the classificatory and systematising science also went so far along this road that mathematical equations were the outcome. Logic merged into mathematics. Weber was writing before the identity of the two had been proclaimed, but he had no difficulty in seeing them as intimately connected because mathematics had long held its position as the most impressive product of pure thought.

As Kant put it, 'mathematics presents the most splendid example of the successful extension of pure reason, without the help of experience' (1933: 576). Mathematics, for him, represented construction on the basis of a priori intuition, it operated through definitions, axioms and proofs which owed nothing to the empirical world.

For Weber, therefore, it was the most natural thing to consider the mathematising of the sciences as an extension of rationality, the growth of the fruits of pure thought. At the same time the application of science to the world through technology and the application of mathematics, even at the simplest level to everyday life, were equally advances in rationality. He gave great weight to these factors in his accounts of the development of Western culture.

As with logic, calculative power could be developed in any sector of social life if the conditions were right. In the case of economic activity calculation became necessary when companies were formed and divisions of proceeds among the individual members had to take place.

In Weber's lectures on economic history, which he gave in the last year of his life, quantitative reckoning became the defining feature of rational commerce and the development of computation from mechanical aids like the abacus, to the Arabic numerals and double entry book-keeping, was associated with the requirements of commerce (GEH: 170). In fact, Weber went on to give rational capital accounting pride of place as the main defining characteristic of modern capitalism, and it was calculability which was the bonding element in his list of further features; trading on the market, a technology which could be reduced to calculation, law on which the trader could calculate, free labour so that costs of employment could be calculated, and the development of instruments of exchange which could facilitate commercialisation (ibid.: 208-9).

It was in the area of economic life that Weber was most explicit in theorising the idea of rationality and in giving it central significance. 'The term "formal rationality of economic action" will be used to designate the extent of quantitative calculation or accounting which is technically possible and which is actually applied' (E&S I: 85). This was actually the case in the highest degree in a money economy which has all kinds of advantages over calculations in kind and indeed Weber preferred to use the term 'market economy' to refer to situations of exchange through the medium of money because uniform calculation became possible.

Formal rationality therefore came to its point of highest development in capitalism and all kinds of attempts to regulate economies in the interests of collective actors, state intervention, nationalisation and socialism, however rational in a substantive or material sense, could never in Weber's view achieve the same degree of formal rationality. What in this context Weber termed 'material rationality' referred directly to rationality in terms of means and ends which we will come to shortly. He was also expressing a notion which has a profound significance in the whole structure of his thought, namely that even within the very concept which is centred on the unity of thought and logic, unbridgeable conflict is also an irreducible element.

4   Rationality as science

Beyond logic, beyond calculation was the real world, the realm of nature and other human beings, which was experienced in daily life. In an important sense that world was ultimately irrational, it was infinitely and irremediably diverse and Weber did not hesitate to employ the Kantian notion of multiplicity (*Mannigfaltigkeit*) as an ultimate idea in this context. The experience of this multiplicity was equally irrational.

The irreducible irrational foundation to reality and experience is as important in Weber's thought world as the rational idea. The one requires the other, but empirical science represented the mastery of reality by the rational idea and the knowledge gained through scientific method the most important foundation for rational action.

Weber's doctrine of scientific knowledge, derived very largely from Rickert, was outlined in his early essays on Roscher and Knies, and was concerned very much to delimit the spheres of the rational and irrational in natural and cultural sciences. We were concerned with his discussion of Knies in connection with the theory of personality, but Weber had an equal interest in the methodology of historical and cultural science. He wanted to combat the idea that the sciences of human action were in any sense more focused on irrationality than natural science.

For Weber scientific knowledge, both natural and cultural, took us further away from irrational foundations. We saw how at the beginning of those essays he outlined the distinction between generalising and individualising sciences. The former proceed to ever more comprehensive propositions about the world, abstract and mathematical, the latter to ever more refined description of the universal significance of an individual person or phenomenon and to identifying its place in a concrete context.

A dominant image Weber employed for illustrative purposes was that of the rock which had fallen from a cliff face in a storm and shattered into countless pieces. The generalising science could account for the fall, and even the extent and degree of the shattering, but there would be a point at which it became senseless to pursue the quest for explanation for the fate of individual splinters.

Scientific knowledge, in the form of laws, generalisations, hypotheses and theories made sense of an ultimately irreducible diverse reality. Similarly, the individualising science crafted a concept of universal significance by disregarding the inessential and relating the phenomenon to the broadest historical context in order to discern its characteristic features. With the individualising science in the sphere of culture there was also the possibility of understanding motives which raised a whole series of further issues and actually enhanced the rationality of individual events in the human sphere for the observer (WL: 67).

But as well as the sciences of reality, Weber acknowledged the scientific status of disciplines which dealt with principles, aesthetics, law or even economics. Here rationality involved the development of basic ideas or values in specific directions. These axiomatic or dogmatic sciences were of particular concern to Weber as a political economist and sociologist, and we shall consider his elaboration of the ideal type concept in this connection later. They even included theology for him, which equally represented the intellectual *rationalisation* of sacred values (Essays: 153).

The point was that for Weber every science began with certain presuppositions. Rational knowledge was constructed on a variety of foundations. Empirical science gave us mastery of the world and our environment, the dogmatic sciences a different kind of control, over ourselves and our values.

The vast resources this intellectualisation provided the human race in the form of accumulated knowledge and technique created for Weber a disenchanted world, one in which the irrational foundations were left far behind as individuals inhabited a vast rational edifice, which they knew in principle to be wholly explicable, but over which they had no control. But the development of this alienating rationality appeared to him to be inherent in any prospects for the future which he could discern.

5   Rationality as action

That rationality could inhere in and be expressed through human action was not merely a fundamental tenet of German idealism. It was a central theme of Western philosophy going back to the Greeks. The Aristotelian account of the virtues was that they occupied an intermediate sphere where the rational and irrational elements in the human psyche intersected. Arising out of education and the acquisition of good habits, the individual expressed virtues through action (*Ethics*, Bk 1, ch. 13). Wisdom was the knowledge of virtue and incontestably rational. But, additionally, prudence was exhibited in practical activities, both in politics and day-to-day business, and involved calculation and familiarity with the details of daily life. In those ways it also was rational (*Ethics*, Bk 6).

The ideas of action in accord with principle and action involving calculation of means and ends were then inextricably bound up with the concept of rationality for Aristotle as they were in the eighteenth century for Kant. The latter's *Foundations of the Metaphysics of Morals* (1785) reflected the eighteenth century's faith in the development of two kinds of law, scientific laws and man made legal systems, and consequently differed in its emphasis from Aristotle's account of virtues encompassed by the life of the citizen of a Greek city state.

So the principles of action now are likened to natural laws, exercising an objective constraint on the human being as imperatives, or commands of reason. But the Aristotelian distinction between wisdom and prudence lives on in these starker Kantian contrasts. Categorical imperatives arise out of reason determining what is good in itself, while hypothetical imperatives relate to the performance of actions technically necessary for obtaining some future good. In either of these senses action was the peculiar property of rational beings, distinguishing humanity from the animal realm.

It is not easy to exaggerate the significance of this nexus of thinking about ideas and action in Western civilisation. To be sure, if action was defined by reference to principle, it arose out of something which was not itself ideal or rational, namely from the body, material needs and desire. But this also meant thinking about rationality established the agenda for any inquiry into the natural causes of human action. Materialist responses to idealists' assertion of the primacy of reason in human affairs still leave the action concept or the idea of practice as the common topic of concern.

Hegel's own so-called 'objective idealism' sought to locate the idea in reality, to view the actual as rational. Marx went further still by treating ideas as somehow secondary to action, reflections or expressions of what people do. The major ideological conflicts of the modern world have therefore involved conceptual shifts around the axes of ideas, action and the material world. But all the main protagonists in these epic struggles to command the human mind accept that, whatever else rationality might mean, it must in some way inhere in action.

Weber took action to be the central concept of his sociology. It follows that rationality became an inherent element of all his scientific work in that discipline. In one sense, it was a simple and straightforward decision to take. It was obvious. But its obviousness was the outcome and product of over two thousand years of philosophical work. Weber was in effect asserting the claim for sociology to be the true inheritor of that tradition of thought.

Let us be clear. Weber did not sit down to read Aristotle and Kant and then devise a sociology to borrow their best ideas and supplant philosophy. What he did do was to take the utterly familiar ideas of the educated classes of his time, to which he unquestioningly belonged, and whose discourse was the product of a long intellectual development, and then respond to the ever more insistent demand that an empirical science should be advanced to give an account of the often bewildering changes which afflicted the times in which they lived.

Kant's response had been to the scientific Enlightenment of the eighteenth century, Weber's was to a world which was absorbing the scientific revolutions of the theory of evolution and modern physics. To a large extent, those changes in themselves were sufficient to sever any direct and explicit discussion of the foundations of the modern idea of rationality. The idea was cut loose from its anchorage in the past. It was embedded in the practical daily activities of businessmen, lawyers, administrators, and ordinary wage workers.

6   Rationality as consciousness

The idea expressed in clear propositions, the precise and incontrovertible deductions of logic and mathematics informing the human action, remained at the centre of Weber's notion of rationality, but as one moves away from that centre and approaches the opposite pole of dark, unpredictable, inchoate forces, arising from nature and the material world, there is a transitional zone where it is difficult to locate the boundary between the rational and irrational with any precision.

We saw that empirical knowledge, while clearly for Weber on the rational side of the divide, nonetheless partakes of irrationality to the extent that it must accommodate experience and sheer brute fact. They can be shaped and interpreted by reason, but their source is from elsewhere. The world of thought and ideas equally has a very broad border territory which it shares with the irrational.

Weber was writing at a time which one intellectual historian of the period, H. Stuart Hughes, has characterised in part by the 'recovery of the unconscious' (1959: 105). Bergson, Freud and Jung were contemporaries of Weber who all sought to facilitate a coming-to-terms with inner forces over which the individual might feel there was no control. Bringing them to consciousness was regarded as the prerequisite for self-knowledge and the achievement of, variously, power, integrity, rational action, or the full life.

Freud's work was included by Weber within a much wider genre of interpretative psychology, practised also by his friend Karl Jaspers, whose massive *Allgemeine Psychopathologie* (1913) Weber cited at the beginning of *Economy and Society* as a basic source for the discussion of *Verstehen*. When it came to the sociological explanation of irrationality, then the kind of psychology Jaspers represented could undoubtably provide 'decisively important services', said Weber (E&S I: 19).

If consciousness is regarded as a prerequisite for individual rationality, it may also sometimes be taken to be coextensive with it. In which case the bringing to consciousness of basic hitherto unacknowledged feelings may locate them within the rational sphere. In his essay on the objectivity of social scientific knowledge he argued that the critical analysis of purposes and underlying ideas could submit them to the postulate of inner non-contradictoriness. In this way they could become the object of reflection to reveal the ultimate axioms and value standpoints from which the individual either unconsciously proceeded, or would have to if he or she was going to be logical (WL: 151).

Motives of all kinds could be revealed through rational reflection and one of the central tasks of sociology was to proceed towards the discovery of repressed or displaced motives. Most people, argued Weber, operated unconsciously, or at least in only a dim half-consciousness, of the meaning which underlay their own actions. All kind of drives or acquired usages that dominated their action needed to be brought to the surface (E&S I: 10).

In this way Weber quite explicitly linked sociology with the task of enhancing consciousness for the methods he imputed to the emerging discipline clearly for him went far beyond what was open to the unaided individual's introspection. All the resources of empirical and axiomatic science needed to be enlisted to amplify and check whatever insight might be available from personal self-enquiry. This point comes close to the heart of Weber's theory of understanding to which we will return in a later chapter.

Weber did not pursue this idea of rationality to its full radical potential. The revelatory functions of reason, combining as they do the Kantian idea of critique with Socratic notions of knowledge of self, can be understood as a transformatory force, for the individual and for society as a whole. It was the kernel of the young Marx's revolutionary theory and has inspired a bewildering variety of nineteenth- and twentieth-century searches for alternative lifestyles.

In a purely theoretical form it has received its most sustained expression in the work of the Frankfurt School and, most recently, Habermas. Such ventures would have taken Weber too far from the chosen path of empirical science and his own sense of identity was too intimately linked with the German intellectual classes to make alternatives attractive.

However, the intellectual affiliations between Weber's idea of rationality and notions of critique and the recovery of the unconscious need to be recognised by commentators. They certainly give the lie to the accusation that he represented technocratic reason. While rationality as consciousness is not an extensively elaborated idea in his work, quite clearly his thinking took him a long way beyond the notion of purposive rationality, or means–ends thinking, or the ideology of technocracy, which far too often have been held to characterise his work to the exclusion of all else.

7   Rationality as structure

Like critique and the unconscious, structure has become the focus for a broad twentieth-century intellectual movement. And just as Weber has been criticised for neglecting the radical potential of reason, so also has he been accused of failing to recognise that individual thought and action is embedded in and dependent on structures of all kinds, cultural and social.

It was in fact a criticism which was the main burden of the most substantial early treatment of Weber's methodology by Alexander von Schelting. He pointed out that the main thrust of Weber's discussion of the method of social science was to emphasise the understanding of the real inner processes of individuals. Unlike his mentor Rickert, Schelting argued, he did not see the understanding of unreal structures of meaning as an equally important focus for social and cultural science (von Schelting, 1934: 353–400).

Talcott Parsons took up von Schelting's criticism with enthusiasm and also asserted that Weber just missed identifying the importance of atemporal complexes of meaning (Parsons, 1937: 636–7). In fact both Parsons and von Schelting moderate their criticism to a very substantial extent by acknowledging that in practice Weber paid considerable attention to the way individual motivation was embedded in larger complexes of meaning and it was only that his methodological statements appeared to give less weight to this vital element in his work.

For the neo-Kantians the idea of system belonged to the mind and meaningful structures inhabited a timeless sphere which was studied systematically by axiomatic sciences, such as law or aesthetics, sciences which Weber termed 'dogmatic'. He considered empirical science could, and indeed had to, make use of constructions from the dogmatic sciences and he reserved for them a vital place in the construction of ideal types. Moreover, the systems of ideas which the dogmatic sciences developed exercised profound constraints and pointed in obvious directions for their adherents and those who had to submit to them. Systems of ideas, while not properly termed 'causes', were certainly key elements in causal explanation of human action.

But Weber was also perfectly prepared to go further and acknowledge the importance of more concrete structures. So often the reservations he has expressed about aspects of sociological methodology have been exaggerated by commentators into outright opposition. Hence his comments on functionalist approaches have been seen as a root-and-branch rejection of them. Weber's actual summing up of a lengthy discussion of their merits needs to be emphasised to counteract that misrepresentation: 'Any form of functional analysis which proceeds from the whole to the parts can accomplish only a preliminary preparation for this investigation – a preparation, the utility and indispensability of which, if properly carried out, is naturally beyond question' (E&S I: 18). As so often with Weber it was not the intellectual gains from a methodological viewpoint to which he objected. He was able to give generous acknowledgement to Freudian, Marxist and functionalist insights alike. It was what he regarded as invalid socio-political inferences from scientific positions to which he responded with vigour and sometimes venom.

In addition to ideal structures and social wholes, Weber drew on a third major idea of structure, namely of an underlying or deeper foundation of action which needed to be discovered by sociological and psychological analysis. Central to Weber's intellectual objectives was the explanation of action by reference to motives, conscious or unconscious, and these were normally to be seen as part of a wider complex of meaning which had to be reconstructed by the observer from a multiplicity of data sources. Indeed, interpretation was precisely the revealing of the structure of meaning in a motive, or the placing of a motive in an ever more elaborated meaningful structure – the emphasis varying depending on the limits placed on the idea of motive.

Unfortunately this third major idea of structure in Weber is one which has suffered most from translation difficulties. There is no easy translation of the German *Sinnzusammenhang*, which Weber employed repeatedly in his discussions of method, and in English it is rendered in a variety of ways according to context in one and the same work. The result is that the English speaking reader loses the thematic unity of Weber's discussion. The most literal translation is 'a hanging together of meaning'. Parsons called it 'the expressive German term' (1937: 482) and translated it variously, 'complex of meanings' (ibid.), 'relations of meaning' (ibid.: 485), 'context of meaning' (E&S I: 58) and 'meaningful system' (ibid.). A more recent German introduction to Weber's work has emphasised, in order to counteract the misunderstandings, which one may infer have been fed back into German commentary, that the idea of *Sinnzusammenhang* is central to Weber's thinking, allowing him to develop his analysis beyond the starting point of subjective intentions (Käsler, 1988: 176–7). Indeed, one may go as far as saying that social science in the Weberian, or perhaps any, sense could not proceed without this idea.

Meaningful structures pervade Weber's empirical work, often in combinations of the three types we have just distinguished –

Protestantism, bureaucracy and rationalism being only some of the most obvious. They are intimately associated with rationality. But we can go further than noticing an association. They are not accidental expressions of Weber's interests. Wherever 'meaningful system' is invoked the idea of rationality is evoked also, and whatever rationality comes into focus then the idea of system follows.

The making of connections between ideas, the identification of entailments and contradictions, in so far as it is cumulative, has as a result the construction of a system in any ordinary sense of the term. For Kant the end of reason was system, knowledge had to form a unity, and that was a system in which all the parts were related to the whole (Kant, 1933: 653). The thrust to system was therefore an inherent goal of rationality.

8 Irrationality

Weber took it for granted that against rationality was counterposed irrationality. This sphere was not simply defined negatively. It had its own shape and complexity. Thus, for example, the emotions were a prime instance of rationality, but constituting a complex and differentiated field of forces interfering with rational thought and action. While, as we shall see, rational action had a special place in Weber's thinking about method, he was emphatic that the sphere of the emotions was as least of equal importance as a field of sociological investigation, precisely because the analysis of rational action invariably came up against these irrational forces (WL: 405). This was notwithstanding the fact that psychology, both laboratory-based and interpretative, had a lot to say on the subject too.

Weber's idea of irrationality was no more tightly and formalistically defined than his idea of rationality. It was identified concretely in historical contexts and provided Weber's more abstract classificatory schemes with ample illustration. It was not a mere abstract possibility. It might appear as the 'greatest irrational force of life: sexual love' (Essays: 343) or as 'the most irrational form of religious behaviour, the mystic experience' (ibid.: 342). In these cases we appear to face a force of uneven and unpredictable incidence, but capable of being documented and recognised in its impact.

In other respects irrationality might appear as an irremediable part of the human condition, as the presuppositions of a rational methodical life, accepted as simply 'given' (ibid.: 281). To this extent, reality itself could be characterised as 'irrational' (WL: 213). As Kant had done, Weber associated emotional irrationality, which arose our of the animal nature of the human being, with a metaphysical irrationality in which reason invariably came up against limits. In this respect the roots of action were always ultimately shrouded in darkness and the experience of life was a pre-rational mystery. He considered the irrational element in religious experience to be ultimately incommunicable and cited William James' *The Varieties of Religious Experience* (1935) approvingly (PE: 233). But true to his Kantian presuppositions he added the rider that all experience to a greater or lesser degree was irrational. In the same way scientific ideas 'occur to us when they please, not when it pleases us' and arise out of imagination and inspiration (Essays: 136).

As well as these momentous forces, Weber allowed for the more mundane irrationality of logical mistakes, errors about fact, and prejudgements. He also gave very great weight to mundane everyday activities which were maintained out of unconscious adherence to the usual way of doing things. Rationality was not confronted simply with forces from below, surging to the surface, but also with the dull acceptance of routine, with tradition.

Without being unduly schematic we can identify four of the major variants of Weber's idea of irrationality – the metaphysical, the emotional, the logically and scientifically erroneous, and the traditional. These could be bonded into and expressed through structures of various kinds, from the tribal group to the nation-state. And it is in the relations between groups, and especially in the modern nation-state, that Weber located a fifth great field of irrationality, that of power and physical force, an irrationality of the 'world' which gave enormous trouble to ethical philosophers or indeed anyone with a conscience.

In one sense violence might be seen as the expression of an instinct, but for Weber more important was its calculated use in conflict between states, and there it became just one resource among others, a fact of life, and in its conflict with ethical principle fundamentally irrational still. It was for Weber, as he explained in his lecture on 'Politics as a Vocation', the prime example of the irrationality of the world, and no amount of sophisticated argument or cool calculation could overcome that fact (Essays: 123).

There is no system here, then. He made no attempt, as Pareto his Italian contemporary attempted, to identify a logical sphere and proceed by elimination to identify the illogical and classify non-logical element in behaviour. In fact the distinction between the irrational and non-rational was one of which Weber made very scant use. He did, on one occasion, speaking of the pure type of economic action, suggest that it made fully evident the non-rational elements of actual economic action, but this is a rare example (WL: 131). On occasion he spoke of the 'anti-rational', as exhibited in the religiosity of boundless trust in God as a barrier to developing anything that could be called religious intellectualism (E&S I: 567). But normally he operated on the basis of a binary distinction between the rational and irrational.

The preference in Weber for this polar distinction does tend to give an accentuated tone to points of conflict between reason and unreason greater than would exist if he used a more open vocabulary. The core of Talcott Parsons' prodigious commentary on the modern founders of sociology, *The Structure of Social Action* (1937), is largely based on pointing out the deficiencies of models of action which depend on treating them as operating one one dimension, scientific/unscientific.

As Parsons says at one point, theories, or elements of them, may not only be unscientific, they may be non-scientific, in that they involve entities or considerations which fall altogether outside the range of scientific competence (1937: 202). To think otherwise was to fall into the positivistic trap. Certainly one can feel that 'facts of nature' would be more appropriately designated 'non-rational' than 'irrational' since they fall outside the realm of reason altogether. A mistake can be seen as a cause of illogicality, while a poem is more properly designated non-logical. Reason has a hard task if the rest of the cosmos is arrayed behind unreason. But then that was how Weber felt. And as he never ceased to reiterate, when it comes to the ultimate elements of a world-view, feeling is quite as important as reason.

9 Conflicts of rationality

The source of Weber's idea of rationality was not explicit engagement with philosophy, but a lifetime's encounter with it in a range of academic and professional disciplines and in the daily maxims of the German intellectual classes. In this sense it is not self-contradictory to say that his knowledge of rationality was *empirical*.

He was more than happy to use the term 'rational' in quotation marks to indicate its location in everyday parlance. He was equally happy to accept that rationality appeared in life in a variety of guises. It was an empiricist's view of rationality, in tune with the thrust to develop sociology as an empirical discipline and with Weber's prodigious appetite for historical and empirical source material.

On the face of it this empiricist attitude to rationality is sufficient to explain the frequency with which Weber not only saw different varieties of rationality, but also conflicts between them. He made no attempt to minimise clashes between different rationalities. Different people could rationalise their lives from different points of view. Hence differing kinds of 'rationalism' developed. Confucianism avoided all kinds of metaphysics and religious foundations and appeared rational in the sense of utilitarian, yet it different fundamentally from the Western utilitarianism of Bentham (Essays: 293). 'Rationalism is an historical concept which covers a whole world of different things', and that, said Weber, should be placed 'at the beginning of every study which essays to deal with rationalism' (PE: 78).

The particular contrast between Benthamism and Confucianism was drawn by Weber as part of a general discussion of the meaning of 'rationalism' with which he prefaced his comparative studies of world religions. This was published first in 1915 (Essays: 267–301). When these studies were drawn together in 1920 Weber wrote yet another introduction to them in which he reverted to the same theme, namely the peculiar character of Western rationalism, pointing out that different life spheres could be rationalised so that 'what is rational from one point of view may well be irrational from another' (PE: 26).

These conflicts of rationality were not confined to the pursuit of differing ends. They went deeper than that. The mastery of the world through concepts was not the same as the methodical attainment of ends, and the differences between English and Continental physics could be traced back to similar types of differences in the comprehension of reality (Essays: 293).

In the sphere of ethics he identified two internally consistent types: the ethics of responsibility and of conscience, each defensible in rational terms but in everlasting tension. The former involved acting with regard to consequences, the latter with regard to following imperatives, each in their own way 'rational' (ibid.: 120). No amount of sophisticated argument could overcome this irrationality of the world, and this was for Weber the 'driving force of all religious evolution' (ibid.: 123).

We shall see that this kind of irreconcilable difference was also reflected in Weber's two types of rational action, and also in his distinction between formal and material rationality. Efficiency may conflict with justice, precise calculation may detract from achieving an objective. Distributive justice may militate against production, while economic rationality may generate inequality. Dilemmas of this kind were for Weber at the heart of the debates raging around capitalism and socialism. And these were not resolvable in any ultimately rational sense. As he put it when discussing money calculation in relation to property distribution: 'Formal and substantive rationality, no matter by what standard the latter is measured, are always in principle separate things, no matter that in many (and under certain very artificial assumptions even in all) cases they may coincide empirically' (E&S I: 108).

Mommsen has spoken of this feature of Weber's thought as 'antinomian', thereby rightly evoking similar dilemmas in Kant's thought (1981). Kant examined such notions as 'everything has a beginning', or 'every complex whole is made up of parts', or 'everything is caused', and he found that every proposition of that kind could be countered by an equally plausible opposite. The result, he pointed out, was perplexing in the extreme: 'For in this domain, however it may endeavour to establish its principle of unconditioned unity, and though it indeed does so with great though illusory appearance of success, it soon falls into such contradictions that it is constrained, in this cosmological field, to desist from any such pretensions' (1933: 385).

Kant's solution to the problem of what he called the antinomies was to argue that they arose out of a misunderstanding of the limits of reason when applied to the real world. Ideas, such as infinity, or universal causation, were not part of experience, they transcended it. Indeed, they could not possibly be experienced, and there was no object in the real world which corresponded to them. They were, however, an essential feature of regulating our understanding of the real world, where their employment would be necessary and without end. This disjunction between the real, empirical world and the realm of ideas, and the regulative function the latter serves for the former, is the core of Kant's philosophical intuition.

Weber shared that intuition. But he was not a philosopher. He was in his own mind an empirical scientist of human affairs. It was therefore not his task to pursue the logic of pure ideas. He was guided by reason and logic, but in this respect they were just as likely to reveal contradiction as consistency.

Both those who in their lives regulated their activities by reason *and* the social and cultural scientist seeking to account for those activities were committed to an endless task of transcending one set of difficulties, and in that very success revealing another. The quest for systematic unity was the goal of science, but the belief that you had ever attained it was contrary to reason.

We shall find that these antinomian dilemmas are retained in the technical scheme of concepts Weber developed for his systematic analysis of the relations of economy and society. As he readily admitted, the pursuit of precision generated new technical problems and in the case of social and cultural sciences was often overtaken by changes in the real world partly induced even by science. But so long as science was valued, there was no escape from this fate.

8

From Premises to Constructs: Modelling Social Life

Preamble

Up to now I have examined the assumptions underlying Weber's work, his world-view, and in Chapter 5 surveyed the stimuli to which he responded. The last chapter explored the idea which I have argued was the focal one for his life and work. But it remained still at the level of assumptions.

For the purpose of clarity I want to distinguish assumptions, premises and constructs. In interpreting Max Weber's work I proceed from the implicit to the explicit. This method adheres to his canons, namely that ultimately ideas spring from sources which the author does not control.

Premises are those ideas which are distinguished from assumptions by the fact that the author examines them for their cogency and defends their use. They are assumptions over which the author seeks to extend some control. As we shall see, Weber's thinking about action and the relation of ideas to the world generates premises in this sense.

Constructs develop from premises as part of the creative intellectual work of the scholar or scientist. They are ideas which are fashioned for a purpose. Weber's ideal types fall into this category. In this chapter and the next I shall go on to examine those constructs by means of which Weber analysed social structure.

1 The most elementary unit of analysis

Weber's search for the foundations of social science was as central to his personality as the Protestant's quest for salvation. The question 'How can I be sure?' has an equivalent place in both his view of science and in a Protestant's faith. The anxious search for certainty, for a sure foundation in a world in which rationality had overturned both traditional knowledge and authority structures was the distinguishing feature of European philosophy from the seventeenth to the early twentieth centuries. It expressed itself in the depth of concern for both origins and destinations, the desire to have some relief from involvement in infinite chains of cause and effect or of responsibility.

The most profound and popular expression of the dilemmas of science and faith in the modern world may be found in Goethe's *Faust*, a drama with which Weber, like any other member of his class, was deeply familiar. Goethe has Faust, the intellectual who has mastered every discipline and found meaning in none, come back from a walk in the country with his dog to find comfort in the close confines fo his study where reason speaks to him and where by translating the New Testament he may find that revelation about the source of life:

> It is written: 'In the beginning was the Word'. Here I am already at a stand – who will help me on? I cannot possibly value the Word so highly; I must translate it differently, if I am truly inspired by the spirit. It is written: 'In the beginning was the Sense'. Consider well the first line, that your pen be not over hasty. Is it the Sense that influences and produces everything? It should stand thus: 'In the beginning was the Power'. Yet, even as I am writing down this, something warns me not to keep to it. The spirit comes to my aid! At once I see my way, and write confidently: 'In the beginning was the Deed' (Hayward's trans., 1834: 50).

Almost at once Faust is confronted with Mephistopheles, the personification of evil, who, when Faust asks him his name, mocks the searcher after essences, who rates the Word so low and yet asks for something so trifling as a name.

The irony of this fable for Weber would not have been lost, since the ambitions of sociology itself emerged precisely out of the belief that the existing sciences failed to make sense without this new-fangled higher order integrative discipline. The overall view, but getting to the essence of things, led Faust to a compact with the

Devil; Weber was drawn relentlessly and in spite of himself towards sociology. Like Faust he concluded that the foundations, the beginning of things, lay with the Deed, or at least with something very similar, namely *action*.

Weber's first version of the foundations of sociology was published in the journal *Logos* in 1913. There he stated: 'The purpose of the consideration, namely "understanding" (*Verstehen*) is ultimately the reason why interpretative sociology in our sense of the term treats the single individual and his action as the most basic entity, as its "atom", if that in itself dubious comparison may be permitted here' (WL: 415).

In the later version, which was published with *Economy and Society* in 1920, action was central to his definition of sociology which became 'a science which attempts the interpretive understanding of social action in order thereby to arrive at a causal explanation of its course and effects' (E&S I: 4). Again only individuals were allowed to be the bearers of action. No one should underestimate the amount of theoretical underpinning by which this definition of sociology was sustained. It remains to this day the most consciously chosen, and the most painstakingly derived of any of the multitude of competing definitions which this now prolific intellectual growth has borne.

Numerous other possibilities for a starting point were available to Weber in the contributions of his contemporaries and forerunners. Holistic theories modelled on Comte's or Spencer's examples were still popular. Society itself was often conceived as the immediate focus. Historical materialism offered the option of the material life of concrete persons, while idealist refutations, such as Stammler's, saw society in the mind. Racial and biological theories came in numerous guises. Weber rejected them all as an inadequate starting point, while acknowledging always the grain of truth in each. The individual actor, whether the particular one, the average or the typical, was the only route to understanding which his sociology sought.

Was he therefore saying all other versions of sociology's basis were in error? The answer to this question does reveal deep-seated ambivalence in Weber's approach to social science. He sought never to be dogmatic about terms. They were matters of convenience and he had no special regard for the term 'sociology'.

However, it is scarcely surprising that he should have felt

wedded to his own conception of an intellectual discipline (whatever it might be called) when he had devoted so much attention to its construction. There is then no doubt that his version of the basis of sociology was invested for him with far-reaching importance. However much a materialist or a biological perspective might have heuristic value, it is clear that Weber felt his own approach had features which gave it a compelling intellectual force. But that force derived as much from a *Weltanschauung*, a view of the world, and the values tied up with that, as from any purely logical necessity.

This is the real source of Weber's ambivalence. It was not so much a problem of terminology. For him that was obviously conventional and relatively superficial. Much more important was the fact that ultimately a view of science, where it should start and what its focus should be, was intimately associated with a view of the world and the meaning of living. The pursuit of any science whatsoever obviously involved choices for the scientist in terms of interest, satisfaction and sense of worth. But Weber's definition of sociology made it that discipline which brought those processes of choice into central focus as the very topic. Put at its simplest, at the most devastatingly obvious, he was erecting a scientific discipline around the question, 'Why do people do things – anything or everything?'

That simple question clearly took for him priority over any other question. It was universal, no modern person could avoid it, and it was the burden of the Protestant Kantian tradition to invest it with the fear of damnation and the hope of salvation. It was that tradition above all which had reason penetrate and reveal the transcendental necessity for individual isolation and responsibility, for moral law and individual choice.

When all the technical definitions of meaning, motive, understanding, interpretation, action and behaviour are put to one side, and that is difficult to do since they have both fascination and enormous difficulties, the sense of the whole operation depends upon that Protestant struggle with causation and moral responsibility, with human freedom in a world governed by scientific laws, with the divine spirit in the animal body.

That was the burden which Weber bore in his science and his life, which set him the task and spurred to achievement. The human act, and the reasons for acting, had to be the biggest problem of all. Since it was rationality which forced one to these conclusions it was the presupposition and the necessary formative element in any consideration of these foundation problems. It is the transcendental presupposition for Weber's question and for the discipline which was to answer it.

The great principled decisions which were his own responsibility became then the subject for his enquiry into the lives of other people. He hoped to discover empirically the grounds for the decisions in others' lives which he found in his own life both so fraught and compelling. Sociology then arose out of rationality and became the discipline which examined the nature and limits of rationality in the world. Encapsulated therefore within Weber's conception of the elements of a social science were the organising concepts of not only his own personality, but also the polar ideas between which the minds of modern people had been tossed from the time of the Reformation.

In the beginning was action. All action was either rational or irrational. Action was behaviour with a motive. Action is to be explained by motives. Motives could be understood by being placed in an ever more comprehensive framework of meaning. But only individuals could act, hence could have motives. The meaning of their acts, however comprehensively understood in context and by others, had in the end always to be a meaning that they could at least possibly possess, whether they understood it or not. Again shorn of technicality, this is the underlying message of the fundamental concepts in *Economy and Society*.

The existential requirement of the Kantian version of Protestantism was that individuals had necessarily to be seen as responsible agents, freely willing their own acts and consequently in charge of and mastering their animal natures. In Weber's hands this becomes the heuristic requirement of his sociology. People are to be seen as individuals, with the property of acting for reasons, willing their own purposes, with an animal nature often hidden from their knowledge but still their own for which they could assume responsibility. The purposes of the actor took on a range and depth of meaning often far beyond what any one of them could momentarily grasp. The scientist as sociologist was thus placed in the position of identifying the measure each person took of the universal tasks which it was humanity's fate to undertake.

In Weber's hands it meant that sociology assumed the task of enquiring into the bases of mutual understanding, the place of ultimate values in human existence, the nature and limits of the capacity to achieve anything, the sources of and directions to which rationality impelled the human spirit over historical time and into the future.

It would be difficult to imagine a more ambitious prospect for any social scientist. Weber couched it in terms of impeccable austerity and dryness, expressed it in fine distinctions penetrable only by careful scholarship. He might not even have been prepared to acknowledge this meaning underlying his scientific enterprise. But his own method, turned on himself, does suggest that the deep meaning of his project was his own search for the meaning of human existence. It is revealed even in the technical specification of his basic scientific concepts. Some of the most fundamental are the ones which involve direct specification of some facet of rationality. As we have noticed, the idea of action involves that intrinsically.

2   The types of action

Weber said he did not wish to provide an exhaustive categorisation of action. However, in his own terms all actions had to be either rational or irrational. It was a theme he was to develop on a series of occasions.

One of the most important statements was included in the editorial he wrote on becoming editor of the *Archiv für Sozialwissenschaft und Sozialpolitik* in 1904. At one point there he states his position at its simplest. '"Purpose" is from our point of view an imagined outcome, which becomes the cause of an action.' Like any cause of a significant outcome this attracts our interest; but 'its specific significance depends on our ability and desire not only to give an account of human action, but to understand it' (WL: 183; cf. Meth: 83).

Weber remained steadfastly by his conception through to his last formulation in *Economy and Society*. Human beings are agents whose intentions are of central importance in the explanation of events. Hence rationality has to be always in view. He therefore found himself offering repeated refinements and clarifications of the idea of rational action from 1904 and by his last account he was identifying four major types of action, two rational and two irrational. They were:

   i)   Purposively rational (*zweckrational*)
  ii)   Value rational (*wertrational*)
 iii)   Affectual (*affektuell*), more specifically emotional
 iv)   Traditional

For each of these he provided a definition and a commentary.

i) Purposively rational action he defined as 'determined by expectations of the behaviour of objects in the environment or of other human beings and where these expectations are employed as 'conditions' or 'means' for a person's own rational purposes, striven for and weighed up as outcomes' (WG I: 12; cf. E&S I: 24). In his commentary Weber pointed to rational calculation as essential to *Zweckrationalität*, weighing means against purposes, side-effects against purposes. Sometimes values would be brought in to determine choices where purposes conflicted but it was also possible simply to respond to subjective needs and consciously to calculate their relative urgency on the principle of marginal utility.

Through all his account of action *Zweckrationalität* had pride of place as analytically it offered the maximum degree of determinacy and intelligibility at the same time. The determinacy arose out of the fact that empirical knowledge, accessible to outside scrutiny and the test of experience, was essential to the correct choice of means to ends. The assessment of suitablity of means to given ends was identified by Weber in 1904 as a central contribution the social sciences could make. Often he likened this to natural scientific knowledge. For means to ends were merely the inversion of cause and effect. X causes Y in the framework of human purposes simply became the condition 'If you want Y do X' (WL: 129; also in 1917, WL: 491). Action based on correct causal knowledge had the maximum of certainty or '*Evidenz*', a key term for Weber indicating the point at which questioning ceased because intuitively the investigator felt that the correct answer had been reached.

Of course, this connection between rational action and science meant that the degree of knowledge an actor possessed became a crucial factor in understanding action. Weber elaborated on this theme in 1913 in his first attempt to outline the basic concepts of sociology, suggesting that there was a whole range of possibilities from the most understandable action where means were correctly chosen to ends by all recognisably valid knowledge, through subjectively correct choice of means but objectively mistaken, to action where ends and means are unintelligibly hidden from analysis (WL: 411). The similarity between this account and Pareto's theory of logical and non-logical action has often been noticed.

But if empirical scientific knowledge, technical correctness, was for Weber a key element in *Zweckrationalität*, an equally important component was the coherence of ends in a world in which means were necessarily limited. From his earliest statements he made it clear that economics was specifically a science of rational action in the sense that it provided for clarity about the implications of choosing between ends where resources were limited. His editorial for the *Archiv* stated the matter simply: We are offering the actor the possibility of calculating the unwanted as well as the wanted consequences of his action and hence an answer to the question 'What does the attainment of the desired purpose "cost" in terms of the foreseeable harm which will be done to other values?' (WL: 150).

Weber's view on this is a statement of what was known as opportunity cost and which arose out of the treatment of the idea of marginal utility by the Austrian economists, especially Menger, Wieser and Bohm-Bawerk. The characteristic of their work was that economic analysis arrived at propositions about the rational use of labour, allocation of resources and pricing which were independent of the physical characteristics of the factors.

For Weber the development of economics, and marginal utility theory in particular, offered purely logical ways of integrating the elements of action (see Schumpeter, 1954: 912–17). In addition to technical correctness in the light of empirical knowledge, logical coherence in the light of the rational models of economics offered increasing scope for purposively rational action. Indeed, the fullest statement of his idea of *Zweckrationalität* is contained in his account of the basic categories of economics as a sociologist would construe them (E&S I: 63–74). The modern development of microeconomics since Weber from his standpoint simply represents the enhancement of the degree of rationality available to the rational actor.

ii) Value-rational action, the second type of rational action, represented a late refinement of Weber's theory. Values had been present in the earlier methodological essays as elements of action, but did not enter as a component of a distinct type until his last formulation. No one writing in the Kantian tradition could think about action except in terms of the relations of ends and means. Hence Weber, at the start of the 'Objectivity' essay, is quite categorical: 'Any reflective consideration of the ultimate elements of human action is in the first instance tied to the categories of "purpose" (*Zweck*) and "means" (*Mittel*). We desire something concretely either "for its own sake" or as a means in the service of what we ultimately desire' (WL: 149; cf. Meth: 52).

Immediately after, Weber goes on to speak in terms of the costs of desired ends in relation to other values. Technical questions are considered less problematical in this context than the question of the relation of science to values and the main features of his theory of ideal types. The place of values in action is subordinated to the question of the relation of values to economic, historical and cultural sciences.

Nine years later, in the first attempt to outline the basic concepts of sociology, the concept of value is given a very marginal position. Pride of place goes to purposively rational action, and in terms of being accessible to understanding and carrying with it the maximum degree of certitude, the purposively rational action which corresponds to the objectively correct type (*Richtigkeitstypus*) is pre-eminent. It is the interplay between that type of action and both error and psychological deviations from the rational which take up the bulk of Weber's discussion of action before a brief glance at the relevance of legal concepts and then an introduction to structural concepts through the ideas of community and association.

There are, however, intimations of the subsequent elevation of value-rationality into the strategic position it later achieves in the last version of the basic concepts. At different points Weber suggests:

- that purposively rational analysis of action at some stage necessarily will come up against 'goal orientations' (*Zielrichtungen*) which are not means to ends (WL: 405).
- ultimate 'goal orientations' may be 'understood', in this case 'empathically experienced', as with the sexual drive, and any

interpretative psychology will come up against them as data (WL: 409).

- sociology can be concerned with the ideas human beings have about the validity of legal norms (WL: 416).
- 'communal action' (*Gemeinschaftshandeln*), where subjectively people orient to the behaviour of others (a formulation Weber later drops) may in the marginal case 'be orientated to the subjectively believed "value" of its meaning content as such ("duty" or whatever), in other words the action is value-orientated rather than expectation orientated' (WL: 418).
- an expectation of communal action is on average better grounded when it is dependent not simply on reciprocal expectations of behaviour but also upon a widespread belief in a legally binding order (WL: 422).
- imitative action may be a form of mass behaviour but it might equally reproduce the actives of others either for purposively rational reasons or from an estimation of their intrinsic value (WL: 431).
- mutual understanding between members of a community can present itself as an almost unbreakable valid 'norm' (WL: 434).

All these elements were later to be incorporated within Weber's type of value-rational action. In his brief commentary on it, he singled out 'the conscious formation of the ultimate targets of action and the logically planned orientation to them' which distinguished value-rational from emotional action. The key distinguishing feature, which separated it from purposively rational action, was the disregard for consequences, the desire to fulfil the demands of duty, honour, beauty, or whatever, for its own sake. From this point of view it was always irrational in relation to *Zweckrationalität* (WL: 12–13; cf E&S I: 24–6). Weber added that such action amounted only to a modest proportion of action generally but it was significant enought to deserve singling out as a special type.

In this way Weber drew attention (albeit modestly) to a conceptual innovation which was quite strategic in his theoretical framework, systematically related to a series of other conceptual modifications which distinguish the sociology of his last period of work from that of the period 1911–14. It will be easier to say something about the significance of these changes after considering his two types of irrational action.

iii) *Affectual action*, more specifically emotional action, was undoubtedly for Weber the original and most fundamental polar opposite to purposive rationality. I have said amply enough about his Protestant Kantian education and upbringing to have shown how this could have been simply self-evident for him. Emotions interfered with rationality, they deflected people, especially sober businessmen and bureaucrats, from their plans and their duties. From this point of view subjectively-conceived purposive rationality, which corresponded to an objective validation of its correctness, served always as a clear reference point when trying to understand other people's behaviour. As an ideal (in the sense of counterfactual) concept it was the most important source of 'ideal types' which I will consider shortly.

At the same time feeling and purpose were inevitably intertwined in human action, constituting the warp and weft of human motivation. Weber insisted that a method of analysis, which found the idea of rationality indispensable for scientific clarity, in no way prejudged the issue of the actual extent of rationality in human action or history (see WG I: 3; E&S I: 6–7). Moreover, given the years of painstaking work he conducted in the sociology of religion particularly, and the prominence he gave to irrational factors in political life, the charge of 'rationalistic bias' is as wide of the mark as accusing the original black-and-white film-makers of being biased towards black.

The very idea of 'understanding' other people, which was the central thrust of his method, Weber argued involved understanding both purpose and feeling, although the quality of understanding was different in each case, and with feelings more onus was placed on our personal experience of like states. Weber was a sociologist of irrationality as equally as he was of rationality. There could be no arbitrary exclusion of vast areas of human motives.

Emotions presented themselves to the world in varied guises. Broadly Weber distinguished between manifested affects, outbursts of joy or anger, for instance, where a need exists to express these in an uninhibited and obvious way, and states of feeling, such as jealousy, hurt pride or a diffuse love. These latter would often be 'abreacted' or sublimated in actions which had to be understood in terms of these hidden motives. At the boundaries of our understanding we came up against deep forces or drives, of which, for Weber, sexuality was the most important, which was an irrational fact of existence and yet expressed in action in so many ways. Often if we could understand these deep forces then behaviour which appeared unintelligible was shown to have a peculiar kind of rationality.

The inextricable relationship of reason and feeling, out of which the unity of the individual was constituted, meant that Weber found no clear dividing line between psychology and sociology. In so far as both were concerned with understanding the behaviour of individuals, they contributed to a common task, but since sociology specifically had as its main focus *social* action, and as we shall see Weber had a very special delimitation of the concept of the social, not all psychology was of direct interest to the sociologist.

However, unlike his contemporary Durkheim, Weber had no reluctance to admit the causal significance of non-social factors for social processes. For instance, different reaction times could easily provide for quite different outcomes of actions which in their meaning were identical (WL: 411). But psychology conceived as a natural science had no closer connection with sociology than any other discipline which identified factors which could affect social outcomes.

Where sociology and psychology were intimately connected was precisely in the idea of meaningful action, action with motives, and the kinds of psychology which put the interpretation of such action as its main objective could render 'decisively importance services to sociology' (WG I: 9). This had to be the case where irrationality was involved and in the 1913 categories essay he cited the 'so-called' psychoanalysis as well as the kind of theory represented by Nietzsche's account of resentment as examples of psychological interpretation of the ostensibly irrational which, however, by pointing to the unacknowledged motives revealed a kind of 'rationality'. 'Displaced motives' and 'substitute satisfactions' were, said Weber, naturally of concern to sociology (WL: 410–11).

In fact only a matter of degree separated affectual action from value-rationality, a question of the extent to which the ultimate targets of action were consciously formed. In consequence there could be no question of neglecting one or the other in a science devoted to understanding motives. It was Karl Jaspers, Weber's friend, philosopher and adviser on his illness, whom he cites at the beginning of *Economy and Society* as a key authority on *Verstehen*. Jaspers' *Allegemeine Psychopathologie* (1913) was intended as a basic textbook in interpretative psychology. Nor was this a token respect from Weber. His sociology of religion revolved around the interplay of needs and rationality and made recurring use of the ideas of hidden motives and ultimate drives as well as universal values.

Weber's emphasis on the importance of interpretative psychology and his own frequent use of psychological argument has normally been neglected by commentators in favour of emphasising his concern to distinguish sociology from psychology. But as so often with Weber, he makes conceptual distinctions only in order to show the intimate substantive connections.

The same thing has happened with his so-called 'rejection' of functionalist perspectives where in fact he stressed their indispensable preliminary uses in sociological analysis. In both cases, however, what comes into question is the capacity of Weber's intellectual framework to take in human action which is not purposively rational.

iv) Traditional action was the fourth category of action which completed the Weberian account of the irrational and which, along with the concept of value-rationality, bears the evidence of Weber's development of his action concept in the years between 1913 and 1920. 'Traditionalism' was singled out by Weber in an empirical context, namely in the rise of capitalism, as the most important opposing attitude to the capitalistic spirit. It meant the desire simply to live as one had been accustomed to live, with a customary level of effort and income, with, for instance, in the case of women workers their often noted reliance on old-fasioned working methods, or, for instance, with a business firm, the time-honoured ways of winning customers (PE: 59–67). As such it would appear that the main thrust of Weber's idea of the traditional was a concern with the philosophy of history and with the emergence of modern society. That it had such connections will become clearer when we consider the master developmental process of rationalisation.

But an ahistorical and analytical element was even more

important in the context of Weber's theory of action. This became clear in the 1913 essay on the categories. One of the most important sections of that was where Weber sought to explain how language communities or market behaviour could work even though there was no external regulation or explicit agreement. Their basis, he argued, was *Einverständnis*, the assumption that one's own action was part of the normal expectations of oneself by other people, an assumption which might or might not be borne out by events (WL: 428–40). Even an association or organisation constructed on clear-cut objectives and rules, when it came to the ordinary behaviour of the mass of its members depended upon this taken-for-granted nature of daily conduct.

> For the 'mass' of the people action which corresponds to some degree to the averagely understood meaning is, as we say, 'traditionally' acquired through usage and sustained mostly without any knowledge of the purpose, or meaning or indeed of the very existence of formal regulations. The actual empirical 'validity' of a 'rational' order therefore depends basically in this respect again upon the common understanding (*Einverständnis*) of compliance in the customary, the habitual, inculcated, the ever self-repeating (WL: 449).

There was no question, then, of traditional action being replaced by rational action in the modern world. Indeed in some ways rationality was removed further from everyday life. The bulk of daily behaviour fell into the category of conventional observation of taken-for-granted norms. As Weber put it at one point in discussing the foundations of law: 'Whenever the regularities of action have become conventionalized, i.e., whenever a statistically frequent action (*Massenhandeln*) has become a consensually oriented action (*Einverständnishandeln*) – this is, in our terminology, the real meaning of this development – we shall speak of 'tradition' (E&S I: 327). In these formulations Weber provided an explicit refutation of the accusation, which was to be made so often, that his view of social order was rationalistic and individualistic. Average everyday conduct for him was carried out without any clear consciousness of its meaning and was a matter of behaving in a way the actor had both got used to and could anticipate would not offend anyone else. It obeyed norms which no one had enacted.

When Weber formulated his fourth type of action in the last version of his basic concepts, he defined traditional action as 'determined by ingrained habituation' and therefore on the boundaries of meaningful behaviour, but it still formed the bulk of everyday behaviour. However, he added the important qualification that tradition could itself become consciously upheld, and then it approximated to value-rational action.

This brief comment provides an important clue to the disappearance of the term *Einverständnis* from his last version of the concepts and the introduction of the new term 'value-rational'. I shall examine some of the implications of this shift in different places in the last part of this book.

3 Ideal types

Action had to be the true focus for a social science in Weber's view. Asking about the method for such a science took him back to the same sources which generated that focus, namely the idea of rationality. Science had to be a matter of the human mind, replicating its organising qualities, the self-same qualities which marked personality and morality. A science of human action was bound to be reflexive, had to operate with the idea of ideas, was a field for analysis, not of mere recorded impressions. A Kantian method for social science opened out a world of possibilities as opposed to a mere accumulation of established facts.

The successors of Kant could no more see science as accumulated technology than they could imagine the human being as defined by an animal nature. As far as the sciences of the natural world were concerned, the Kantian view of rationality was that it was the organising or regulative power of human ideas which precisely guaranteed the *scientific* as opposed to the mere everyday nature of knowledge. But those arguments set up a fundamental cleavage between nature and the world of human action, where the mind's creative force was to establish goals and incite a striving for perfection. It was this rational faith in human effort which one commentator on Kant, Lucien Goldman, has seen as the most important legacy for subsequent generations: 'Nothing deserves the name of philosophy which is not aimed at the liberation of man and the realisation of true community' (Goldman, 1971: 228–9).

Kantian inspiration has motivated the major and often giants of modern thought. It underlies the utopianism of Marx, the negative dialectics of Adorno, the critical rationalism of Popper and the idea of a society of free and fully communicating human beings most recently advocated by Habermas.

What all these have in common is a faith in the capacity of the human mind to transcend the limitations of present existence and to imagine conditions or states of the world more in accord with rational requirements. The differences between these thinkers are often exaggerated out of all proportion to their fundamental similarity. For all of them empirical social science can at best be an aid in a process of self-improvement, even if that self is often conceived as society rather than the individual. As Goldman points out, the Kantian inspiration offers a liberation from the present. We can say then that social science is attached to the counterfactual, rather than the factual.

It was Weber's special talent, not to say burden, that he was never carried away into a liberationist philosophy, even thought he adhered so closely to Kantian principles. He discovered no escape from this world through rationality; on the contrary, he saw it more as a means to come to terms with irresistible forces and the unrelenting pressures of modern life. For one of his pietist upbringing, visions of brighter futures could only offer the temptation of false optimism. The Kantian structure of thought was put to a different use and resulted in a formulation which remains the most important single account of the nature of social science concept construction.

Weber renounced the temptations of the prophetic or critical modes of thought, but at the same time generalised their core of validity to argue that all accounts of the world were essentially based upon the capacity of the human mind to think of it as full of alternatives and differing possibilities. The world around us is not a matter of what is, but of what might be, or indeed what might have been. That in turn depends upon the self-consciousness of human beings and their capacity to pose alternative forms of action and to choose its future course. Possibility and potentiality are therefore built into existence because it is our existence, which we make for ourselves to whatever degree of power we possess.

This has been expressed here in a way which Weber never did. Already it begins to take on the tone of prophetic inspiration which he so much despised. Rarely did he descend to invoking the collective 'we'. For he had profound doubts about any academic attempt to promote a view of the 'world' in general. What he did recognise was that any account of social life by the historian, social scientist or any serious scholar was inherently bound to make use, or to generate, concepts not of the world as it is, but as it might be, or even could not be although it had to be *seen* that way. Indeed the whole of the social scientific enterprise was characterised above all by the counterfactual nature of its assumptions and the ideal nature of its concepts. For this reason Weber argued that any social science was bound to be conducted through 'ideal types'.

Once again it has to be said. Weber did not invent the term 'ideal type'. He borrowed it from a scholar he admired greatly, Georg Jellinek, who laid the foundations for the study of comparative government, and then Weber adapted it to his own specifications. As such he has made it his own trademark term. It conveys in the most concise possible way what for him was the essential nature of social scientific method.

Once he had adopted the term it became a constant feature of Weber's work, taking on a wide variety of nuances and becoming the all purpose intellectual resource. It had to be, because in a sense he could not see any necessary limits to its employment, since it summed up for him the necessary feature of any social science concept formation whatsoever.

This cannot be stressed too strongly. With ideal types Weber was not offering some special technical invention. We do not have the 'Weber ideal type' as we have the 'Phillips curve', or the 'Likert scale'. We do have particular ideal types Weber constructed, as of bureaucracy or action, or the Protestant ethic, but each of those has to be discussed in its own terms, by the method which was adopted in the particular case. Ideal types are for Weber the pervasive feature of social science and indeed historiography. They are simply unavoidable and the only question is how and for what purpose should any particular type be constructed.

Those are ambitious claims for any intellectual construct but many miss the point that in one sense the term is not even specially technical. If after all such diverse terms as Protestantism, authority, Marxian theory, the state, Bismarck, can all be used to refer to ideal types, then we have to expect ideal types to possess some highly generic features. These are in fact conveyed very adequately by 'type' and 'ideal'. A type is a class of objects which itself belongs to a more inclusive class or group. So 'traditional action' itself can be exhibited by an act of worship, or the wearing of an academic gown, or the opening of a shop at 8 am every weekday, but all exemplify that one type of action, which is just one of the four possible types in Weber's typology of action. 'Type' then is no more technical than 'example' or 'class'. It has a necessary everyday use in the ordinary classifications of either the natural world or social life.

Similarly 'ideal' has ordinary connotations. It refers to the mind's products, to images, representations, thought, beliefs or ideas. It is difficult to get by without such terminology. What then are 'ideal types'? Imaginary classes of objects, events, etc.? Very close, but in Weber's elaboration of the term the context of debates about method in his own time gave it a special point. For, as he said at the end of his essay on 'Objectivity in Social Science and Social Policy', 'the implications of the fundamental ideas of modern epistemology, which ultimately derives from Kant' are that 'concepts are primarily analytical instruments for the intellectual mastery of empirical data and can be only that' (Meth: 106). Something very general is being said about accounts of any world, natural and social, in that statement. Yet for Weber the ideal type expressed the special nature of concepts for the *social* world. In the passage which followed, he gave an indication of the crucial difference.

'Ideal type and historical reality should not be confused with each other', Weber asserted. By implication we can observe the confusion is not so serious with the natural world. But the concepts we employ for mastering historical reality have to be constructed precisely and clearly 'just *because* the content of historical concepts is necessarily subject to change' (ibid.: 107). Crucially Weber sought to demarcate the historical or cultural sciences from the natural sciences by stressing that the world of culture was 'our' world, was continually changing *through* human action, and the concepts we use are thus continually bound to be transcended: 'Moreover there are sciences to which eternal youth is granted, and the historical disciplines are among them – all those to which the eternally flowing stream of culture perpetually brings new problems. At the heart of their task lies not only the transiency of *all* ideal types *but* also at the same time the inevitability of *new* ones' (ibid.: 104).

He distinguished the ideal types of the cultural sciences from the type of concepts as employed in the natural sciences by their very departure from the idea of summing up the features which united a set of phenomena. The average or generic type could be used for the natural world precisely because the empirical phenomena of that world revealed repeating patterns across time and space. It made sense to operate on the basis of identifying classes and types of phenomena and finding their average characteristics, especially since the phenomena were not themselves changed by the conceptualisation.

We might sum up the point by saying that the thunderstorm is not changed, nor its prevalence affected in the slightest by our classifying it with atmospheric electrical phenomena. The philosophical point that our concepts for the natural world are all products of the mind remains just that, a philosophical point. The ideal nature of our concepts for ordering the natural world does not change the reality of the world.

Cultural reality was different. The aims and purposes of human beings constituted that world. A view of the world could shape that world. 'The cultural problems which move men form themselves ever anew and in different colours (ibid.: 84). What Weber called 'the flow of life' provided an endless set of questions, problems and viewpoints. Classifications were therefore bound to be transcended by events and this applied to attempts to order the past since the questions asked of the past changed with the preoccupations of the present. Order was therefore not found in cultural life as it was in nature. It was constructed around reference points, which themselves changed over time, and which are themselves subject to a wide variety of interpretations by participants and observers alike.

Weber instanced mediaeval 'Christianity'. 'A chaos of infinitely differentiated and highly contradictory complexes of ideas and feelings', he called it (ibid.: 96). The mediaeval church succeeded in giving it a relative unity. But we can only apply a 'purely analytical construct created by ourselves. It is a combination of articles of faith, norms from church law and custom, maxims of conduct and countless concrete interrelationships which we have fused into an "idea" (ibid.). In talking about 'Christianity' with any degree of precision and consistency, we are bound to use an ideal type, a complex of characteristics brought together into a consistent whole for the purposes of analysis.

4　Rationality in ideal-type construction

The scope of the idea of the ideal type is no less than any disciplined knowledge of human affairs. Some commentators have sought to delimit its field of application prematurely. Talcott Parsons made much, for instance, of the contrast von Schelting had earlier made between generalising and individualising ideal types, between, say, the generalised concepts of economic theory and the individualised concept of the Indian caste system, and suggested that these fitted ill with each other (Parsons, 1937: 601–10).

But this is to misunderstand the generality of Weber's purpose. He placed no limits on the varieties of ideal type – they could be a legal norm, or a personality type, or an institutional complex, or the Austro-Hungarian Empire. It was absolutely remote from his intentions to construct an inventory of ideal types. In his terms that was senseless. Above all he was seeking to convey his deep conviction that social science depended upon the construction of clear, unambiguous concepts, without which disciplined thought and communication between scientists was impossible.

The clarity and discipline Weber required necessarily meant that rationality entered into the construction of ideal types, and the types which sought to outline the features of rationality in social life became themselves the most prominent concepts in Weber's social theory. Purposively rational action rather than affectual action appears as the anchor point for his typology of action, just as bureaucracy and legal rational authority appear as the anchorage for his institutional analysis.

As we have seen, Weber strongly denied the accusation that his method was rationalistic in the sense of imputing rationality where it did not exist (E&S I: 7). But for him rational method and science were identical with each other. Ideal types of the irrational were therefore also constructed rationally, that is coherently, precisely and without contradiction; ideal types of rationality were doubly rational and the dividing line between simply providing points of orientation and contributing to a science of action became very thin indeed.

Indeed for Weber the most important source of ideal types in the social sciences was knowledge inspired by the practical needs of government and commerce. Law and economics for him were sciences organised around rational principles of action. A legal regulation or ideas like the rational economic agent or the theory of marginal utility were not social facts to be ascertained by empirical research in the first instance. They only became social facts if people observed them in their behaviour and adopted them as principles of conduct.

Law and economics as intellectual disciplines were what Weber called 'axiomatic sciences', concerned to advance the rationality of their core ideas. The largest ideas, concepts such as state, church, law, markets, were all the subject of continuous ratiocination, refined and disputed by theoreticians, put into practice by professionals, observed or flouted by the mass. These ideas provided the greatest single source of 'ideal types' for the social scientist who was concerned to examine the empirical social world.

The most profound of Weber's subsequent commentators and critics, Alfred Schutz, identified the latent problems in this conception of ideal types. The purpose of ideal types in Weber's account was to permit the empirical social scientist to work with clear reference points in studies of actual social behaviour. Questions of degrees of conformity to a type of action can only be settled by knowing in advance what is being chosen as the basis of comparison. But if ideal types are themselves generated in social life, and not merely by social scientists, it is the process of type production itself which becomes an empirical issue and ideal types cease to have some privileged methodological status.

Schutz was in no doubt about the importance of the ideal type concept. However much he was bound to dispute with him the immense significance of Weber's contribution could not be over-emphasised. 'Repeatedly Weber refers to the problem of the ideal type as the central problem of every social science. Our investigations have demonstrated how thoroughly justified that view is. For the worlds around us and in the past can only be grasped at all ideal typically' (Schutz, 1960: 258). But Schutz extended the implications of Weber's concept. In effect he democratised it by arguing that the fixed conceptual reference points were not the preserve of social scientists, or of axiomatic disciplines, they were the necessary product of the everyday social activity of ordinary people.

The effect of Schutz's intervention on the development of sociology in the Western world in the 1960s and 1970s was immense, inspiring a generation with the belief that everyday lives could be illuminated by the method of a phenomenological sociology. Law, morality, economic exchange ceased to be the preserve of special sciences, but constructs generated in daily interpersonal relations.

The work of Cicourel (1964) and Garfinkel (1967) in particular made rationality an on-going practical accomplishment of daily life rather than a transcendental, even divine, necessity as the Kantian tradition was inclined to believe. It took sociology a long way away from the developing institutionalised theoretical rationality of economics and law. It appeared effectively to have made Weber's preoccupations with the ideal types, provided by the axiomatic disciplines, obsolete. An empirical sociology, such as Weber wanted, surely had to begin with the people, not with the professionals.

In this way the democratic stereotype of the discipline which pervaded public consciousness in the 1980s acquired its real basis in the 1960s. The sociologist, penetrating the rationality of ordinary living, adopting the lifestyles of the subjects of research in order to grasp their secrets, appeared to assume, whether wanting it or not, the role of champion of the people, notwithstanding the fact that the people remained at best suspicious, at worst overtly hostile to these covert intruders.

Schutz found his inspiration in a suppressed side of Weber's theory of ideal types, in the unexplored identification of typological procedure being a feature of normal and not merely scientific life. I do not believe Weber would have followed the same route. In his concept of rationality there is a resistance to the idea that it had ordinary, mundane roots.

There were a number of mutually reinforcing ideas which determined his adherence to ideal types from professional life. While he was always ready to acknowledge differing rationalities, they still appeared to be inherently scaleable. We might say that just as colours may differ in hue, they are still capable of being ordered by intensity. For Weber rationality could be intensified. Moreover, as we shall see, it could develop over time. Furthermore, scientists, theoreticians and professional experts could set their minds to developing it. And their efforts bore fruit; their ideas were implemented and the world in part moved forward through their efforts.

Rationality was a force and, other things being equal, greater rationality had more force than lesser. The reason the empirical social scientist might use the analytical ideas developed by economists and lawyers was because they *did* have power. Therein lies the grain of truth in the otherwise shallow comment on Weber that his sociology merely served the interests of the ruling class. If it was their ideas which shaped the world, then it followed that those were the best starting points for empirical research.

Having stressed the source of Weber's ideal type notions, we should not, however, forget their function, namely to allow the empirical social scientist to reveal that the world was *not* a replica of them. Weber stressed that it was ideal types which showed how the world might be, and by using them as our reference point we could show what life was like in *reality*. That intellectual quest for reality took one away from the purity of ideal types and always in the direction of 'multifarious nuances of form and content, clarity and meaning . . . a chaos of infinitely differentiated and highly contradictory complexes of ideas and feelings' (Meth: 96).

In this way Weber stood poles apart from the radical interpreters of the Kantian tradition, from Marx to Habermas. Far from a true social science revealing the potential for liberation, distilling the utopia from the accidentals of life, it began by imposing even greater order on the world than the confused aspiration of individuals could manage, and ended by showing just how chaotic life really was. Weber offered understanding where others offered vain hopes.

9

The Structure of Collective Action

1 The social relationship

One of the most important facets of Weber's argument for the necessity of ideal types in social science was his insistence that collective concepts for social life, ideas such as the state, or church organisation, ultimately always referred to the actions of individuals.

This concern for the relation between such concepts and individual motivation went back as far as his doctoral dissertation on the 'History of Mediaeval Trading Associations' (1889). There he examined the development of the idea of a limited liability company as opposed to societies with full personal liability as it emerged from the commercial requirements of the period. In his preface to this work Weber states that his purpose was to obtain a more concrete idea of the motives which were essential for this development (GHM: 2). Did these collective concepts indicate quite new legal ideas generated by the needs of the time (*Bedürfnisse des Tages*), or were they modifications of pre-existing ideas, was the question he posed at the beginning. Whichever it was, he was emphatic that a term like *societas*, however it was legally conceived, had to be interpreted in terms of the people to whom reference was being made (ibid.: 13).

As a professional lawyer Weber was unable to subscribe to any doctrine of the relation between individual and society which made the latter an uncontested terrain. It was essentially conceptual, a web of norms, beliefs, expectations, contracts, even illusions, but always one where the professional intelligence could penetrate to point up implications, consistencies and inconsistencies, and points of difference between ideal and real behaviour.

158

Legal rules for the *societas* with far-reaching consequences for economic development were forged in the heated atmosphere of the mediaeval court chamber, but the contestants were impelled by the requirements of their customers and competitors and the rigours of economic necessity. 'Society' was not a pure set of ideas compelling adherence; even less was it some material reality, a king of substratum for individual behaviour. The concrete reality to which the term referred was the messy behaviour of individuals. It was for purposes of analysis only that we could turn to the logical constructions, such as the lawyers produced, for our ideal types.

This is the train of thought which underlies the sociological concepts which were outlined at the beginning of *Economy and Society*. They begin with individual action and trace a course through to the state and political organisation, covering intermediate concepts such as social relationship, conflict and organisation, in which every term is defined by reference to another in the set of terms and in which ultimately all can find their reference in the behaviour of individuals.

The method of exposition therefore leans heavily on two resources of legal thinking, namely the idea of a closed and gapless system of concepts and the idea of personal responsibility. But those two features of legal thought Weber was used to seeing as aspects of rationality in general. The resulting paradox is that the person who, like Nietzsche before him, rejected the idea that a closed system of concepts could capture the reality of social life, nonetheless produced the most impressive set we have. But that bitter truth Weber took to his heart and acknowledged as the very meaning of science: 'Every scientific "fulfilment" raises new "questions"'; it asks to be 'surpassed and outdated' (Essays: 138).

The concept Weber elaborated immediately after his presentation of the types of social action was the social relationship:

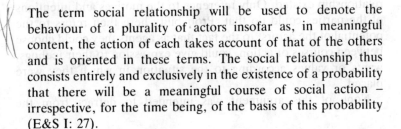

The term social relationship will be used to denote the behaviour of a plurality of actors insofar as, in meaningful content, the action of each takes account of that of the others and is oriented in these terms. The social relationship thus consists entirely and exclusively in the existence of a probability that there will be a meaningful course of social action – irrespective, for the time being, of the basis of this probability (E&S I: 27).

It is clear that Weber regarded this concept as the testing place for the most basic of his methodological principles. It is the most general example of the relationship between action and structure because he clearly quite deliberate allows it to cover an indefinite number of individuals, from the individual father and child at one extreme, to the millions of citizens of the modern state at the other. Common to all such cases is the positing of a state of affairs, of something existing, the evidence for which is only available intermittently over a period of time.

Moreover, it is a state of affairs which is wholly dependent upon the meaningful action of the parties toward each other. Social relationships, therefore, as objects of scientific inquiry have a peculiarly open texture; as observers we can only say that there is a probability that certain kinds of action will take place under certain circumstances, and that is the only sense we can give to the 'existence' of the relationship. What exists in the continuous sense is the probability, not the specific action.

Weber's use of the idea of probability here requires comment. While he was familiar with the developing ideas of statistical probability of the period this was not primarily what he had in mind.

This can be illustrated in any number of ways. In a friendship a birthday card may mean more than daily conversation; but the failure to send a card may be compensated by a visit. Giving assistance at a time of unanticipated crisis can cement a relationship, whereas failure to keep a promise may cause a rift. In all these expressions the contingent nature of the events is plainly visible in conditions like 'may'. There is no certainty, but the meaning of friendship covers these possibilities, often only brought to realisation by fate or circumstances.

While Weber allowed for and indeed encouraged social research which examined the statistical regularity of certain actions, it was not by this route that one established that a particular social relationship existed. Only reference to the motives and intentions of the parties could do that. Probability here then refers to the potential of the actors, to the fact that as agents they could choose between courses of action, could give expression to their feelings, wants or values according to the situation in which they were placed.

None of this argument was intended to detract from the

significance of standardised and regularly repeated uniformities of social action which were a prime feature of social life and a main focus for sociological investigation. But Weber insisted on the variety of ways in which such uniformities were generated. He distinguished between usage and custom where the motive to conform was unthinking adherence; law and convention where the fear of the reaction of others underpinned conformity; all the regularities of market-type behaviour where rational calculation gave the same action outcomes to independently motivated individuals; and finally, the standardisation of behaviour which might emerge from rationalising values. Such distinctions were the widely acknowledged elements of the sociological discourse of his time. It was not his intention to move the focus of attention, rather to enhance its clarity and precision.

2 Legitimacy

It was for the purpose of clarity that Weber introduced one of the distinctive and strategic conceptual pivots in his system of sociological categories immediately after discussing the empirical uniformities of action. 'Action, especially social action which involves a social relationship, may be guided by the belief in the existence of a legitimate order' (E&S I: 31). This statement is as important for Weber's sociology as the more famous definition of action which we explored earlier: 'We shall speak of action insofar as the acting individual attaches a subjective meaning to his behaviour – be it overt or covert, omission or acquiescence' (ibid.: 4).

The importance of the concept of legitimacy is best appreciated by considering the marginal presence in Weber's system of a concept of 'society'. He not only stood out against those who wished to make a holistic idea the beginning and end of sociological analysis. That was incompatible with his insistence on the centrality of the responsible agent. But this was not inconsistent with having at least ideal types of collective bodies, such as a church or a bureaucracy and Weber was well known for his adoption of such tools of analysis. He was also taking a stand against allowing even that kind of methodological usefulness for a concept which suggested that there was a material ground to human behaviour in membership of a collectivity.

We shall see in a closer examination of Weber's idea of the social that in this he diverged fundamentally from Marx. Attachment to a collectivity was not even usefully understood for sociological purposes as material or natural, certainly not in any sense biological. For Weber that attachment had to be a matter of belief, i.e. ideal, and from that point of view terms like nation, state, church, even class, could have clear-cut ideal definition. But in that sense society had no precise referent, it was the vaguest invocation of all, beloved of those who preached solidarity, who mixed morality and science illegitimately. So society did not even gain 'ideal type' status in his scheme.

When, therefore, we consider through Weber's eyes the broadest settings of social action, the wider social fabric, we do it with the aid of an accessory to action, *belief*, and in particular 'belief in the existence of a legitimate order'. Social order is made to depend on the belief in social order, and moreover, not merely a cognitive belief, but one bound to a view of what ought to be the case.

In sociological terms this meant that some of the actors involved at least had to regard the order as binding for their own actions. The rules had to become the basis of their own actions and they had to feel obliged to adhere to them. Not uncharacteristically Weber instanced the civil servant's sense of duty as an example (ibid.: 31). It was this binding nature on the participants which Weber terms 'legitimacy'.

It would be easy, but equally wrong, to infer from the place of legitimacy in Weber's account of social order that he was proposing a theory of society which made its stability dependent upon the sharing of common values. In fact his own thinking developed specifically as a counter to a theory of that kind propounded by Rudolf Stammler, a professor of law who had acquired considerable fame by publishing a refutation of Marx's materialist conception of history and substituting for it a theory of the ideal determination of society, in particular through the ideas of law and justice (1906). It was here that Weber insisted most vigorouly on his fundamental presupposition, namely that social relationships and, even more, all social collectivities, had to be understood in terms of the multiple types of motives which individuals brought to the situation.

While belief in legitimacy was a major factor in enhancing the stability of a social order, for a great deal of the time individuals were oriented towards it in terms of expediency, either from fear for the consequences if they departed from it, or from the advantages they perceived if they conformed. Equally for much of the time people adhered to an order simply because they were accustomed to do so and could see no good reason for doing anything else.

In brief, Weber regarded the maintenance of social order as another case which required the elaboration of his elementary motivational types. While he concurred with Stammler in accepting that a social order consisted of relationships governed by rules, those rules in no way implemented themselves. Much of the time individuals were trying to get round them, the rules could conflict with each other, they could be open to differing interpretations, and over and beyond those points people had additionally to be given the special task of enforcement.

People could live for rules or from them, could abide by them or fight against them. And those conceptual possibilities were all subject to empirical investigation. Precisely because social order was contingent upon the whole variety of individual orientations, so documenting and explaining the actual variations provided a massive task for the social researcher. As with ideal types in general, the concepts of social order which Weber construed so carefully only provided the guidelines and categories for investigating real courses of action.

But, given the variety of motives, rules became the common point of orientation for the parties to a social relationship. And where the rules were invested additionally with the quality of legitimacy, and that quality itself was justified by individuals, regarded as 'right' on some grounds, then the motives for accepting the order were correspondingly strengthened and its endurance more securely guaranteed.

Those justifications for attributing legitimacy to a set of rules, or order, Weber classified into (a) traditional, (b) affectual, (c) value-rational and (d) legal, with the latter subdivided into the voluntary agreement and the rules imposed by a legitimate authority. It is a classification which bears important and necessary resemblance to his typology of action, but it has gone through a series of

conceptual levels to reach this point. The importance of distinguishing these levels is such that it is worth identifying them briefly
as follows:

Motives	meaningful basis of behaviour
Action	behaviour from motives
Social action	action directed towards other people
Social Relationship	the possibility of mutually orientated action by two or more persons
Order	social relationships governed by rules
Legitimacy	belief in the rightness of rules, possible meaningful orientation for motives.

Weber's argument takes us through these stages in sequence, each
one taking on an ever more specific delimitation of the field which
so many others have simply called 'society' without ever breaking
the thread which tied them to individual motives. Indeed, by
means of the idea of legitimacy, he secured an intimate linkage, a
loop back between motives and beliefs, providing the conceptual
possibility for a common order to arise out of various and
conflicting individual motivations, without ever postulating common will or attributing reality to collective ideas except as
symbolic points of reference.

Weber's theory of social order depends on two distinctive
solutions to the question of the existence of supra-individual social
entities. As we saw, he solved the problem of the 'existence' of
social relationships by reference to the idea of persisting possibilities of action. But that was a solution only adequate for
relationships seen in relative isolation from each other. For the
wider social order, those possibilities of action could have
generated unpredictable chaos without a common point of
orientation. That problem was solved by the introduction of the
idea of legitimacy, and stipulating its intimate connection with
individual motivation.

Ideas were then essential elements within Weber's theory of
social order. The ideas that participants possessed helped to

explain the course of their actions. But in turn those ideas did not take shape spontaneously; the social order was not a product of pure reason but more of an arbitrary imagination which could be shaped and directed willfully by those with power. There was a material reality behind the collective concepts which expressed the social order. But it was not that to which those concepts ostensibly referred. Almost always they depended on the power of some over many. Time and again underlying the posited common appeal of collective concepts was a reality of coercion.

3 Power and authority

'In the great majority of cases actual action goes on in a state of inarticulate half-consciousness of actual unconsciousness of its subjective meaning' (E&S I: 21). For Weber rationality was *not* the hallmark of everyday life. Ideas and beliefs became crucial elements in the orientation of social action only under certain conditions. The primary (both historically and logically) type of social relationship was one based simply on the feeling of the parties that they belonged together. The conscious formation of a relationship for mutually advantageous or common purposes was secondary even if of world-historical significance in terms of the transformation of modern society. Weber's thinking here was quite explicitly broadly in accord with Tönnies and many others who contrasted *Gemeinschaft* (usually translated 'community') with *Gesellschaft* ('association') and who saw traditional primary relationships being supplanted by secondary, calculative relationships under modern conditions.

The mundane, everyday world was not primarily a world of ideas. By definition almost, it was material, if material was construed to comprise the behaviour, motives and actions of human beings. That was the world of irrational facts. But ideas, the stuff of the rational, were also the products of daily life, and returned to shape and direct it. No simple formula can cover Weber's exploration of the relations between the material world and ideas, or the real and the rational, precisely because it was the totality of his intellectual investigations.

Weber is renowned for having identified the belief in legitimacy as a core structuring element in all kinds of social organisation.

But in no way does that warrant the suggestion that he was offering an 'idealist' interpretation of history. He was insistent that his sociological investigations were designed to reveal the real relations ideas had to social action, rather than the ideal stipulations of philosophers and theologians, or even lawyers. In this way his empirical science was Nietzschean in its emphasis on the way ideas could be harnessed, manipulated and used to benefit particular groups and be imposed on the masses. 'Not ideas, but material and ideal interests, directly govern men's conduct' (Essays: 280). It is an approach which elsewhere I have called 'bourgeois materialism' (Albrow, 1975). (But that too is a rhetorical device.)

Finally, ideas themselves sprang from mysterious roots, and that applied at all levels, from faith in a saviour to scientific achievements of the highest order. The causes of the origins and diffusion of new ideas were therefore a prime concern for any empirical sociologist. The most rudimentary observation of regularities in social life must see them as based on organic necessities, says Weber in a discussion of custom and convention (E&S I: 321). Only later does a belief in binding norms arise. The causes of innovation under these circumstances are for Weber likely to be the deviant experiences of individuals who have been capable of exercising special influence on others.

Even duty, that sublime concept in the Kantian world-view to which Weber was in thrall throughout his life, arose out of a sense which was probably shared by domestic animals, the result of coercion and discipline. The concept was the later development, primary was the feeling that had been induced by others. In this respect Weber was entirely in accord with the savage demystification of morality which Nietzsche had initiated and which was displayed in *The Genealogy of Morals* (first published 1887).

Belief could not act alone to change social relationships. Within them there was always the potential for force, coercion, fear and submission. For Weber, as for his more influential (in this respect) colleague Simmel, it was axiomatic that conflict was just as much a social relationship as cooperation. Even in that type of relationship known as 'communal', based on the feeling of belonging together, so often coercion is a fact.

He was particularly alive to the types of coercion which were exercised within erotic relationships. Coercion could, of course, take place through violence. 'Violent social action is obviously something absolutely primordial' :E&S II: 904). Every social group from the household upwards made use of it from time to time if it could. But over historical time the means of violence became concentrated and at the disposal of the state. What Weber called the political community was distinguished precisely in that it was a body prepared and able to use violence both against other bodies and against its own members, and additionally it was able to exercise this power within a defined territory and over the multiplicity of activities within it.

Force then was an elementary component of social relationships and the way it was exercised and organised was fundamental for the wider shape of social relations. But it was still only one way in which power in general might be exercised. Weber's definition of power has become justly famous: the chance that one or more people within a social relationship can assert their will, even despite the opposition of others, and irrespective of the basis for this chance (E&S I & II: 53, 926; two separate definitions are amalgamated here).

As with all of Weber's definitions it contains a wealth of fine distinctions. Even the word 'even' counts because Weber allows for power in this way where resistance is not exhibited. Furthermore, power is in terms of realising one's own will for any conceivable purpose and not in terms of imposing one's will on another. The result is that Weber's definition is not of the zero-sum type, where gain in power for one party must be at the expense of another.

At the same time, power per se has no generalisable relationship to social phenomena. As he says, it is 'sociologically amorphous'. For sociological analysis, much more important is the fact that power is normally structured in social relationships in a particular way, namely that one or more persons accept commands from others. In this way Weber introduces the key concept of his account of large-scale social structures – *Herrschaft*.

Herrschaft has given translators considerable trouble, partly because its meaning is deeply based in German historical experience and in particular has all the connotations associated with the personal relations of rulers and ruled under feudal conditions. (See E&S I: 61 for Roth's discussion.) As he frequently did, Weber took a term which had this maximum scope and then progressively narrowed it for purposes of analysis. At times he used it for the kind of power which an economic monopoly position gave where the obedience of one party to the other's requirements was secured out of sheer self-interest. That was something very different from the situation where obedience was viewed as a duty. But *Herrschaft* could cover both cases. The latter he termed *Herrschaft kraft Autorität* and 'authority' has been the most frequently used translation, largely because it is around the latter connotation that Weber centred his discussion.

Herrschaft was a form of power but sociologically structured because it involved relations between definite sets of people: it was 'the probability that a command with a given specific content will be obeyed by a given group of persons' (ibid. I: 539). As such, authority was one of the most important and widely found features of social action, appearing in such diverse settings as the school, the office, the politics of language or the feudal relation of lord and vassal.

The idea of authority has at least equal strategic significance in Weber's conceptual framework as the idea of social order and in terms of empirical interest a larger part to play in his work. It represents the completion of his consistent determination to provide a set of conceptual tools for the analysis of society without ever departing from the principle that only individuals can act and that collective terms must always be seen as ways of referring to the actions of individuals, however large the aggregates involved.

4 Groups

From the point of view of the wider social structure, the idea of social order was sufficient to express the prevalence of similar practices and the possibility of coming to common understandings with indefinite numbers of people. But the concept itself said nothing about the diversity and differentiation of practices and the boundaries between people. Further assumptions were required to do justice to the variety of ways social relationships were organised into larger structures.

It is no accident then that Weber introduces the idea of authority at the end of an exposition of the ways social relationships could be organised, to be open or closed to newcomers, to be administered as 'organisations', and to have a variety of claims over members. In these contexts he was happy to talk of 'structures', and we can easily discern the same interests in the relations of the individual to the group as he had shown in his doctoral dissertation, even as far as a discussion of representation and responsibility which introduced distinctions reminiscent of those made in that early work.

Weber was hard-headed: both as a trained lawyer and as a social scientist. Vague talk about the existence of groups and society took one nowhere, he felt, if you wanted to identify what people did and why. Hence collective terms for which there were no clear empirical referents he regarded as bogus scientifically, and, when used in public life, as rhetorical tools to arouse emotional responses.

Groups then, in the Weberian perspective, required individuals to be orientated to them, to give commitment to them and to provide for their continued existence. As far as large groups were concerned this meant essentially that an authority structure was necessary to determine whose will was to prevail in group decisions. It was a corollary of Weber's individualistic starting point that specific mechanisms were required to ensure that the potentially chaotic aggregate of purposes was coordinated. Essentially this meant at a minimum that there had to be a leader.

We have then the ostensible paradox, but paralleled in German political history, that the theory which began with the irreducible necessity for individuals to be viewed as the sole agents in human history, also was emphatic that group structure depended on leadership. Weber did not see it as a paradox; rather the focus for the central processes of group formation.

As always the nuances of these ideas are beautifully captured in Weber's definition of the *Verband*:

An organised group shall be defined as a social relationship (*Beziehung*) which is either closed to or limits the entry of outsiders, where the observance of its order (*Ordnung*) is guaranteed by specific people whose behaviour is directed towards its very implementation: a leader and if necessary an administrative staff which normally has delegated powers (WG I: 26; my translation).

This is the most general definition of a structured group which Weber provides and can be regarded as the most succinct statement of his political sociology. It is precisely articulated with his concepts of relationship and order, and provides an entry point into his analysis of bureaucracy.

The reason he chose this definition of an organised group was because he observed that the dominant modes of social structure of modern times were basically organised on a tripartite basis: leaders, administrators, ordinary members, and that those who exercised authority enjoyed a largely self-perpetuating power position. With his friend Michels he shared a pessimistic view about the potential for democracy in large social units, if by democracy one meant the ability of the members to determine the decisions of the organisation as a whole.

What Michels called the 'iron law of oligarchy', Weber termed the 'advantage of the small number' and he saw this as fundamentally related to secrecy. 'Wherever increasing stress is placed upon "official secrecy", we take it as symptom of either an intention of the rulers to tighten the reins of their rule or of a feeling on their part that their rule is threatened' (E&S II: 952). As soon as a group passed a certain size (never fully specified), Weber argued that processes came into play such that it was completely wrongheaded to use the same criteria of democracy as one did for the small group of peers.

With the large group, its existence and the bonding of members to it depended upon a series of very real, but nonetheless intangible features for which it was the task of sociological analysis to render a precise account. Weber's identification of these features came as the result of painstaking conceptual analysis illuminated by a wealth of historical examples. In briefest summary we may suggest the main ones:

> How is the order of the group maintained? That is, how are members motivated to uphold the order?
>
> How is belief in the legitimacy of the group's order secured?
>
> When and how are leaders selected/do leaders gain control?
>
> Why do people obey the leader's instructions?
>
> How does the leader select staff?
>
> What order governs the organisation of the staff?

How do people come to accept instructions from leader and staff as legitimate?

These questions are all capable of being answered sociologically, that is, in terms of the way actual people behave towards each other. But however much Weber determined to interpret these questions in such a way that they were susceptible to rigorous empirical investigation, there is no concealing the profound conceptual problems he was seeking to clarify.

All such questions revolve around the issue of authority and consent. As we have just suggested, the idea of the autonomous human being freely deciding to follow rules of his or her own making, which the Kantian foundations of Weber's thought made axiomatic, was limited in the real world by the fact that some people dominated others. How was the autonomy of the individual to be reconciled to the requirements of large organisations for conformity, coordination and control? That was not only a philosophical problem. It was a practical one for leaders, a matter of self-searching for members, and something for empirical sociological investigation.

5 Charisma

Authority structures were complex and involved a myriad of processes and motives. But Weber did attach a causal priority to a crucial element. He resolved the autonomy/control problem by belief in legitimacy. In exploring that factor we can come close to the centre of his analysis of how society works. Both the rules which people uphold in their relations and the obedience they give to others are strengthened and secured above all by a faith, by thinking that it is *right* to obey, that the other person has a right to give orders. That belief is more important than any motive of self-interest or fear or presumed advantage, or any sense of shared values.

'Belief' is not a technical term in Weber's conceptual armoury. It is nonetheless of strategic importance. Too often it is simply treated as identical to 'idea'. More properly it could be identified with 'faith'. For the belief in legitimacy could just as easily be expressed in the unrelecting devotion of a disciple to a prophet, as it could in the execution of a governmental minister's instructions by a civil servant. The latter could refer to minutes, regulations, statutes and the law, all obviously 'ideas' but the former could only offer the testimony of his or her eyes and ears. In each case, however, agents relinquish independent judgement over the content of their own actions. 'Thy will be done' becomes the basis of their own actions and that is sufficient basis for action provided legitimacy is maintained. Ultimately belief in legitimacy is at the irrational rather than the rational end of the spectrum of reality. That applies even with the most rational form, namely legal-rational legitimacy associated with the modern bureaucracy. But to understand that, we need to consider the diametrically opposed form, the charismatic.

'Charisma' was a property, or more specifically a gift, which was imputed to the person of the leader by the followers. It was a quality which compelled obedience. It was therefore a power, we might even say the power of power. Psychologically the follower felt bound to give recognition to this power, it was a *duty* to acknowledge its proof (cf. E&S I: 242). Weber took the term from Rudolf Sohm who had studied authority in the early Christian church, but he argued that the principles of leadership through God-given grace were generalisable to a range of cases far more extensive. He applied it to Napoleon, to the cult poet of his time, Stefan George, to Jesus Christ and to the Chinese Emperor.

In the last thirty years this term has become part of the everyday analysis of political commentators and a normal word in the vocabulary of the politically educated. That is in itself a testimony to Weber's identification of a key component in political structure, namely the attraction a leader has for followers which goes beyond any rational explanation. It is a mystery which becomes a fact in the situation. In so far as this idea has currency today, there is an implicit recognition of Weber's intuition of the limits of rational analysis. The charisma idea depends on the linkage of three elementary factors underlying all of Weber's work: power, faith and duty. The last is the product of the first two.

Quite obviously charisma belong to the sphere of the irrational. Is is therefore not difficult to speak of faith in the legitimacy of the charismatic leader. But the irrational foundations of all authority are somewhat concealed to the English reader since *Legitimitäts-glaube* is always translated as 'belief in legitimacy' which underplays the fact that *Glaube* equally means faith, and we are talking here of 'believers' and the faithful rather than scientific credibility. Weber says: 'Above all we have to grasp: the foundation of *every* authority and therefore every compliance, is a faith: "prestige" faith in favour of he or she who rules' (WG I: 153).

Even legal authority, Weber continues, is never purely legal: there is a tradition of belief in it. And there are negative charismatic qualities in the sense that modern regimes may lose their efficacy and be ripe for charismatic overthrow. A huge amount of commentary has been devoted to Weber's legal rational authority and the bureaucratic administrative staff which serves it and dominates the administrative systems of the modern world. The intricacy of the rules and regulations surrounding this has been explored many times (the reader can look at my own account in *Bureaucracy* [1970]). But for Weber rationality always comes up against irrational limits.

6 Morality, obedience and democracy

The head of a legal-rational system is regularly chosen in non-rational ways. The very obedience which is owed within the system has irrational roots. For the believer in legal-rational authority, just as the believer in charismatic or traditional authority, has to relinquish independent judgement about what is right and wrong in the acts which are commanded. That is intrinsic to Weber's definition of obedience: 'the content of the instruction is taken to be the maxim for conduct for its own sake and in respect of the formal relation of obedience, without heed for one's own view about the rightness or wrongness of the instruction' (WG I: 123). This is the reason for the fact which has puzzled so many commentators, namely that there are three kinds of authority as compared with the four types of action (Albrow 1972). Weber's formulation is clearly a deliberate evocation of Kant's ethics. Moral agency is relinquished as far as the content of doing one's damned duty is concerned.

Such an analysis not merely emphasises the irrational facets of social structure. It also highlights the inherent limitations of the idea of democracy under the conditions of mass social organisation. Weber devoted a considerable part of his political sociology to identifying the alternative ways in which limits could be placed on authority, but in the end he felt forced to rely on the judgement and sense of responsibility of the leaders. It was the defects of the German leadership of his day which depressed him so much, rather than any belief that a different political system could produce better results.

I have stressed throughout this brief account of the building blocks of Weber's social theory that the way he cuts these from the raw material of social experience expresses his own moral theory. The problem of the existence of society and its relation to individual action is not a preliminary methodological topic to be solved with a few well chosen definitions. The very nature of that existence, the kind of reality to be accorded to the social, is what every individual determines in every act and is what the social theorist interprets.

For the individual to comply with authority is to contribute to the on-going production of a certain kind of reality, certainly real in its consequences. So long as a person lives, the compliance with an order contains an element of the voluntary, however great the coercion involved. At one point Weber uses the Latin tag *coactus tamen voluit* ('although coerced it was still his will'), and comments, 'Even the most drastic means of coercion and punishment are bound to fail when the subjects remain recalcitrant. In many spheres such a situation would always mean that the participants have not been educated to acquiescence' (E&S I: 334).

That acquiescence is intimately connected with the ways in which individuals can be induced to shift the sense of right and wrong from the content of their own acts to obedience to others. Equally power holders themselves seek the justification of their own power. In Weber's words: 'Indeed, the continued exercise of every domination (*Herrschaft*) (in my technical sense of the word) always has the strongest need of self-justification through appealing to the principles of its legitimation' (E&S II: 954).

The relations of power and legitimation are clearly dialectical in Weber's account, that is, each requires the other and develops in conditions of mutual determination. The dynamics of mass social organisation centre around the outcome of those relations. Certain external conditions also provide important inputs to those processes, in particular the size of the populations involved and system of material production. But in the broadest sense, the political process, which is the making of social structure, is at the centre of Weber's account of a science of the social.

Economy and Society was written as an outline of the interconnections between economy and society. His fundamental sociological categories were developed to identify the elements of society which clearly were not reducible to economic processes. Again I shall return to this issue in a later chapter an in particular to the hotly debated matter of Weber's response (or non-response) to Marx. At this point it is sufficient to point out that the power of Weber's analysis was acknowledged implicitly, and sometimes by direct reference, by the Marxist writer in the twentieth century who did most to contribute to the modification of the elements of economic determinism in historical materialism, namely Antonio Gramsci. His account of hegemony, of the way the ruling class managed to gain the acquiescence of the masses in its view of the world and to share basic assumptions of social order, was a backdoor route for the assimilation of Weberian ideas into Marxist theory.

The assimilation of Gramsci's idea by intellectuals of the left in Western countries in the 1960s and 1970s made it all the easier for them to adopt crucial elements of Weber's account of legitimation. Weber became a common property for theorists from left and right after a period in the 1950s and early 1960s, culminating in the centenary conference in Heidelberg in 1964, when he was seen by some as a prime representative of bourgeois liberalism (Stammer, 1971). It is now not unfair to say, especially since the Habermas account of the legitimation crisis of late capitalism, that Weber has become the dominant influence on political theory of the twentieth century.

But that acknowledgement of Weber's key position has not been accompanied by an adequate understanding of the intellectual strategy underlying his account of domination. Unlike Gramsci, whose concern was political commentary and whose account of hegemony was largely descriptive and intentionally inspirational, Weber's purpose was precisely to reveal the conceptual and real relations underlying systems of domination in a society with mass social organisation, and always to bring those questions back to the motivation of individuals – particular, typical or average.

He did not take it for granted that hegemony produced the individuals it needed. But his pessimistic vision rested upon an analysis which showed that for large-scale social structures to function, it was necessary for a rationality appropriate to them to supplant autonomous individual rationality. Impersonality did pervade modern life, but that was not to be laid at the door of industrial capitalism per se. That phenomenon of the modern world, however threatening to individuality, only shared in an overall process of rationalisation which made the dream of an end to class society a utopian irrelevance.

10
The Historical Development of Rationality

Preamble

The purpose behind the development of ideal types was to assist in the description and explanation of social reality. But that reality already contained its own organising principles – which came indeed from the same source which generated ideal types, namely rationality.

Weber vehemently rejected the accusation that his method was rationalistic. It was indeed the case that he emphasised irrational factors in social life. But any appreciation of the past or other cultures was tied to their accessibility to the observer – and the rational was the most easily understood.

More than that, rationality clearly exhibited cumulative development. The more rational ideal types of action and social structure were the more they were adequate for interpreting recent times. It was a fact that markets, bureaucracy, the state, industrial production, all exhibited more complex levels of rationality in the modern world.

Weber's sociology is historical and comparative precisely because it is through rationality that human beings transform their own world. It is a complete misunderstanding of the thrust of his work to imagine that his ideal types were designed to serve as models of how society works. They might be derived from disciplines which had such objectives, e.g. an economist's model of the market could serve as a rational ideal type for the sociologist, but only to highlight the sociologist's search for an account of change in the real world, not to substitute for it. The point is that all such models are ephemeral in part because they transform the world in which they are applied.

177

For Weber the tasks of sociology are descriptive and explanatory and it is a matter of fact that society is organised differently worldwide and has been transformed over time. The largest and most comprehensive framework within which that transformation is to be understood is to this date to be found in the 'rise of Western rationalism'. Wolfgang Schluchter has very effectively presented this in his book of that title (1981).

Any presentation, therefore, of the empirical social research which Weber undertook must present it as findings in relation to the rationalisation process. This applies whether one is looking at the psychology of the industrial worker, the development of Western music, the influence of Confucianism, or the rise of the legal profession, to name only some of his fields of enquiry.

It is beyond the scope of this book to produce an account of Weber's findings. The task has been to show how he arrived at this scientific purpose, to reconstruct the argument which led him in this direction. It is not even possible to demonstrate in any detail the fruitfulness of his approach. Randall Collins has made a very useful contribution to this effect with his recent survey of some central themes in Weberian sociology (1986). He testifies to the vitality of the approach.

In this chapter the concern will be to uncover some of the repeated issues which arise in differing contexts in Weber's account of the rationalisation process. The result will be to suggest that none of those issues is closed and that the scope for their future examination is unlimited.

1   Formal and material rationality

Weber grounds his analysis of modern society not in the particular power configuration which characterised capitalism, in ownership of the means of production, but in the participation of individuals in systems of action bonded by an institutionalised rationality over which they had no control. It was a sociology addressed to the fates, or the life chances, of particular individuals, rather than towards the collective power of a class. To effect that analysis he had to draw on a distinction as old almost as Western philosophy, the difference between form and content, between, in his terms, formal and material rationality.

At this point it is necessary to recall the full extension of the idea of rationality as we explored it earlier, from rationality as idea through to action and structure. It is inherent in the analysis of communicable ideas to presume first of all that there are principles that are shared by the communicating parties, that they can recognise the same things as the same, that they can know what the other is talking about even when they say that what they have is only an idea. Second, those principles are, by being shared, not alterable at will, but take on an independence from the parties. Third, there is potentially no limit to the number of parties who can employ them for communication. Fourth, a limited number of principles permit an unlimited number of things to be said and understood.

Such notions all contribute to understanding rationality as the ideal structure of the human mind, with a constraining power over it and at the same time an independence from particular minds. What you think or say is merely an employment of those general principles and makes sense only in so far as they are employed. We all can share in this universal resource. What appears to be locked away in the recesses of our own minds turns out to be public and inexhaustible. That private light of revelation which accompanies the first proving of the Pythagorean theorem burns for everyone else too. But the theorem remains eternally unmoved by use or enthusiasm.

Rationality, the idea of the idea, or the form of thought, orders particular ideas and provides the enveloping system within which people think and act. Whenever the doctor prescribes a medicine, the accountant draws up a balance sheet, the electrician makes a circuit, the airline pilot checks his altitude, or the school pupil does an exercise in arithmetic, they all make use of a set of principles of enormous extent, intricately related, codified in textbooks, learnt by painstaking application, being constantly developed and providing the basis for rational action. These are the principles for effectiveness in practical affairs. They may make the difference between success or disaster, they provide the basis for competent work. And they cannot be flouted or modified with impunity. They constitute what Weber called formal rationality.

He had his own special interests in formal rationality. He was particularly intrigued by the way lawyers over the centuries had developed codified principles which became the basis of their professional qualifications and control of legal processes. He examined in some detail the relation between that formal rationality and the requirements of the capitalist system. He accorded enormous significance to the development of money as a formal means of exchange and to the rise of double-entry book-keeping as a means of calculating profit.

Above all he was impressed by the formal rationality of bureaucracy, with the systematic keeping of records and the development of office procedures which ensured system, continuity and control. It was the schooling of the bureaucrat for this system and the knowledge acquired in the job of the way it operated which guaranteed to bureaucrats a permanent power position within the modern organisation. By contrast the ordinary member of an organisation or the citizen of the state was powerless when faced with this expertise. At the same time, the bureaucrat was a mere cog in a machine, unable to interfere in the operation of the gigantic machinery.

It should be clear how well the idea of formal rationality sustained Weber's analysis of domination. The formally rational acted as a necessary and compelling framework for most spheres of life in the modern world. When it was associated with authority, and in particular linked to legal rules, then structures of domination were immeasurably strengthened. Individuals worked within structures according to meanings over which they had no control, implementing orders which came from elsewhere. In such a context it was to be expected that individual requirements were neglected. But that was not altogether without mitigation.

Weber contrasted with formal rationality, material rationality, and here two related, but different, ideas are associated. The form of an argument may be contrasted with either the motives or purposes behind it, or alternatively with the specific topic or content which it is being employed to present. So the formal rationality of bureaucracy may be contrasted with the real practice and personal motives of the individual bureaucrats who may be implementing a procedure. Alternatively, it may be distinguished from the specific policies which are being implemented in accord with the bureaucratic rules. In the former case subsequent literature has concentrated on what has been called the informal aspects of organisation. In the latter case Weber himself drew attention particularly to the fact that material welfare might be promoted by bureaucracy as a policy (he had the Bismarckian social legislation in mind), but that the formal procedures might well make it difficult to realise the purposes of the policy.

In every case Weber emphasised that formal and material rationality were potentially always in conflict. Just by keeping to the letter of the law did not mean that justice in the individual case would be attained. On the contrary, the very effort designed to ensure the integrity of procedure and the impartiality of the judge, might mean that obvious miscarriages of justice could take place. Rules of evidence, for instance, might be organised to be effective overall but in individual instances could result in ruling out clearly decisive information.

In the most general terms, individual rationality, the pursuit of happiness and satisfaction on this earth by particular people, was never necessarily in harmony with the growth of formal rationality. The achievement of particular purposes was never guaranteed by general methods. For Weber this was a matter of both regret and at the same time heroic celebration. Echoing Nietzsche, he rejected happiness as a proper goal anyway, whether for the individual or for the state. At the same time the growth of formal rationality posed problems which it was near the limits of endurance to bear.

In these matters the dividing line between Weber's world-view and his sociological theory melted away. He was at the closest point to his own engagement with the world as a scientist working within the formal frame of scientific knowledge and at the same time following the dictates of his own conscience. He could not do otherwise. For him there was no denying the obvious fact: formal rationality had vastly increased. Its scope was extending all the time. By contrast, individuals could claim mastery over smaller and smaller sectors of life.

2 The growth of rationality

The most celebrated statement of Weber's position on the growth of rationality was contained in the introduction he wrote for the collected edition of his essays on the sociology of religion. Its importance is even greater than might appear from its position in English translation as an introduction to the *Protestant Ethic*, which had been written in 1904–5. The collection of essays was prefaced by a brief account, written in 1920, of the general thrust of all his work in the sociology of religion which had occupied him through to the end of his life. It amounts to the most succinct summation of the deeper purpose of Weber's life's work. He began: 'A product of modern European civilization, studying any problem of universal history, is bound to ask himself to what combination of circumstances the fact should be attributed that in Western civilization, and in Western civilization only, cultural phenomena have appeared which (as we like to think) lie in a line of development having *universal* significance and value' (PE: 13). He proceeded to enumerate a set of cultural achievements of the West which all raised the 'question of the specific and peculiar rationalism of Western culture' (ibid.: 26). These included such diverse things as empirical science, systematic theology, rational jurisprudence, rational harmonic music, the gothic vault, trained administration by officials, the state, the rational pursuit of profit, the capitalistic organisation of free labour.

He acknowledged that forms of rationalism existed in non-Western culture, and he had examined in some depth the rationalism of imperial China, for instance. Moreover, even such irrational phenomena as mystic contemplation could be rationalised. So really the question was what determined the specifically Western form of rationalisation. Here he argued it was important to consider 'the ability and disposition of men to adopt certain types of rational conduct. When these types have been obstructed by spiritual obstacles, the development of rational economic conduct has also met serious resistance. The magical and religious forces, and the ethical ideas of duty based upon them, have always in the past been among the most important formative influences on conduct. In the studies here we shall be concerned with these forces' (ibid.: 26–7).

In other studies, especially of law, politics and economics, Weber was concerned with those rationalised structures directly. 'For our study, the increasing penetration of enacted order is but one especially characteristic component of that process of rationalisation and association, which we shall have to pursue in every sector as a most essential driving force of development as it makes comprehensive advances into all kinds of communal action (WG I: 195; my translation). Here Weber was examining the reciprocal support given to each other by market organisation and the monopoly of force in the hands of the state. He is employing the distinction between community and association, and seeing the latter as part of the whole process of rationalisation.

Weber allowed for rationalisation to be possible in any sphere of life, and moreover, in contradictory directions. In particular the great religions fostered the rationalisation of lifestyles towards the goal of salvation. In the case of Confucian China there was even a comprehensive secular rationalisation of life. But the formal rationalisation which extended over so much of Western life required a methodical personal lifestyle which was subordinated entirely to impersonal goals. It was the rational inner-worldly asceticism of the Protestant which provided the adequate motivation to infuse the structures of capitalism and, we may add, bureaucracy.

Weber's bureaucrat also had to work with dedication and impersonality, not letting personal feeling interfere. The bureaucratisation of domination fostered the development of a certain sober, rational, professional personality type (E&S II: 998). The systems of examination to prepare individuals for office nurtured the same kinds of qualities. In other words, people were produced who could fit into bureaucratised structures of domination, where the rationality belonged to the system as a whole. Of all the features of rationalisation in the modern world, it was the central importance of bureaucracy which seemed to Weber to guarantee the ever widening scope of formal rationality. Bureaucracy 'destroyed structures of domination which were not rational in this sense of the term . . . with rules, means-ends calculus and matter-of-factness predominating' (E&S II: 1002).

'Bureaucratic administration means fundamentally domination through knowledge. This is the feature of it which makes it specifically rational' (E&S I: 225). But this knowledge was linked to a whole series of other institutional conditions which included precise communication networks and also predictable money resources. In this way, Weber identified a causal nexus of capitalism, bureaucracy and modern communication, which for him made it unlikely that a socialistic system could compete. In fact, it was only the capitalist entrepreneur who could maintain a relative independence from bureaucracy and this because of the specialised knowledge acquired in economic activity. That relative independence, however, also provided a support for bureaucracy and itself often depended on the development of internal bureaucracy within the capitalistic organisation.

Weber's remarks on the institutional foundations of capitalism and socialism are among the most intriguing in his whole analysis of modern social structure. They were written before the world had had experience of socialist regimes and the whole experience of those regimes in the last seventy years would suggest that their problem arose precisely in the areas Weber identified as crucial, namely the production of a sufficiently rational basis for the interrelations of state and economy. The knowledge basis of capitalism was for Weber an essential prerequisite for use of resources by a bureaucracy and he was sceptical that socialism could find an adequate substitute for it.

Modern capitalism represented the confluence of a number of originally independent streams of rationality in Western culture. In the 'General Lectures on Economic History' (GEH), which he gave in Munich, after the end of the First World War, he depicted a relentless torrent of rationality arising out of these mutually reinforcing streams. Roman law assisted the development of the state as well as jurisprudence suitable for capitalism, rational book-keeping permitted capital accounting and the calculation of profit, market freedom removed irrational limits on the market, the labour contract made possible the rational division of labour on the basis of technical efficiency alone, technology and pursuit of inventions served commercial ends, the mass of free citizens provided the basis for mass demand and the need for developed rational administration. The masses themselves had to be imbued with a sense of the worth of work and the need for discipline. Everyday life had to be rationalised.

The modern labourer worked under conditions which were pre-tested in the army. Next to the army, the modern factory was the great inculcator of discipline. American scientific management represented the highest point yet in the rational conditioning and training of work performance. The psycho-physical apparatus of the human being was completely adjusted to the demands of the outer world, the tools, the machine. Centralisation of the means of control, the mechanisation of production and the extension of discipline were coordinate elements in the relentless growth of rationalisation and the standardisation of individual behaviour (Essays: 263).

'Relentless', 'unavoidable', 'inevitable' are adjectives Weber frequently used when describing the universal progress of rationalisation. It was an all-embracing process, not merely conceptually, as with the notion of the growth of human reason, but practically, in material terms in the extension of methods of production and administration which were dominating the world. It had very concrete referents. Moreover, new inputs to strengthen the process occurred all the time. The development of weaponry could aid in the rationalisation of warfare, the development of postal and news services aided in a general process of democratisation. The railway he called 'the most revolutionary instrumentality known to history' (GEH: 221).

There is no doubt that Weber saw himself as engaged in nothing less than an interpretation of the specific nature of modern, namely Western, culture and considered that rationality held the key to understanding. It is an interpretation which has been criticised particularly for what Gouldner (1955) called 'metaphysical pathos' and for the pessimism about the fate of the individual which recurs so often in Weber's writing. Unfortunately this has diverted attention away from the method and logic of Weber's account and also inhibited any attempt to replicate it for the contemporary period. After all, the individual processes which he subsumed under the heading of rationalisation have continued unabated since his time and at a rate which probably would have amazed even him. If we take just two examples, the development of biological, especially genetic, engineering and the use of computerised data bases, in both areas necessitating governmental enquiries and legislation throughout the Western world, we can see rationalisation raised to new levels (Albrow, 1987).

It is possible to replicate his account. Less easy is the identification of the underlying principles which generate it. The rationalisation process was a historical fact for Weber. He presented it as such. He never reached the point where he was able to offer an account of the underlying causal processes. Unlike Marx, he has no equivalent to the laws of the concentration of capital or of the decline in the rate of profit. We have plenty of intriguing statements like 'not ideas, but ideal and material interests, directly govern men's conduct' (E&S I: 280) or 'everywhere bureaucratization favours mass democracy' (E&S I: 226) but an underlying model which would link these propositions is never made explicit.

This too has given support to those who would suggest that the basis for Weber's account is metaphysical prejudice. But this neglects the care Weber took to give clear empirical referents for his account, and it also ignores the many indications that for him the process did not take place in a vacuum, that it was conditioned and limited by real circumstances and that he too would have wished to penetrate still further into the underlying mechanisms. He left moreover a number of indications of the direction in which he would have been inclined to search for those. We need to follow some of these leads in order to complete a picture of Weberian social science which does not leave it in an apparent metaphysical cul-de-sac and which shows that it retained its empirical basis to the end.

3 The boundaries of rationality

As we established earlier, Weber accepted as part of his intellectual ambience that rationality and irrationality were simply counterposed. A ceaseless exchange took place between them, however, and what began as a simple dichotomy at a conceptual level turned out to be a complex interchange when viewed historically. But viewed historically, or empirically, irrationality had prior place.

That position was sustained by the implicit alignment of a series of dichotomies in the Christian-Kantian world-view. We live in the 'world': beyond that is 'spirit'. The world is 'real': as opposed to the real there is the 'ideal'. The real is manifested in 'facts': 'ideas' belong to the sphere of the ideal. Facts are 'irrational': ideas spring from the 'rational'. It is the fate of the human being to be the bridge between these dichotomies. Living in the world the individual aspires to the idea. The person is both animal nature and spiritual essence. Human history is precisely the story of the struggle between those two sides.

Nothing could be further from the truth than to see Weber's account of the rationalisation process as the inevitable unfolding of the power of rationality. The material world was always recalcitrant, always placed limits on what could be done. Moreover, the grounds of human behaviour were themselves always ultimately irrational and that could never change, however much rationality advanced. That was axiomatic, built into the basic assumptions of Weber's thought and method. The key question was where the boundaries were located.

Once again we have to stress that this was a question to be solved empirically. And Weber was open to possibilities on this from far beyond what have since been customarily established as the boundaries of sociological explanation. For instance, when it came to the rationalism of the West and the peculiar disposition toward a practical everyday rationalised existence as compared with the East, Weber explicitly refused to rule out the possibility that biological differences might one day be shown to be important (PE: 31). On the other hand, and quite consistently, he was vehemently opposed to those who claimed that they had been able to identify racial differences as the basis for social differentiation (SSP: 457–60).

The springs of action had ultimately to be irrational. However rationally pursued, the preferences, tastes, interests which human beings possessed were the starting point for economic action. In this respect Weber simply adopted the economic theory of his time. About tastes there could be no argument. Values too, however far they were rationalised, were chosen on unprovable grounds. There was no rational way in which reason could bridge the gap between different ultimate values.

So too with belief: ultimately belief in science also was a kind of faith, while belief in the law, however rational the way law might be developed, sprang from deeply imbued traditional acceptance of ways of thinking and acting. When it came to power relations, then this was inherently a sphere of the irrational, in which outcomes were determined by force, strength, resources, weight of numbers. But rationality here could become a potent weapon too.

Conflicts of rationality too were regularly solved in irrational ways. Weber always showed himself acutely aware of the fact that the very rationalisation of a sphere of life could bring it into conflict with other spheres. The rationalisation of the economy brought it into conflict with the rationality of the state. This was the theme of his inaugural lecture. Economic liberalism was endangering the integrity of German culture, and hence its political strength. But in this case we have seen that for Weber, in general, economic and political rationalisation were in tune with each other. Although again, in the case of socialism, he saw the conflict as acute.

In fact Weber offered no systematic resolution of these dilemmas. They remained open in his work as ever present possibilities with no determinate solution. What he did regard as pious nonsense was the thought that these conflicts could ultimately be bridged in a harmonious resolution of divergent wills. Neither the utopianism of French calls to solidarity, nor the English belief that somehow compromises were ultimately rational, appealed to him intellectually. The represented so much fudging of the real intellectual and practical problems.

One of the most prominent explorations of these issues occurred in an essay Weber wrote in 1913 on the economic ethics of the world religions. For him the great religions were all characterised by the effort to make the actual world comprehensively meaningful. It is always intellectuals who have pursued this active quest for a rationalised image of the world. But their premises remain irremediably irrational, however far they are pushed into the recesses of the system of thought. 'The various great ways of leading a rational and methodical life have been characterised by irrational presuppositions, which have been accepted simply as "given" and which have been incorporated into such ways of life' (Essays: 281).

In typically hard-headed style Weber attributes the basis of these presuppositions to the character of the social strata which were of decisive importance during the formative period of the religion. And that character was determined by their social and psychological interests. In fact rationalism in religion is always pushed ultimately to finding mystic experience and the fact that contemplation time and again has been the ultimate resort has had vital consequences for the conduct of economic life. Of course, for Weber the peculiarity of the Protestant Ethic was that its irrational foundation was a belief in predestination which worked in the world and assisted in its transformation. But this most rational methodical religious response to the world was based on irrational foundations.

However irrational the foundations, Weber explicitly rejected the view that their rationalisation was of no significance. That, he said, was contrary to the factual evidence. He goes on to point out that the conception of a supra-mundane God decisively influenced the way salvation has been experienced. 'The rational elements of religion, its 'doctrine', also have an autonomy' (Essays: 286).

An empirical account then of rationality, of the way ideas are effected and effective in the real world, does have to allow for them to have an influence on events. Weber's whole method required that ideas should be one element among many which helps us to understand and explain the course of social action. We need to explore how far he was able to specify just what the contribution of ideas might be.

4 Ideas as Explanatory Factors

From 1904 to his death, Weber's work revolved around the theme of the rationalisation of the West. For him it was the largest historical fact, something which stared every historian in the face. But, despite what his critics have said, he was not prepared to be satisfied with what could easily become an overarching philosophy of history. It was an empirical process and it was open to a deeper interpretation as well as causal explanation.

Weber had a deeper purpose than summing up the course of history. The question to which he returned throughout the period was how far ideas had contributed to that development, and precisely what causal part could ideas be said to play. Nothing was further from his intention than to replicate the Hegelian approach, in which the idea, rationality, came to consciousness in the course of history. Talk of the power of ideas in history was for him so much confusion of idea and reality. Ideas were not the true reality lying behind events and working their way through history (Meth: 94). They only existed in the minds of human beings and could only be effective through them. But they were nonetheless in principle determinate elements within the course of human action.

Nothing should be allowed to detract from the magnitude of Weber's project. It was matched only by the prodigious nature of the scholarly enquiry which he conducted in this pursuit. Whether he wrote of law, or religion, or sexuality, or bureaucracy, of the economy or music, he reverted time and time again to his core problem: in what way precisely could ideas be said to contribute to the overall process of rationalisation which was detectable in every sphere. His intended contribution was, as he said at one point, to the 'typology and sociology of rationalism' (Essays: 324). For it was Weber's conviction that the question of the contribution of ideas was not one to be resolved by *a priori* argument. It was *not* a philosophical question. How ideas became factors in *reality* required the investigation of their location, in the ways people act.

Weber was fully convinced that he was proposing a specialised method for taking the fraught issue of the relations of ideas to the material world out of the realm of dogmatic system building. Often quoted is the penultimate sentence of the *Protestant Ethic*: 'But it is, of course, not my aim to substitute for a one-sided materialistic an equally one-sided spiritualistic causal interpretation of culture and history' (PE: 183). He goes on to say that, while he was in that essay concerned with the influence of religious ideas (*Bewusstseinsinhalte*), he had not gone on to attempt to deduce everything characteristic of modern culture from Protestantism. 'But that sort of thing may be left to the type of dilettante who believes in the unity of the group mind and its reducibility to a single formula' (PE: 284).

It was not a question of making a choice for one or other side of a dichotomy. Any rigorous scientific treatment of the problem involved the dismantling of that crude distinction and the building of a sophisticated set of concepts appropriate to viewing human beings as agents. This has not been widely appreciated, for two main reasons. The first is that Weber is so often seen as the bourgeois response to Marx. But this is to overestimate the extent to which Weber's intellectual agenda was set by that requirement. The second reason is of altogether different origin, although it is compounded by the tendency to align Weber with an anti-Marxist position, and hence to simplify his thought. The problem here is that the complexity of his vocabulary is often lost in English translation.

Weber employed as many different terms as possible to render nuances in his analysis of the complex of factors involved in human motivation. The quotation above is a good illustration. *Bewusstseinsinhalte*, literally contents of consciousness, has been translated 'ideas'. That is not a mistake, but something is lost, because the English 'idea' is a term of vague and all-embracing scope. It therefore also is used to translate such terms as *Vorstellung*, which is more 'mental image' or 'representation', *Gedanke*, which is more a thought, or *Begriff*, concept. *Idee* in German, which Weber does use, tends to carry more precise associations, a mental content verbally formulated. As Weber employs it, he certainly makes full use of these nuances as compared with the other terms. *Vorstellung* is not yet *Idee*, just as *Glaube*, belief, is not yet *Wissen*, knowledge. The contents of consciousness are not all organised: thoughts, images, impressions, jostle with each other for attention, and as for the unconscious, this is almost raw material.

Much of the contents of consciousness could be interpreted psychologically, and Weber had no hesitation in drawing upon relevant psychological interpretations for much of human motivation. Emotions were strongly linked with interests in much of Weber's accounts of motives. In these respects ideas in the strict sense play no part. We can recall his famous statement, 'Not ideas, but material and ideal interests, directly govern men's conduct'. Such interests stem from experience, they arise out of the social and psychological position of whole strata. They are not material in the Marxist sense, but they are very real in the Weberian sense as arising out of life situations. His conception of life situation was more comprehensive than simple economic position or relation to the means of production. But this is very far from identifying 'ideas' as the key factor. Indeed, Weber's emphasis on interests was designed very much to delimit just what scope ideas could have in the determination of conduct.

Ideas were important precisely because they represented the organisation of mental contents. In them rationality worked to provide shape and to give them the quality of providing a focus, a common reference point, a means for the orientation of action. Passions, yearnings, desires, remain as unfocused discontents or unhappiness. Ideas can provide directions for these, in Weber's words, 'like switchmen, determine the tracks along which action has been pushed by the dynamic of interest' (Essays: 280). Most important, for instance, were the specific world images provided by religious intellectuals as the form within which the suffering masses could express their suffering. It is here that rationality comes fully into play. The desire to be saved was an inarticulate yearning until intellectuals provided images of what one was to be saved from and what one was to be saved for. These images were intellectual constructions, open to rationalisation.

Ideas are not then a hidden power. They always have a specific content, are communicable, have varying degrees of coherence, have to be worked out and are relatively more or less appropriate for particular life situations. Some ideas will spread very rapidly if the situation is ripe for them, e.g. Protestantism among the free citizenry of the sixteenth century, or socialism among the industrial proletariat; other ideas, like rational capitalism in imperial China, can make little headway. But they have to be reckoned with in any assessment of human motivation.

5   Rationality as a force

There is a great variety of ways in which Weber gives expression to the influence of ideas on action, and more specifically to the importance of rationality. These are uncodified, certainly not part of a systematic model, although they could probably be made to be so with diligent work. For the moment it is possible to distinguish at least four major facets to Weber's account of the power of ideas and rationality.

i) The need for a unified world-view. This is what Weber also calls 'metaphysical need for a meaningful cosmos'. Here he emphasises that under conditions where there is already a differentiated social structure, and especially where there is disparity of wealth and suffering, there is a need to produce a unified image of the world, and intellectuals, prophets and priests normally provide this through ideas.

The ordering of Gods, and finally the idea of one God, was generated to meet this need, and Weber suggests that there are not too many alternative ways of conceiving of God's relation to the human world. But the differences as conceived by the intellectuals and theologians have been critical in determining the direction of action towards salvation. Here then ideas have a symbolic and psychological function for the masses.

ii) The metaphysical need to produce the meaningful cosmos is felt particularly strongly by intellectuals, but their needs are different from the masses in this sense that the production of ideas has more importance than the actual salvation content. Weber is very ambivalent about intellectuals. They represent for him a psychological type: undisciplined they can degenerate into the coffee-house type, content simply to exchange talk about ideas; disciplined they can, as scholars and scientists, occasionally produce a really important idea. In both cases, however, Weber acknowledged an inner need to engage with ideas, not shared by the mass of the population.

iii) Ideas serve functions: they also have power, and here Weber is quite explicit, by virtue of their consistency and internal logic. In this connection Weber speaks of the *ratio*, the Latin term for reason, argument or proof. Eduard Baumgarten has pointed out that this is the key concept within one of Weber's pivotal statements in his sociology of religion, the *Zwischenbetrachtung*, the theory of stages and directions of the religious rejection of the world (1964: 472). At its outset Weber says:

For the rationality, in the sense of logical or teleological 'consistency', of an intellectual-theoretical or practical-ethical attitude has and always has had power over man, however limited and unstable this power is and always has been in the face of other forces of historical life. Religious interpretations of the world and ethics of religions created by intellectuals and meant to be rational have been strongly exposed to the imperative of consistency. The effect of the *ratio*, especially of a teleological deduction of practical postulates, is in some way, and often very strongly, noticeable among all religious ethics (Essays: 324).

We find the *ratio* cited by Weber in connection with the development of the idea of a single God, with universal claims. Here he links it with the rationalism of professional priests or a more mundane striving for order (E&S I: 416). That linkage to interests is important for it shows how careful Weber was not to overestimate this power of ideas. When he refers to it in the 'Objectivity' essay, for instance, he says that 'however important the significance even of the purely logically persuasive force of ideas', still events in men's minds are more psychologically rather than logically conditioned. Again we ought to stress, the power of ideas here is not as a kind of crypto-agent, but more like a natural force, a light which illuminates or blinds. Or to use an example Weber employs to illustrate immediate understanding: $2 \times 2 = 4$. We might say that human beings have little choice in the matter and that the reason they say $2 \times 2 = 4$ is because 2×2 cannot equal anything else.

iv) *Ratio* has a hold on human beings. In turn they can employ rationality to effect technical solutions for their problems, and those solutions become a very real part of people's life situation. Most of the examples Weber gives in his introduction to the sociology of religion are of this kind. The solutions will become part of an institutionalised system of knowledge, such as architecture, medicine, law, accountancy, and through professional practice will become an inherent necessity for the conduct of life in the modern world. Human beings are constantly seeking to build their stock of technical solutions in every sphere of life and Weber devoted a lengthy study of music to the problem of the relationship between psychological and technical moments in its development. He regarded it as an especially challenging field in which to work out his analysis in depth.

According to Eduard Baumgarten he exasperated the *Verein für Sozialpolitik* in 1914 by presenting his analysis of music as a proof that it was possible to write a value-free account of technical progress in a sphere of value. They did not want to listen and he incorporated his ideas into the value-freedom essay (Baumgarten, 1964: 483). Silbermann points out that it is precisely the obviously irrational source of music which made it so attractive to Weber as a topic for the elaboration of his theories (1963: 460).

Silbermann also draws attention to the way Weber weaves his general sociological perspective into the account of music. The idea of the greater rationalisation of Western music compared with music in other cultures is the overarching conception which holds the piece together and within which he examines the interplay of emotional and rational moments. He examines the way those work through social relationships to the extent of showing how the organisation of status groups and their requirements dictated the direction of musical development.

But it was the meaning of rationality as applied to music which was the focus of Weber's critical acumen. In examining that, he made a central distinction between what he called rationalisation from within, which referred principally to the development of a system of tone intervals and the accompanying notation, and rationalisation from without, which concerned the technical refinement of musical instruments. In his view the rationalisation of tone intervals was attempted in other cultures (he cited examples from East Asia), but only in the West was the scale tempered to meet the harmonic and melodic needs of musical expression. What Weber called the 'tonal ratio' operated as a formative principle in Western music even if the theory often lagged well behind the practice. 'The relationships between musical *ratio* and musical life belong to the most important historically variable fields of tension in music' (WG II: 920).

The rational development of harmony was influenced by the technical development of instruments, but here socioeconomic factors played a more important part. The piano developed very much as a bourgeois domestic instrument, within the capacities of only modestly gifted people and also able to fit into the confined comforts of the home. It had, said Weber, disadvantages for singers, and accounted for the greater impurity of tone among singers of the North trained in the home as compared with singers of the South. Technical developments, then, always were to be seen in terms of the purposes of definite people.

Technical rationalisation, the development of means to ends on an institutionalised basis, would appear to contrast with inner rationalisation which far more was the shape given to inner need. Here Weber does suggest that there is something in the Western experience which results in greater intensity of rationalisation. At one point, for instance, he suggests that the harmonic rationalisation of music is always in tension with melodic realities, and that the overcoming of this irrationality (which always recurs) is a constant stimulus to further development (WG II: 880). Such remarks were interwoven with an extraordinary accumulation of ethno-musicological material from different periods and cultures.

Weber was using music as the test bed for ideas which he was developing throughout the sociology of religion. There is a constant interplay between inner drives and needs and the institutionalised channels in which they are expressed. Those channels are developed by specialists who acquire an interest in their rationalisation, which in turn influences old needs and creates new ones.

These ideas never reach the point of becoming a formal model of development. The complexity of considerations, which Weber took into account as he accumulated more and more case material, made that an ever receding possibility. Everything suggests, however, that he had concluded that rational structures of all kinds were not only stronger in the sense of providing technically better solutions to enduring problems, but that they evoked, and enlisted, the motivation which contributed to their further development. Western rationalism on this account contained an inherent dynamic. The twentieth century has not yet proved Weber wrong.

PART III

Explorations in Weberian Social Theory

The most exalted of all would be: to comprehend that everything
factual is already theory.
(Goethe, *Maxims and Reflections*, no. 575)

Preamble

Weber has generated a distinctive approach to social theory because he links the requirements for understanding other people to the necessity to establish facts about social life. The explorations which follow seek to show that Weber's social theory is distinguished by its insistence on the empirical moment as a constitutive factor in social life, however far that life is guided by theory, and that sociology as an extension of the everyday need for facts, however complex, has a continued and developing role to play.

If we follow Weber's arguments on understanding, on the empirical study of values and the relations between society and the market, we will find that in his insistence on facticity and his discussion of common understanding (*Einverständnis*) a series of questions is removed from speculation and opened up for empirical research. Even the question of whether society exists or not becomes a manageable empirical problem.

At one level Weber's work is tied to how the world is and is therefore in a trivial sense ideological, but since it grasps the changing nature of that world and offers explanations for those changes, it provides an ever developing potential for self-understanding.

It is in fact the statement which comes closest to grasping the central implicit thrust of sociology today, while at the same time its interpretative power has yet to be put to full use. This book will be justified if it succeeds in extending the appreciation of that power.

11

Understanding and Social Structure

1 Human agency

For Weber a science of social reality was concerned with the analysis of actual events and real structures. The living individual had to be seen as the source of social action, as an agent. By explaining actions by reference to the motives of individuals and not to abstract or ideal entities Weber held to a particular notion of reality. The human being was real and it was in human beings that the scientist should search for explanations. '*Hinter der Handlung steht der Mensch*': 'behind the action there stands the human being' (WL: 492), was Weber's most succinct expression of this dominating idea.

That, we should recall, was the animating spirit behind the immensely complex articulation of concepts which Weber elaborated to trace the linkages between individual action and the most all-embracing social structures. This must be stressed to remove the crude misinterpretation of Weber's approach which sees it as a denial of the existence of such entities as the state. The point is that for the empirical sociologist the state *exists* as a complex of actions guided by certain beliefs.

We have to seek therefore to explain changes in society by reference to what people do and why they do it, allowing always of course for the fact that material factors of all kinds in the environment and in the organism will also exercise an influence on outcomes. But the social scientist turns to people and their qualities first. Moreover these are concrete and real. On average they exert enormous force: think of the disciplined energy and skill of a workforce. In individual cases they can exert a controlling power over millions of people: the charisma of a Lenin or a Gandhi (Napoleon and the Dalai Lama were examples Weber chose).

This ought to be sufficient to rebut the other crude judgement on Weber's method, that it is a prime example of abstract individualism, when by that is meant the assumption that the social scientist need operate only on the basis of the minimum of features attributed to the individual, no more than the ability to set goals, make choices and calculate correctly. That approach Weber recognised and applauded when it came to economic theory. But he distinguished it sharply from an empirical approach to social life.

It is, of course, proper to point out, as I did in the first part of this book, that Weber's insistence on the importance of human agency was itself based upon Kantian ethics and arguments of an extremely formal and abstract kind. In this sense the imputation of responsibility to human beings for their own action is not itself based on experience. It is transcendental as a general principle. But in every individual case a dividing line has to be drawn between what can be deemed within the power of the individual and what is an extraneous factor over which no control could reasonably be expected.

It is this Kantian emphasis on responsibility which probably accounts for the rather exclusive emphasis on motivation as an element in explaining the course of human action in Weber's comments on the nature of sociology. In fact, other aspects of his work would suggest that in addition to motives we have to take account at least of beliefs (knowledge and values) and powers or capacities as properties of individuals if we are going to be able to explain the outcomes of their actions. The concentration on purposes and feelings in his basic definitions betrays the moralistic origins of his individualism.

Notwithstanding this qualification, the point about imputing responsibility to the human agent is precisely that it is then sensible to talk of human acts as causes of events. The empirical social scientist therefore, far from reducing human responsibility, actually seeks very precisely to attribute it to where it belongs. This corresponds not only to legal assumptions in imputing responsibility to individuals, at least in respect of criminal acts, it corresponds too to everyday assumptions when seeking to answer such questions as 'Why do people save money?' or 'Why do people work hard?' Explanations are sought in action and the motives behind that action. And in finding explanations for why people act as they do we conclude that we therefore understand them.

This is the juncture where we can see the intimate connection between Weber's individualistic method for social science and his doctrine of *Verstehen* or understanding. The reason Weber insisted on *Verstehen* as his method was because this was what one meant by explaining human action. Motives were the meaningful causes of action and an interpretative sociology sought to gain explanations of action through identifying such motives (and we might add beliefs and capacities).

From this standpoint there is nothing particularly problematical about social causation. Causality for Weber involves two elements, the idea of an effect and the idea of regularity, and this applies across the sciences (WL: 135). In the essay on Stammler he carefully dissects the differences between rule-following in the Kantian sense and regularity in the sense of repeated occurrence. There is no special difficulty in coming to judgements about people observing the law normally because of a fear of consequences if they were not to do so. For Weber that is an explanation of social behaviour which depends equally on observed frequency and interpreting a rule. It is an explanation which involves understanding of both rules (ideas) and motives.

Of course, understanding a rule, such as a law, was different from understanding people through motives. Weber recognised fully that the rational understanding of rules, such as a lawyer possessed, was different from an understanding of why people obeyed the law. Moreover, the first was an understanding which aided empirical investigation. But he consistently emphasised that this was distinct from and an adjunct to the understanding which a science of social reality sought.

The subject which for Weber was most intimately linked with sociology or empirical social science, where the difference was really only one of emphasis, but where the material was basically the same, was history. What he said about the centrality of the human agent applied equally to both disciplines. The generality of their interest was different but each drew from the other. Neither was reducible to scientific laws nor deducible from ideal principles. The human being was at the front of the stage in each.

Weber certainly engaged fully with the technical literature of his day on theories of understanding and scientific methodology. He located his own approach in relation to them. But it would be a complete misunderstanding of his position to suppose that he somehow drew from the theories of language, interpretation of art or hermeneutics and from ideas of causality in physics and biology to produce a distinctive amalgam called 'interpretative sociology'. His method was to start from the unshakable everyday assumption that people are responsible for their actions. To that extent his approach can be termed phenomenological, but that was not a term which he employed.

Interpretative sociology as empirical social science is neither idealist nor materialist. It relates to both ideas and the material world without deriving its methods of study from any of the disciplines which focus on those spheres. In association with history it has an intellectual independence which is appropriate to the dignity and autonomy of the human agent.

Understanding is central to the discipline, not as a derived method from some other academic sector. It is in fact a foundation for any possible social relationships. The method for the discipline is therefore derived from the intrinsic nature of the subject matter. We have to examine it now in that light.

2 The meaning of understanding

We understand sentences, mathematical equations, statements of fact, poems, people playing cards, someone opening a door; we understand why people do things, sometimes we even claim to understand ourselves or why we live our lives on this earth.

In all these cases the understanding we claim may be challenged by another person. How do you know you understand? The response will normally refer to a 'meaning'. That which is being understood will be taken to refer to something else. It may be an idea behind a word, a feeling behind a poem, physical events behind an equation, a purpose behind an act. Very often, perhaps more often than not, reference to meaning will be made through language, and so the response to a query about the meaning of a statement may well be another statement. But the meaning of an equation might well be expressed through another equation.

It is equally legitimate to ask for meaning behind a meaning. Having revealed a purpose underlying an act the respondent may well be asked again why he or she had that purpose. The further response could refer to another purpose or to a feeling. There is no point in logic where the questioning has to stop, nor any necessary end to the quest for meaning. If the questions stop, it is for practical purposes.

While there are unending series of questions which may be asked about meaning across innumerable spheres of human life, there are nonetheless spheres of reality where such questions appear to the modern mind to be meaningless. the natural world is not held together by meaning. We no longer ask for the meaning of the thunderstorm; we explain it in terms of electro-magnetic forces.

Meaning questions make sense in human affairs. There their scope is vast. It is in fact the sphere of human culture. Any systematic enquiry into history or the forms of human expression and life in society is based on questions of meaning. In Weber's words: 'The transcendental presupposition of every cultural science (*Kulturwissenschaft*) is not that we find a particular or indeed any "culture" valuable, but that we are cultural beings, endowed with the capacity and the will to take up a conscious stand towards the world and to endow it with a meaning (*Sinn*)' (WL: 180). But to speak of a 'transcendental presupposition' did not for Weber consign the discussion of understanding to the abstract realm of Kantian philosophy. For transcendental presuppositions are important precisely because they are the frame for ordinary everyday experience. Weber was interested not in pursuing philosophy but in empirical social science. Understanding and meaning were, as part of the fabric of everyday existence, a subject for such a science, even though equally specialised 'dogmatic' sciences, such as aesthetics or theology, might seek to explore particular spheres of meaning and develop their own technical theories.

For Weber, then, the analysis of understanding as a general concept, namely what meaning we can give to 'understanding', was important as a preliminary to investigating meaning as it was shaped in real social life and as a way of approaching the fact that social life itself depended on some degree of mutual understanding. In this sense the special disciplinary approaches to understanding, which were already far advanced in theology with Schleiermacher (1768–1834), philology with Boeckh (1785–1867), or even the attempt to found a general philosophical standpoint in *Verstehen*, as Dilthey had done, were much too focused on high culture, on highly refined sectors of meaning to give him his guidelines for researching into social life (see Outhwaite, 1975). To this extent he sympathised with the brilliant phenomenological speculations of the young economist, von Gottl (1901). We have to understand what ordinary people mean by purpose, need, investment and so on, and not just economists' definitions.

3   Immediate and motivational understanding

In *Economy and Society* Weber acknowledged the importance of his contemporary George Simmel's distinction between the understanding of the meaning of an utterance, a reference to something objective, and understanding the motive which led a person to make the utterance or to act in a certain way, the subjective meaning. In tune with his whole emphasis, however, he expressed reservations about what he considered to be Simmel's overreadiness to associate 'objective' meaning with the validity of the sciences. In everyday life it was necessary to come to a judgement about what a command, for instance, might mean on the basis of the actual reality in which a person was placed. This was 'objective' but not dependent on science. Only if there were doubt about this meaning would questions of the motive for the command come into question and then 'subjective' understanding come into play. These arguments were advanced in his essay on Knies in 1905, but were still important enought for Weber to allude to them in the final version of the basic concepts of sociology (WL: 93–5; WG I: 1–6).

In the basic concepts Weber distinguishes between two main kinds of undertanding. He took, for instance, the equation $2 \times 2 = 4$, and stated that we had an 'immediate' understanding of that (*'aktuelles' Verstehen*), but we might also understand why someone was using that equation if they were doing the firm's accounts (*'erklärendes' Verstehen*, explanatory understanding from motives). That distinction applied to behaviour too. Lifting a gun to shoot an animal, taking a key to open the door, carried a meaning which could be read immediately, without the need to search for motives. However, it was the placing of that immediately understood behaviour into a motivational context which provided an explanation for it (WG I: 4).

Weber's use of this distinction has given rise to considerable controversy. In particular Alfred Schutz's critique has revealed ambiguities and opened up directions of enquiry so that precisely the way in which understanding can be claimed for such actions as taking a key to a door can become the focus for investigation. Those few paragraphs at the beginning of *Economy and Society* provided the spur to the phenomenological movement which made the construction of meaning itself the topic rather than the datum. That movement has rendered important insights into a range of social phenomena. Deviant behaviour and professional socialisation are just two examples. But the virtues of its narrower focus are offset by a neglect of the wider rationale for Weber's position which is to be read from his whole work and not from those few paragraphs.

Weber's 'immediate' understanding is undoubtedly problematical. It refers to the common sense unreflective acceptance of obvious everyday statements and actions as having a meaning. That acceptance, however, becomes a premise for the sociologist, not out of a desire to ignore the problems, but because it is a premise for everyday life and because social relationships are constructed on its basis. Utterances and actions are then the primary data for sociologists precisely because of their posited, even arbitrary, quality as both 'objective' and 'meant' by the people who speak and act.

In the same way Weber treats the understanding of feelings as being either 'immediate' or explained through motives. The anger of a person is understood from the raised fist. It is understood and explained by reference to the frustration of a broken love affair, or the wilful disobedience of an order. Of course, ethnobiological and comparative cultural analysis could seek to determine the universality or otherwise of the raised fist as a sign or expression of anger. Nothing in Weber's account detracts from the importance of such an enquiry. But it takes investigation in a different direction from the one he chose, which was to take the raised fist as meaning anger and then to ask why the person was angry.

Unfortunately this aspect of Weber's theory of understanding has not been appreciated. By and large sociologists have accepted the phenomenological critique and concluded that Weber was proposing a defective or limited theory of meaning in his ideas of *aktuelles Verstehen* (immediate understanding). But he was not concerned to explore how we understand $2 \times 2 = 4$, or opening door behaviour, or angry gestures, however intriguing those questions might be. His concern was to start with some facts which are at the same time meaningful to the people concerned, in the first place the agent and those around. Facts of 'immediate' understanding therefore function in Weber's thought as social facts do in Durkheim's, the data the scientist seeks to explain.

This would all be much clearer were it not for the fact that this aspect of Weber's thinking has been obscured by ineffective translation. The following appears in the Henderson and Parsons translation which Roth and Wittich reproduce:

> Thus for a science which is concerned with the subjective meaning of action, explanation requires a grasp of the complex of meaning in which an actual course of understandable action thus interpreted belongs (E&S I: 9).

This renders Weber's distinction between immediate and motivational explanatory understanding opaque and neutralises the force of the connection he then makes between them. A more literal and effective version would be:

> 'Explanation' for a science which is concerned with the meaning (*Sinn*) of action means just this: grasping the complex of meaning (*Sinnzusammenhang*) within which, in accordance with its subjectively intended meaning, an immediately understood (*aktuell verständliches*) act belongs.

That 'complex of meaning' to which he refers here he exemplifies entirely by explanations from motives.

In brief, this amounts to saying that, for the purposes of empirical social research, when someone says $2 \times 2 = 4$ both the ordinary listener and the social scientist will assume that the speaker means what is said and understands what it means; when someone 'opens the door', that they know what they are doing and mean to do it; when someone appears to be angry, that they will acknowledge that they *are* angry. These are commonsense everyday assumptions. They can, of course, as Goffman and others have not tired in pointing out, be invalidated by trickery, fraud, insincerity, self-deception, indoctrination, or innocent imitation. Does rote learning create understanding?

These are certainly not unimportant issues. Weber pointed out the difference in meaning which $2 \times 2 = 4$ would have to mathematicians and the masses. He acknowledged, 'In the great majority of cases actual action goes on in a state of inarticulate half-consciousness or actual unconsciousness of its subjective meaning' (E&S I: 21). (In the German 'subjective meaning' is in quotation marks.)

But the initial presumption for people in everyday life and for the social scientist must be that people's expressions of judgement and feeling and their actions *belong* to them. It is a presumption conveyed in such ordinary sayings as 'being in possession of one's faculties'. It is the assumption of Kantian ethics. It is enshrined in legal doctrines of personal responsibility.

It is even possible for the analyst to reveal to people what they do not know they possess: the axioms hiding behind their ideas, the real feelings signalled in their gestures, the motives behind their actions. That means both a recovery and an expansion of self and personality. In that sense the personality becomes stronger as it takes more and more responsibility for itself.

In Weber's sociology and essays on social science there is an effortless shift back and forth between questions of meaning as far as understading other people's actions and words are concerned and meaning as it is experienced in life. These issues he explored most in his sociology of religion. Basically we can suggest that he felt there was a deep similarity between the organisation of needs, motives and actions, on the one hand, and between the organisation of thought, meaning and expression, on the other. The loss experienced in acting in a way which no longer fulfils deeper needs has as its equivalent the use of words which cannot convey the individual's true thoughts. Since both actions and expressions gain their potency in the context of social relations Johannes Weiss is right to suggest that a theory of communication between people is implicit in Weber (1975).

4   Whose meaning?

In his essay on Knies, Weber lays the foundations for a commonsense theory of understanding in social science. He does this by defining his own position in contradistinction to that of Simmel (1905), Munsterberg (1900) and Gottl (1901). As against Simmel he held that everyday judgements of meaning were as 'objective' as those of theoretical sciences; as against Munsterberg he held that the understanding of 'subjective' experience could be entirely scientific; as against Gottl he asserted that the relation between concepts and the cognitions which they shaped, was the same in the natural and the social sciences (WL: 67–105).

The burden of his concern was to establish that it was possible to base an empirical social science on the same kind of data as the historian might treat, namely commonsense reports of what people do and say. Sociology differed from history only in its concern to generalise rather than to offer explanations of unique series of events. It was this direction of intellectual interest which led him to define his position in contradistinction to the others.

At the same time he drew from them. The terminology of *aktuelles Verstehen* was derived from Munsterberg but with different consequences. *Aktualität*, the immediate world of the here and now, was available to the agent, to those around, and even more importantly, for a science, to third parties. Later Munsterberg was to take full cognisance of Weber's position as one of the founders of social survey and attitude opinion research in the United States, holding a chair at Harvard.

Weber was modest about this side of his work, even though according to Marianne Weber the essay on Knies cost him dear in time and worry. She traces a direct line between it and the early categories essay and the final version of the basic concepts. He prefaced his last account with a disclaimer of any originality. She, however, talked of 'his own doctrine' (1975: 312) and there is little doubt that she is right in this estimation because, although Weber felt that he was simply drawing into the open the practice of working social scientists, there is no doubt that the existing theories of *Verstehen* were inadequate to this task or even distorted it.

The importance of Weber's approach was that he directed attention away from epistemology, considered as a psychology, from the processes involved in knowing and understanding, and towards the logical conditions and practical necessities for saying that we understand. In this respect the important thing about a historical or social fact was that agents, those around them, and third parties might agree on it.

However, even 'facts' were, said Weber 'to speak with Goethe', imbued with 'theory' (WL: 275). Already they involved a degree of conceptual construction. That for him was a decisive point in favour of a German critique (J. v. Kries) of John Stuart Mill's theory of causation. After the essays on Knies, Weber examined the issue of social and historical causation in a detailed critique of the views of the historian Eduard Meyer. There, in anticipation of much of Karl Popper's work, Weber argued that all attempts to identify causes relied upon abstraction and hypotheses, a conceptual isolation of elements of reality and that these were part of the apparatus with which any understanding of ordinary life was achieved. Explaining a simple concrete fact drew upon a whole fund of 'nomological knowledge' (WL: 275–7). Simple regularities were not just discovered in the data, they appeared against a background of the rules of experience.

Weber's emphasis on understanding through motivational explanation was not then, as for so many of his contemporaries, a way of separating the social sciences from natural sciences. On the contrary, he was careful to rehearse a theory of causation which was homologous for the two spheres. To do so he had to posit a field of 'facts', albeit already constructed in the sense that they represented a common store of meaning for all parties. The world of everyday life, of common sense, took for granted that there could be 'objective' facts, although as we shall see later, Weber had a strong sense for the arbitrariness of these constructions and, moreoever, the extent to which they could be imposed.

We can infer that there is already a strong common or social element in Weber's idea of *aktuelles Verstehen*. He makes explicit reference to this in stipulating what a meaningful course of behaviour amounts to. 'Adequacy' (no more was required) at the level of meaning was achieved by behaviour which corresponded to the 'average habits of thought and feeling as judged by us to be typical (we can customarily say "correct")' (WG: 5). It was this which had to enter into causal explanation before one could begin to speak of 'sociological rules'. Statistical regularities remained only as conditions or stimuli or hindrances for action.

This aspect of Weber's theory of understanding has consistently been ignored by commentators since von Schelting and Parsons, who criticised Weber for not being able to conceptualise anything between the ideal complexes of meaning in his ideal types and the psychic reality of the individual. Both acknowledge that in practice Weber showed ample understanding of the reality of complexes of meaning at a broader cultural level.

In this way two Webers have been constructed: the Weber of method and the Weber of empirical sociology. This has in itself justified the subsequent fragmented appreciation of Weber's work and consequently the lack of understanding of both sides. For each depends on the other. If this book succeeds in demonstrating the intimate connection between his method and his empirical research it will have done sufficient to prompt a complete recasting of the dominant interpretation of Weber in modern sociology.

He made his intentions clear enough on the first page of his basic concepts. Meaning was used in his text in two broad senses. The second was an ideal-type construction. The first was factual and was divided into two broad types: (i)   the historically specific case of a single actor, (ii)   on average and approximately in the case of a given plurality of actors. All related to subjectively intended meaning, but we will recall the qualification Weber made about 'intended'.

More importantly he said that these concerns for meaning distinguished empirical sciences from dogmatic ones which were concerned with 'true' objective meaning and he gave the examples of logic, ethics, jurisprudence and aesthetics. These were contrasted with sociology and history. Since in his view history was concerned primarily to explore specific courses of action and events, clearly sociology was particularly concerned with average meanings.

Far from being a marginal concern or on some views excluded from his thinking altogether, 'average or approximated meaning of a plurality of actors, has a doubly strategic position within Weber's sociology. It enables one to impute meaning in individual cases. This is an interest shared with the historian but normally used differently. It is the basis, for instance, of being able to ask sensible questions of individuals in a social survey, something with which Weber was thoroughly familiar from involvement in major surveys of industrial workers. But, additionally, it was an unconditionally vital element in any 'sociological' generalisation and generalisation was half at least of the purpose of sociology.

What Weber was not prepared to do was to jump to asserting the wholly social nature of meaning and action. The reasons for this we will explore in a later chapter. For the moment we may simply observe that for him such a jump appeared so often to involve the false imputation of a necessary unity and harmony underlying human affairs and this he regarded as pious wishful thinking.

'Common' understanding often involved conflict, force and fraud. It was not that culture was not a human product. For an empirical science that was axiomatic. Moreover, it was a product which arose out of the social relations of human beings. To assert more, however, would be to endanger the irreducibly personal contribution that at least potentially every individual human being could make to the everlasting flow of events.

But of course, above all, certainly transcending and providing the presupposition for the sociologist's imputation and/or discovery of average meanings, they were the stuff of everyday life. The capacities and contributions of the sociologist were only those of the ordinary person write large. As we have seen, the social relationship depends on the orientation to a meaning, broad structures of relationships are orientated towards a belief in their validity – an order 'when action is orientated to definable "maxims (on average and approximately)"' 'WG: 16). We shall look at aspects of Weber's analysis of these in subsequent sections of this chapter.

For the moment we need to stress that meaning arose for Weber in multiple settings and could be looked at differently depending on its relationship to people. We can distinguish at the least:

1. the actor's intended meaning
2. meaning to the other person
3. meaning on average
4. meaning in terms of a dogmatic system
5. meaning in ideal-typical terms
6. meaning as discovered by social scientist/historian
7. meaning to self
8. institutionalised meaning.

We have briefly considered (1), (2) and (3). Meaning in (4) was important for Weber in two respects. In the first place, dogmatic systems exercised considerable influence through the work of intellectuals and their 'employers'. Secondly, by their clarity they could provide the basis for (5) meaning in ideal-typical terms. This would be a case for knife-edge distinctions, but it was one to which Weber often alluded. A Christian ethical doctrine developed in utmost clarity by a theologian could be employed as a yardstick by the social scientist in ascertaining the degree of compliance with it and its effect on the behaviour of religious believers without the social scientist having to share the beliefs of either. Weber was well aware of the potential moral ambiguities involved in this position and it has given rise to fervent debate.

Ideal types, of course, could be developed by social scientists for the purposes of clarity and to assist in their empirical explorations. Weber certainly regarded the work of economists as being of this order. He was also aware that such types would be used by policy-makers precisely because of their rationality. He gave, however, little or no attention to the possibility that his own ideal types might be used not so much by policy-makers but by others seeking inspiration and the general question of social science type concepts and their effect on everyday responses to the world was not an issue which occupied his thought. It has, to be fair, only become salient in a time of widespread sociological education.

He did, however envisage that social scientists might reveal meaning which was not apparent to actors (6), although unconscious meaning was for him still 'intended subjective meaning' and he was quite explicit on this point. It was in accord with his Kantian view of personality. Once such motives are discovered they are appropriated by the person and are potentially under control. To this extent Weber shared the assumptions which were later to ground the emancipatory doctrines of the Frankfurt school.

Here again he was fully alert to the moral issue which arose from such knowledge and he strenuously fought those who argued that the discovery of repression provided a moral justification for desublimation. He was also alert to the contribution historical materialists had made, even though he rejected their one-sidedness. By and large it did not seem to occur to him that his own work might enhance or change the understanding of social life. That was partly modesty, partly the pessimistic conviction, that the knowledge he conveyed tended to show just how overwhelming the forces of social life were in relation to any individual effort to change them, and how collective effort time and again had the opposite effect to that which was intended.

However, meaning to self (7) was a facet which occupied Weber, particularly in his sociology of religion. For along with the meaning of an expression or deed, which was conveyed to another person as it was expressed, there was also its meaning to the actor. While Weber is not explicit about this in his methodology, and it is not distinguished from 'subjective intended meaning', he does talk of the deliberate attempt to express anger as well as the spontaneous outburst, and very broadly action which does not correspond to the actor's basic needs, he considered would appear meaningless to the individual. Salvation religions particularly arose to express and substitute for basic deprivations in daily life.

If the meaninglessness of life in traditional societies had in major cases been transcended by salvation religions, such as Hinduism or Christianity, it was nonetheless the case that in modern society the quest for meaning had led through science to truth which offered no meaning in life. As we saw in the first part of this book, Weber was only able to cope with this train of thought by acknowledging the quest for knowledge as a basic drive to be satisfied and therefore establishing the scientist as a personality type.

It was by this route that Weber reached the theme of the iron cage, which has so often been likened to the Marxist theory of alienation. For the meaning of so much of the action of the individual in the modern world makes sense only in terms of (8), structures of a formally rational kind, but of which the individual controls and understands only a minor part. That the structure made sense was only a matter of faith to most individuals and the satisfaction of emotional needs was uncertain. Under these circumstances Weber saw that the potential for charismatic movements was ever-present.

5 Structures of meaning

Weber is in no doubt that human beings live their lives in and through structures of many kinds. His only reservation on that point derives from his commitment to empirical science and to Kantian humanism, namely that those structures only have reality in so far as they operate through the actions of human beings.

With that important clarification, one can say that the whole of Weber's work is concerned to explore the relations of action and structure.

Undoubtedly translation into English has meant a serious loss of focus when it comes to the vocabulary of structure in Weber's writing. It contains a rich imagery which is difficult to render in English. Three terms are used. Most frequent is *Zusammenhang*, which has no good literal translation. Parsons used 'complex', 'context' or 'system' (E&S I: 58). It appears most frequently as *Sinnzusammenhang*, a set of meanings which belong together, or a structure of meaning. It could occur also as a causal *Zusammenhang*. In general, the sense is of a structure revealed, one which analysis makes clear.

More overt is the *Gebilde*, which is the generic term Weber uses for such phenomena as church, state, federation, limited company, which are collective terms for a multiplicity of human actions organised in a certain way. This is also normally translated 'structure' and here the emphasis is very much on the reality which is imputed to it by the participants.

Finally, there is *Struktur*, used more sparingly and normally to refer to definite hierarchical arrangements, as in a bureaucracy or in feudalism. But there are additionally an enormous number of occasions when Weber uses variants on these terms or other terms altogether. For instance, he sometimes talks of systems, as on the occasion when he equated his *Gebilde* with Dilthey's 'purpose systems' (WL: 33), or when he talks of the spirit of capitalism as a 'complex' of *Zusammenhänge* (RS I: 30). He speaks of conceptual or theoretical *Gebilde* and counts his ideal types to be such constructions. He talks of 'linkages' (*Verkettungen*) of motives (WL: 413). He speaks of logical structure (ibid.: 197) or a complex of motives (with reference to personality) (ibid.: 47). This vocabulary is employed in the discussion of a variety of types of social structure.

1. Actions are understood by reference to motives. For Weber motives *are* 'structures of meaning' (*Sinnzusammenhänge*). By that he means they are not physical events, although they may be accompanied by them. They are meaningful grounds for behaviour. They might include (and these are all Weberian examples) undertaking a scientific demonstration, fighting an

enemy, earning a wage, jealousy, hurt pride, striving for profit, fear of physical compulsion, duty, desire for salvation, resentment, sexual frustration.

These are not elementary psychological data. Their links with experimental psychology in particular are open, although the connection with interpretative versions, such as those of Freud and Jaspers, may be closer. These are already complex, socially interpreted entities which make sense within a larger framework of motives.

Of course, for Weber rational action orientated to clear purposes was most easily understood and could take pride of place within a chain of motivation. But all such motives could figure within causal chains. The imputation of such motives to people was always, in the first instance, a hypothesis which could be tested by reference to the relevant facts, essentially the presence or absence of plausibly associated motives and circumstances. Getting the right explanation of a person's behaviour meant seeing it in the wider context. In brief, understanding here means putting a complex of meaning (motive) within a wider motivational context which is already structured by customary expectations.

2. Social relationships may involve any number of people, from the two who constitute a friendship to the millions comprised within a state. In the basic concepts Weber generalises the notion of *Gebilde*, or rather sees it as a special case of the relationship, where parties orientate to a meaning imputed to their potential or hypothetical interaction. Here Weber is concerned to draw attention to the range of possibilities where meanings may not coincide and where motives for participating may diverge. Each of the parties to a friendship, for instance, may interpret 'friendship' differently, but equally they may also have differing attitudes towards what they interpret friendship to be. These levels of meaning will be in continual flux even in a structure which has an enduring character.

3. The idea of an 'order' (*Ordnung*), a set of obligations which are held by the participants to govern their relationships, is a major source for the organisation of large-scale structures (*Gebilde*). This set of obligations can be expressed in a number of maxims which guide individual contact. Those ideas can themselves be organised in degrees of sophistication, so that meanings can be imputed to the actions of individuals as referring to, or

being on behalf of, others. The idea of representation, for instance, allows one and the same act to carry two meanings, for the interests of both actor and group. The idea of legitimacy establishes the rights in this field of imputed meaning.

4.   Regularities in action, repetitions, continuities, similarities, uniformities, are all important for Weber in terms of establishing meanings, to which individuals can orientate. He seeks to make precise distinctions between usages, customs, fashion, convention and law, the degree and type of normative regulation being the decisive factor in making such distinctions. Of great importance in the modern world, however, is the development of uniformities of a market kind, where for instance people set prices in relation to their calculation of other people's behaviour without reference to obligations to others. The observation and analysis of this kind of self-interest is, says Weber, the foundation of the modern science of economics.

5.   Structure in the sense of a set of positions defined in relation to each other, hierarchies, networks or groups appears in his concept of closure where group boundaries are maintained against outsiders and where procedures are developed to maintain distinctions of honour and prestige within a group. It plays an important part in Weber's sociology without occupying the prominence in his basic concepts enjoyed by the idea of order, but the reason for this is not because Weber was inclined to minimise the importance of this sector of sociological enquiry.

He allocated special and intensive separate treatment to the distribution of power, on the one hand, in the analysis of domination, authority and legitimation in which his analysis of bureaucracy is embedded and, on the other hand, in his highly influential analysis of class, status groups and political parties. These are explicitly separate and highlighted sections of *Economy and Society*. It is here, however, where one is most sharply confronted by the issue of the boundaries of meaning, by questions of force and control of material factors which require special consideration in the next section of this chapter.

6.   These structural ideas are not haphazardly related in Weber's mind. He makes frequent reference to the different *levels* on which these structures operate and repeatedly draws attention to the importance of construing the relationship between those levels correctly.

One of his first attempts to conceptualise this problem of levels was in *The Protestant Ethic and the Spirit of Capitalism*. The capitalistic organisation of an enterprise had to be distinguished from the spirit in which it was conducted. That spirit was a set of motives which, however, had to be distinguished from their theological bases in Protestant ethics. Those relationships are not worked out in any formal sense there, but it was problem to which Weber returned repeatedly.

So we have to distinguish the basic need or drive, say, the sexual drive, from the motive, say sense of pride, which may be expressed in a social relationship, say marriage, which in turn will be regulated by a legal order, a set of rules enforced by the state and its agents. It is the interplay of these levels which makes sociological analysis so complex and makes human action so open to misinterpretation.

In two areas particularly Weber pays very explicit attention to the problem of levels of meaning. He several times stresses that motives and psychological bases for action are different, which does not mean that the relation between the two is not vital and fascinating as indeed Weber acknowledged, especially in relation to sexuality. Secondly, he developed the most elaborate theoretical scheme of all in respect of domination and legitimacy so that a clear-cut difference could be seen between the motives for adhering to a legitimate order and the reasons for attributing legitimacy to the order.

It was not just in the sequences of action that Weber was pointing to meaningful connection. He was equally stressing the simultaneity of operation of multiple complexes of meaning. He illustrates this in the categories essay in this way:

> The individual can participate in a variety of types of social action in one and the same act. An act of exchange, which someone completes with X who is the representative of Y, which is perhaps the 'organ' of society, contains 1. a language; 2. a written association; 3. an exchange association with X personally; 4. similarly one with Y personally; 5. similarly one with the social activities of the members of the society; 6. as an act of exchange is orientated to the expectations of potential action on the part of others aware of the exchange (competitors on both sides) as conditions of the act and to the corresponding assumptions of legality (WL: 438).

This sixth idea of structure is then a higher order one than the other five, holding them together and at the same time identifying discontinuities and tension.

Under the circumstances, if Weber's analysis of meaning is construed in this way, it can only seem extraordinary that he should have ever been accused of neglecting structure. Perhaps a lot of the time it is just attributable to failure to read a difficult and fragmented text. But not always. Weber's analysis in the categories essay concludes with the case of the modern individual who is the bearer of meanings which are dictated by the large organisations and structures of knowledge which the rationalisation process has engendered. Eduard Baumgarten asks at this point, 'who is the subject of these phenomena?', when Weber's methodology insists on a reduction of all interactions to individual orientations (1964: 604).

Weber's concept of the structure of human understanding, and thus of action, rests on a number of limiting assumptions which prevent him from promoting it as the dominant methodological idea. Ultimately understanding for him always takes place within a non-meaningful context. Complete structures are unreal or exist only in the human mind: in social reality they are necessarily incomplete at the level of meaning. His commitment to empirical science dictated these limits and we turn to them in the following section.

6   Facticity and the limits of understanding

It was in the context of his discussion of the scientific functions of ideal types that Weber repeatedly warned against imputing an excessive degree of structure to social reality. Ideal types, in contrast with reality, were coherently constructed, with their parts logically or explicitly related to each other and therefore presenting a wholly understandable structure to the analyst. The ideal type of rational action particularly provided a shaft of light in the surroundings of dark and hidden motives.

He illustrated this point in his 'Objectivity' essay by reference to mediaeval Christianity. It can, he said, only be reconstructed in ideal-typical form if we are going to give it any conceptual sharpness. For it existed as ideas in the heads of a countless and changing mass of people. A complete representation of that would be a chaos of highly differentiated and contradictory structures of thoughts and feelings. If we use 'Christianity' as a stable concept in this chaos 'it is a combination of articles of faith, norms from church law and custom, maxims of conduct, and countless concrete interrelationships which we have fused into an "idea" (Meth: 96). The difficulty of doing this means that new ideal types are constantly being constructed thereby to highlight different aspects of the historical reality. Sometimes we can find relatively clear-cut ideas in historical reality, as for instance with Calvin's doctrine of predestination, but even there we have to remember that it is primarily the psychological force rather than its logic which will have been most important in the minds of the historical actors.

Long before functionalist theory was faced with the problem of functional autonomy in the sociology of the 1950s or Marxists faced the issue of relative autonomy in the 1970s, Weber had built into his method the principles which would guarantee that what might now be called the degree of structuration was itself a matter for empirical specification. Since Weber's structures are structures of meaning, this implies that it is where limits are placed on meaning that structures are fragmented and problematical. The limits are often tightly drawn.

The reason for these tight limits is that Weber's theory of understanding is itself phenomenological rather than epistemological. That is to say that he was much more concerned to establish when and why people say they understand than to develop a theory of how they understand. In this respect again he stays with the empirical world. The fact is that people say they understand words, deeds, calculations, and it can be demonstrated in everyday social interaction that other people accept that they understand. Actual, immediate understanding carries with it an acceptability, an intuitive necessity which Weber calls *Evidenz*, which in English is best rendered as 'self-evidence'. It does not call for further explanation in the minds of actors, although a scientist can never take it for granted. That need for explanation, which for Weber often becomes a dominating personality characteristic in the intellectual, is only aroused in daily life when the taken-for-granted regularities of life break down.

The brief remarks Weber makes about language reinforce this approach to understanding as a matter of adequacy for practical purposes. A language community, he says, exists within a circle of people where on average an utterance can be made with a fair assumption that it will have a meaningful effect and thus be 'understandable' (WL: 432). In the basic concepts, he talks of language developed through tradition, facilitating every kind of a social relationship, but not in itself creating community (WG I: 23).

In Weber's depiction of everyday life much of what goes on is like the speaking of a language, unthinking, unreflective and a mere acceptance of ways of doing things because no reason for an alternative presents itself. There are regularities in everyday life, but they do not stem from the conscious application of rules, such as Stammler tried to infer and posit as the basis of society. Customs exist, everyone expects that they will be observed, but conformity is not demanded (ibid. 15). As we shall see in the next chapter, regularities of behaviour arising from, although not dictated by, material and biological conditions were for Weber prior in both logic and history to normatively regulated action.

This acceptance of a standard way of doing things applies also to modes of action which originate frequently in the imposition of rules by a person or persons on other people. Sanctions may well have been imposed originally but in the end people accept a way of doing things without realising its origin in force or in argument. Here Weber likens the early learning of the child to the position of a person subject to despotic power. 'The multiplication table is imposed on us as children in just the same way as a rational decree of the despot "*Einverständnis*" and "*Verständnis*" are not identical' (WL: 447). Understanding of the meaning of instruction is not the same as the ability to carry it out. In the end, he says, '"*Einverständnis*" is simple adaptation to the customary, simply because it is customary' (ibid). Rules will be followed because no reason has been found not to follow them. A person does something in the expectation that others will behave in a certain way and that expectation has a good chance of being satisfied because the others take it as a valid expectation.

This is Weber's definition of *Einverständnis*, normally translated 'consensus', but better rendered as 'common understanding' because it involves no prior agreement, nor indeed any prior contact between the persons involved (ibid.: 432). Both languages and markets operate on this basis, not by any prior establishment of rules, even if rules can be inferred from the way people speak and act. But so equally do systems of authority, and the most elaborate systems of legal rules, constitutions and state apparatuses, depend ultimately on the everyday assumptions of legality. Out of this springs Weber's analysis of legitimacy belief, in the end a faith.

In these respects the mass of people in modern rationalised society are in no different position from that enjoyed by people the world over historically. They adapt to ways of doing things without any knowledge of the meaning and purpose which may have lain behind them. Only in two main respects are they different and in each case again faith is involved: the belief that the conditions of everyday life are in principle ascertainable by someone and that in principle calculation provides a basis for behaviour (ibid.: 449).

Weber's treatment of understanding in everyday life is characterised by an emphasis on the limits of meaning which is summed up by the term 'facticity'. *Faktizität* appears on several occasions as does the related *faktisch*, usually translated 'factual'. It appears in phrases like 'Factual regularities of conduct (customs) can, as we have seen, become the source of rules for conduct (conventions, law)' (E&S I: 332). It refers here to the natural attitude which treats human behaviour as a matter-of-fact occurrence. In this respect we can infer a close affinity with that idea of *aktuelles Verstehen* which we examined earlier: the understanding of words and deeds as having an immediate and obvious meaning. We can say that the factual regularity with its average meaning is the basis of immediate understanding. It takes on an obviousness too, a self-evident quality (*Evidenz*). It arises out of experience, it is grasped with the immediacy of intuition or apperception (*Anschauung*).

The facticity of meaning does not destroy meaning. People still use language to refer to things and to people. Meaning involves reference and expression through mutually accepted means and that is intrinsic to human culture. But meanings for everyday life are so standardised, so much based in experience and unquestioningly accepted that they are treatable, in the first instance, as empirical facts by the social scientist because they are facts for ordinary people.

If facticity fixes meaning, it is also the case that it is also the only way in which meaning can become real. At the beginning of his sociology of law Weber asks what is the meaning of a legal order in an empirical sense. 'It refers not to a set of norms of logically demonstrable correctness, but rather to a complex of actual (*faktische*) determinants of human conduct' (E&S I: 312).

In the case of law, the existence of a coercive apparatus guarantees that the maxims of the legal order become the basis for everyday conduct, even if resort to coercion is rare. From this point of view few people need to have any rational understanding of legal norms, nor do they have to have a value commitment to them. The motives for obeying the law can be many and various. For most of the time, then, observing the law is a matter of '*Einverständnishandeln*'. 'The broad mass of the participants act in a way corresponding to legal norms, not out of obedience regarded as a legal obligation, but either because the environment approves of the conduct and disapproves of the opposite, or merely as a result of unreflective habituation to a regularity of life that has engraved itself as a custom' (ibid. I: 312).

Meanings are fixed in conduct and it is conduct which ensures that they are so fixed. They also may be fixed in natural objects by human intervention. Artefacts are only interpretable in terms of their relation to human purpose. But the scope of facticity is still wider. For meaning arises out of irrational roots in the human being. The quest for understanding motivation pushed to its limits always comes up against understandable but basic facts in the form of drives:

> The ultimate 'goal directions' which can be grasped as self-evident (*Evidenz*) and in this sense are 'understandable' (empathically relivable) and which are the limits of an interpre-tative psychology (say, the sexual drive) are, however, still only given, which have to be simply accepted as such like any other constellation of facticities, including one quite devoid of meaning (WL: 409).

This passage and others like it identify the interface between the meaningful and non-meaningful, between culture and nature in Weber's sociology. It is the sector of drives and needs based in the human body, which forms part of the experience of every individual and is therefore reasonably imputed by everyone to others. At the same time it is prior to consciousness, and however much the individual seeks to satisfy and control drives and needs, they offer independence and resistance to the will. This is the sector of 'irrational understanding'. Our curiosity may be satisfied by an answer like 'sex', 'hunger', 'curiosity', to the question, 'Why did they do that?', but it places a limit on interpretative understanding which can only be supplemented by experimental psychology, physiology or some other natural scientific approach if further explanation is required.

Weber saw equally a limit to understanding in another direction, namely where the ultimate values which a person pursued were outside the experience of the observer. The salvation doctrines of religions were in particular a sector where it was difficult for the non-believer to share the sense of obviousness which the beliefs had for the believer (WG I: 2). At the same time Weber felt that, provided the axioms of the belief system were taken as given, then the directions which developments of doctrine and corresponding conduct took could be rationally understood. Here he was certainly seeking to rationalise his own work on the predestination belief.

7 Power and compromise

One of the axioms of his own sociology was that if the analyst examined any sector of action, then it would be possible to arrive at underlying principles which were irreducible, but at the same time irreconcilable in any rational way with any other sector. The principle of power which guided politics was bound to come into conflict with the rational maximisation of the utility principle which underpinned economics. Love was bound to conflict with eroticism. Beauty, truth and goodness likewise were in permanent tension.

These tensions were necessarily resolved in everyday life, but not in any rational manner, rather as the outcome of conflict and compromise, temporary matter-of-fact accommodations, unstable especially in face of the drive to rationalise any one of the sectors at the expense of others. In this sense the very structure of the life-world (to borrow Schutz's term) is a facticity, the outcome of a process of conflict and compromise in which people struggle, but over which as individuals they have no control, no more than an investor can control a market, or a player can control a game.

Here we have the answer to the question Baumgarten posed (see p. 218). *There is no subject* for the phenomena which arise out of the interactions of a myriad of individuals. No person, nor even organised group, can determine a market or even the modern state. Those are structures which regulate the outcomes of struggle and all the parties to them. All individuals who orientate to them contribute to their continuity and change, even if it is an unthinking acquiescence to the *status quo*.

Weber was not concerned to offer a political message in his sociology. His intention was to remain as far distant from that purpose as possible, for only in that way could his scientific integrity be preserved. But there is a transcendental message there. It is that everyone, as an individual, bears some modicum of responsibility, however small, for the maintenance and change of the structures in which they participate.

Not that Weber had any illusions about the scope for individual action in changing structures or its likely success. His emphasis on facticity in relation to meaning is also an emphasis on power. Structures of meaning not only can be imposed, they regularly are. The domination which is exercised through the school imposes orthodox ways of speaking and writing (WG I: 123). The masses in modern society are disciplined into obedience which offers neither resistance nor criticism. Weber's sociology of domination is equally a sociology of knowledge in which leaders generate meaning, disciples disseminate it, intellectuals interpret it, officials administer and enforce it, and the mass of believers conform (WL: 448).

The scientist might well be able to explore meaning in social relationships with much greater effect than was possible for the average person. But nonetheless the boundaries of meaning were only pushed back, never removed altogether. The choices between conflicting values remained, were even sharpened in their significance. Irrational commitments, acts of faith, were equally required of scientist and labourer. Rationality offered no solutions to the questions of how one should lead one's life.

For Weber human society is based on understanding, but perfect understanding does not produce the perfect society. Indeed, there is no ideal of perfect understanding underpinning his appreciation of the necessity for shared meaning as a facticity, the relationship will either disintegrate or become a self-destructive attrition of power. Under those circumstances both or all of the parties may find the appeal of the charismatic leader irresistible. He or she offers new meaning and therefore the renewal of social relationships.

analysis. In his terms the understanding which people share of events in the world and of each other is always a matter of assumptions for practical purposes and never grounded in an ideal. Understanding is based on the daily experience of those assumptions tested against facts. And where understanding might be uncertain there we may have to construct the facts.

Weber's analysis of understanding leads not to a concept of perfect communication, but to the recognition of power as the ultimate determinant of meaning. For if that assumption on which *Einverständnis* is based, namely that other people will take your expectations of them as a meaningful basis for their own behaviour, breaks down, Weber offers no rational solution. We can infer either the cessation of the discordant activities (agreement to differ) or the imposition of meaning by one or other of the two sides or by a third party.

The need to treat meanings as objective facts, the requirement of facticity, means that the possessor of power in a social relationship holds the vital resource for creating the conditions for communication, namely being able to define what is or is not a fact, in practice and in the daily experience of the parties.

Weber was even less interested in equality as an ideal than he was in happiness. But for those who are interested in establishing societies of equals his analysis has much more of substance to offer than regularly comes from those who are committed to the ideal. If we take his account of understanding as the starting point we can see that power inequality is more likely to result in established meaning. Equalities of power are likely to generate mutually destructive conflicts over meaning unless the parties disengage from the attempt to relate to each other, or unless they can each identify it as being in their own separate interests to create a factitious understanding. Here rational analysis can bring advantages to both parties.

Weber saw that under the conditions of mass democracy there was an ever present possibility for the emergence of the charismatic leader able to focus the frustrations of the masses in the structure which they felt were alien to them. Weber's own account stresses the basis for this in mass feeling. In fact his own theory of understanding takes us in a similar direction.

Where for one reason or another the parties to an equal relationship (in terms of power) are unable to reach a rational

12

The Empirical Study of Values

Preamble

Even a cursory reading of Weber will show that 'the problem of values' is not an irritating issue in methodology. Values are there from the beginning. It is not a question of science being able to proceed provided values are not allowed to intrude. Values define human purposes, including science, they pervade human existence, and something called objectivity can be established only with great difficulty within the vast frame of meaning of which values constitute such a major part and which is normally called culture.

For this reason we shall treat Weber's discussion of values both as a whole and as an integral part of his general social theory. Values have quite as central a part in his scheme of thought as they have in Parsons', and they have a far more elaborated conceptualisation in Weber's account.

In many respects Parsons foreshortened our view of values as a topic for social science and set up a barrier to the full appreciation of its scope. We can recover that by returning to Weber. And since values have returned as a key element within contemporary political strategy and ideological dispute, the chances are that his contribution may at last be fully acknowledged. He too was writing in a period when similarly 'values' were invoked and declaimed from all sides.

1 The spirit of the age

In the Germany of Kaiser Wilhelm before 1914, 'values' (*Werte*) was not simply a term drawn from a technical social science nor even was it the catchword of political debate. It was a key word for the whole period. It was the trademark for the dominant philosophical movement of the time, neo-Kantianism, and at the same time the target for attempts to subvert the established order spearheaded above all by Nietzsche.

It was then part of the new language of a new age. Just as in the late twentieth century 'image', 'computer', 'communication' have become keywords which signal the specificities of the age and take on new weight and meaning, so in the late nineteenth century for the first time 'values' became a similar pivotal term.

Value as the standard of exchange, the underlying measure of worth reflected by money prices, for instance, was of course a much longer standing idea in Western thought. But in the middle of the nineteenth century in Germany, emphasis moved from the common standard of exchange to the qualities of the desired object, to the abstract standards by which objects or states of affairs in the world were judged good or bad. Instead of value, focus shifted to 'values' in the plural. Instead of the common standard of exchange the irreducible and irreplaceable was emphasised.

The intellectual preparation for this was laid, of course, by Kant. The rift between nature and morality, and the insistence that the moral world was one where principles of higher abstraction ruled, are presuppositions for being able to talk about values. But Kant himself did not reach the point of identifying the diversity of values as a feature of human life, and therefore speculating about 'values' in general rather than 'value'.

The neo-Kantians themselves traced their inspiration back, after Kant, to an almost exact contemporary of Marx, Hermann Lotze (1817–81), Professor of Philosophy at Göttingen, who saw the principles of the cosmos built upon interaction, and in the interaction of human beings and nature the creation of a realm of values which take their place in human consciousness but have their own logic and reality.

But, of course, the widest dissemination and popularisation of the discussion of values came as the result of Nietzsche's self-appointed task of subverting the values of Kantian-Christian civilisation. His attack on all that the respectable German bourgeois Protestant held dear for the first time undermined the confidence of a group whose ethos had been based on the premise that the world was constructed around timeless principles and made it vulnerable both to the excesses of a youthful generation and to the claims of alternative cultures.

The value crisis of the late Victorian period was not then simply the product of the encroachments scientific discoveries were making into territory long held to be the preserve of theology. That, of course, was important, but not in isolation. Nor was it the recognition of the threat of a new class, the industrial proletariat, although the 'social question' as it was called was the first preoccupation of the political leadership.

There was turbulence at a deeper level of consciousness. It was a profound unease about the purpose of human existence, about the truth or validity of the standards for everyday life. It was brought about by shifts of an unprecedented kind in the boundaries of culture and by a social experience which was unsettled and contradictory.

Indeed, if one attempts to understand the impulse to discuss values, it becomes clear that they can only become salient as a general issue when their taken-for-granted status has been threatened. The denunciation of sexual misdemeanours, for instance, only makes sense in a context where a value of, say, chastity or fidelity or self-control is held, not only by the preacher, but by a sufficient number of listeners. In that context the discussion will not be about 'values' as such but about 'fidelity', etc. Values in general become a topic of concern at the point where no presumption could be made about particular values being held.

From this point of view the neo-Kantians were not only involved in establishing the presuppositions for any valuing and in identifying the possible range of human values. They were also seeking to provide some kind of common point of orientation for people in a world which was increasingly threatening and unintelligible.

That was clearly the point of view of Wilhelm Windelband (1848–1915) who, as Professor at Heidelberg, was one of the most influential representatives of the new School of Values. His widely read *History of Philosophy* concluded in this way:

In place of the 'autonomy of reason' we have the arbitrary will of the superman – that was the road from Kant to Nietzsche which the nineteenth century trod. It is exactly that which defines the task for the future. Relativism is the renunciation of philosophy and its death. Philosophy can thus only survive as the doctrine of universally valued values. It can no longer intrude in the work of the special sciences to which now psychology too belongs. . . . It has its own field and tasks with those universally valid values which constitute the masterplan for every cultural function and the backbone for any particular life of values. But it will only describe and explain these in order to do justice to their validity. It treats them not as facts, not as norms. Its task therefore is to develop as 'legislation', and not the law of an arbitrary will, which it dictates, but as the law of reason, which it brings to light and comprehends (Windelband, 1907: 564).

But reason cannot compel adherence. It was Weber's programme precisely to treat values as facts, or rather to examine people's orientations to values in their lives. To do that, he had to address the question of the nature of values.

2　The nature of values

Weber's concern was to understand the real world. In that sense he was not a philosopher. Weber would have agreed with Rickert on that point. But equally he was more profoundly convinced than any of the other founding fathers of modern sociology (apart from Simmel) that the kind of highly refined conceptual discussion associated with philosophy was indispensable for the pursuit of any genuine science of the social.

The grounds for this approach were ultimately simple even if also profound in their significance. Ideas engaged with, helped to shape, in a sense became part of reality. They did that, however, only in and through human beings. In themselves they were not real. The scope for sophisticated interpretation of this conundrum was limitless. It called for prolonged and serious scholarly argument.

His interest was ontological. He sought to define the contours of reality, but that took him towards empirical science and away from an outline of abstract concepts, and certainly away from any fixed formula about the relation of the material to the ideal. His denial of that intention must be understood not as a ritual disavowal of Marxism, but rather as a statement of a quite distinct intellectual purpose from that associated with either materialist or idealist interpretations of history. He actually took the relation of ideas to the material world to be problematical in every respect and the whole of his work explored that relationship at as many levels as possible. No simple formula was to emerge from that exploration.

That values were of central importance Weber had no doubt. To talk about human culture was to talk about values. But what was their position in relation to culture and to the material world? Could values be located in time? Did values have properties which could be discovered? Were values intuited? Could values be learnt, or developed, or destroyed? Did values affect behaviour? Could they be measured?

Those were all serious questions, answered implicitly or explicitly in the series of papers Weber wrote from 1903 onwards, so misleadingly called 'methodology'. They were papers exploring the scope and relevance of values within the project of empirical social science. Just as much substance as method is contained in them.

The vocabulary Weber employed in his account of values is rich in nuance and fine distinctions. It was possible to engage in value analysis, interpretation, discussion, consideration; values could operate as axioms, decisions, feelings, standards, postulates, viewpoints and theories; values could be organised as hierarchies, orders, systems, spheres and realms; values could conflict, compete, collide; they could be intensified, subjected to critique and placed in relation to anything else; people could be sensitive to them, could judge things by them, evaluate, have faith in them or disbelieve them, be free from them or discover them around and in their lives; values had content, mechanisms, and could change. On the other hand, the validity of values could not be proven empirically and faith in values could never be other than irrational.

The examples Weber gave of values exhibited a similar diversity. As a scientist he gave allegiance to 'truth'. Other values might, however, compete with that, such as 'duty', 'personal loyalty', 'honour', the religious or political cause. The lawyer could show the same kind of commitment to legality or justice (not the same thing and often in conflict with each other). The value of beauty could inhere in artistic creations, the value of love in marriage. The idea of the nation was a powerful value motivating great political conflicts of modern times. Religion could be the guardian of other-worldly values; equally, and more often, it has been the focus for mundane values, such as health, wealth and longevity. Rationality itself could be elevated to the level of the highest value: equally irrationality, especially in the form of eroticism, could be given an equivalent position precisely because it could offer the very opposite.

The main context for the clarification of the concept of values was in Weber's discussion of historical description. Historical reality was infinitely complex and diverse. Reality was always particular. It was the reflecting subject who introduced order into it. In the first place this was done by focusing on or selecting facets of events, people or periods because they aroused concern. Now this could be achieved simply by unguided feeling, by interest or, more explictly, by reference to values.

In these considerations Weber drew explicitly on the formulations of his friend Heinrich Rickert (1863–1936) whose theory of value-relevance (*Wertbeziehung*) was developed to account for the construction of objects of historical concern. Cultural products, be they as large as Christianity or as specific as Goethe's *Faust*, were created by and only understood in relation to values which they embodied. What belonged or did not belong to these historical phenomena was determined by the values of their creators or interpreters. They were indeed value-objects.

This doctrine of value-relevance opened the way to speaking of the objectivity of value judgements. For if the criteria were explicit enough, if the value were specified clearly, then the object in the real world could be judged in respect of its correspondence to those criteria irrespective of whether the person exercising the judgement gave any personal support to that value (WL: 123). But when Rickert linked that idea to the further idea of an objective hierarchy of values, Weber could not follow him. The implication would have been that there was one way to write history: as it was, Weber was convinced of the irreducible multiplicity and conflict of values, precisely because it was through culture that human beings were creative agents, not simply choosing from a fixed range of values.

In the 'Objectivity' essay Weber came to the point of offering some of the most succinct formulations on this theme:

The concept of culture is a value concept. Empirical reality becomes 'culture' to us because and insofar as we relate it to value ideas. It includes those segments and only those segements of reality which have become signficant to us because of this value relevance (Meth: 76).

Order is brought into this chaos (of judgements about events) only on the condition that in every case only a *part* of concrete reality is interesting and *significant* to us, because only it is related to the *cultural values* with which we approach reality (ibid.: 78).

Values, then, were possessed by people, by ordinary people and great personalities alike, by the historical actor and by the historian. When shared, they could provide the common reference point for interpreting events as well as guiding action in the present. They were central, therefore, to our understanding of social reality.

If we want to understand Weber, then we have to come to terms with the centrality of the value concept for him. And we have to appreciate the profound sense of history associated with that concept. For he was writing only two generations away from the very birth of professional history writing and reflection upon what that meant for Western culture.

He was not so far from the time when Hegel announced that it was only the West which had a history and that history consisted in the emergence of the idea of reason. Weber sought to deprive that Hegelian idea of any metaphysical force. There could be no question of a realm of timeless values overflowing into the realm of historical appearances (WL: 62).

But equally for him it was sheer dogmatism to attempt to eliminate ideas, or values more particularly, as elements within the historical process. Everything depended on getting the precise nature of ideas and values right, and then seeking to identify their location within any scheme of historical interpretation and explanation. We shall see that Weber was determined not to exaggerate their importance.

To sum up: as an element in Weber's social theory, and just one element, however vital, we can identify values in the following respects. As ideas they exist in human consciousness, are abstract and general, and hence communicable across time and between individuals. They therefore have a continuity as well as an open and ever reinterpretable character. They provide the criteria for organising and making sense of the events of the world around and find their concrete daily expression in judgements of what is good or bad in that world.

Equipped with this understanding of his concept, we can turn to Weber's use of it in his empirical sociology.

3　Values and the sociological categories

Weber saw sociology as an empirical discipline. It was concerned to give an account of and explain real phenomena, in this case social action. Actions were real, values were not. Hence the empirical study of values could only be construed as the way value ideas became incorporated in the actions of human beings. The only sense in which values could be said to exist was in the myriad and momentary conceptions of value possessed by innumerable human beings.

Yet values were involved in the very definition of action, in providing the idea of meaning in human behaviour and in the direction of scientific analysis of behaviour and action. We shall consider the problems which arose from this co-determination of action and value at a later stage. For the moment it is sufficient to point out that as far as a scientific discipline called sociology was concerned, it meant that there were innumerable possible starting points, no single definitive approach and certainly no one necessary conceptual framework.

The implications of this can fortunately be observed in a very specific way in Weber's work because he made two attempts to provide a conceptual framework for sociology, in the essay of 1913 (WL: 403–50) which provided an analytical background for what was subsequently published as the second part of *Wirtschaft und Gesellschaft*, and in the basic concepts which prefaced the last written, first part of the *magnum opus* (E&S I: 3–62).

The 1913 version is, it must be said, less developed as a categorical framework. It is presented more as continuous prose with an argued theme than the later version which sometimes reads like a lexicon. Moreover, it has a more restricted range of concepts. Most notably, as compared with the later version, it lacks the concept of social relationship; the concept of action largely operates on the dimensions of purposive rationality and emotion, and value-rationality does not appear. Action orientated to other people is called *Gemeinschaftshandeln*, and action orientated to an order is regarded as a variant of this and called *Gesellschafthandeln*. A very prominent place is accorded to the concept which does not appear in the later version, namely *Einverständnis*. As we saw above (pp. 220 ff) it meant the assumption that you and other people were in accord, or working on the same premises. For Weber both markets and linguistic communities depended on such assumptions.

But there is a considerable risk involved in assuming that social relationships operate through *Einverständnis*. The whole process of negotiating a relationship where interests and values differ may be suppressed by participants and observers alike. Conflict may be ignored or regarded as deviant. Intellectual clarity alone requires that suppressed premises are brought into the open. No assumption of shared interests or values need be made, which is not to say that empirically they might not be discovered.

We can go on to assume that it was this intellectual clarity which led Weber away from the concept of *Einverständnis* and towards the concepts of social relationship and value-rationality. Using them it was possible to conceive of the parties to a relationship summing up their understanding of it in terms of maxims of behaviour expected of the other and for the behaviour of each to be purposively or value-rationally oriented to these. Instead of assuming a potential identity of meaning in a relationship Weber was now inclined more to finding irreducible differences of emphasis.

Value-rationality similarly operates in a far more explicit way in respect of social order. Here, instead of relying on the formulation that the binding nature of an order becomes taken-for-granted by the mass of those involved, Weber distinguishes between different types of inner guarantee of legitimacy, distinguishing emotional attachment from beliefs in religious reward and from belief in validity as an expression of ultimate values. He then also proceeds to distinguish different types of legitimacy belief as distinct from motives for obedience.

In discussing motives for observing a legitimate order, he says at one point that the relationships between law and ethics do not pose a problem for an empirical sociology. There was no difficulty in identifying norm conceptions which varied from the self-imposed without external sanction to those where sanctions of a severe kind were imposed as with law. Whether one called self-imposed norms 'ethics' or not depended on the particular conception of ethics prevalent in the group being studied.

Values also entered in for Weber when it came to membership of groups. Groups could well restrict their membership to those who professed a strict faith, while economic activity could itself be orientated to ultimate values as was the case with socialist values. The motivation to work could be strongly enhanced too by value commitment. Certainly Weber's thinking about the assumptions behind socialism was one of the elements which clearly induces him to make orientation to values an explicit part of his conceptual scheme.

Finally, Weber recognised that values might be institutionalised as ultimate justifications for social structures. In particular, he was concerned about the case where they were employed as justifications for law. Attempts to define a 'natural law' foundation for legal enactment fell within this category. In general he felt that such attempts were less reliable as a basis for the continuity of a legal system than the purely technical rational coherence of a system of positive law, but he recognised the historical importance of appeals to natural rights or to 'justice'. It was an empirical question just how effective such claims were in securing the basis of a legal system.

When Weber wrote his 'Objectivity' essay, he concluded quite emphatically that any empirical science of society and culture had to be guided by value ideas in its selection of material (which was Rickert's idea of value relations), and also that such ideas were empirically ascertainable as elements in human action. Only their validity was unprovable in empirical terms (WL: 213). We may then wonder how Weber, at one stage anyway, certainly in the early version of the categories, gave such a restricted place to values.

Almost certainly it was because as that project was first conceived it was precisely the micro-foundations of social order in the behaviour of individual human beings which was the explicit focus. In that setting, values easily became simply conceptions of value, precisely because values as such could not have any other existence in the real world. But in interpreting the development of Western society as a whole, those value conceptions of myriads of individuals had to be summated. That could only be done by treating values as continuants. If we take the rationalisation process as a whole, then it only makes sense by reference to values persisting, changing, developing, over the centuries.

4 Values and the rationalisation process

Weber dared to attempt nothing less than a demystified version of what Marx and Engels had dismissed as the German ideology, an account of history with ideas as the focus. Where Marx and Engels wrote of ideas and thoughts, Weber, in tune with the period, wrote of 'values'. But his emphasis was wholly on the demystification, namely the precise specification of the way values could be included within a causal account of the development of Western society.

The context in which Weber felt most frequently obliged to clarify the place of values in the writing of history was in the discussion of the ideas of progress to which he returned on several occasions from 1903 up until the end of his life. That idea, he noted early on, was a substitute for a religiously-based conviction that history had a God-given meaning, an attempt to find a scientifically-based equivalent (WL: 33). Resorting to the idea of progress carried within it the hope that somehow values would be discovered to have their basis in reality instead of in the aspirations of human beings.

In the essay on value freedom he engaged in a lengthy examination of the relevance of the idea of progress in three respects, in personal emotional development, in the arts, and in the overall process of rationalisation. In brief, he did find it possible, albeit with the greatest circumspection, to speak of the diversification of values and increase in capacity of the individual mind. There was no need to call that 'progress' because it was open to empirical specification and, if one did, there was the danger of neglecting the price paid for this development.

As far as art was concerned, the only 'progress' which could be given unambiguous empirical specification was technical in nature, the solution of problems such as the Gothic vault, for instance, provided. The same was true for music and painting: technical progress could be assessed objectively, whether this meant better art was always dependent on subjective evaluations. And it was this which was generalised in the rationalisation process, which Weber quite clearly states to take a specific form in Europe and the United States and to be a prime focus for sociological and economic analysis.

But Weber knew he was operating here at the margins of clarity. This was for him the boundary of knowledge in his own time. Those who opposed technical progress were not fools. Even where indisputably correct technical advances were made, this by no means justified them in respect of all possible values. The Buddhist, for instance, rejected purposeful conduct altogether – that could not be proved wrong (Meth: 38). Nor could the rationalisation of such a sphere as banking be proved right in any absolute sense. Tracing rationalisation as an overarching process, therefore, had to be problematical.

At this point we have to content ourselves with identifying two points which internal evidence suggests were exercising a persistent and troubling hold on Weber's intellectual imagination. The first was the idea of *Wertsteigerung*, variously translated as value-growth, intensification, or increase, and therefore lost as a technical term. The second is *Eigengesetzlichkeit*, similarly lost in a variety of renderings such as 'autonomy', or 'inner logic', or 'self-determination'.

Steigerung was also involved in the process of developing ideal types, namely bringing hidden premises of action into the open, completing ideas which were only half-formed and producing a coherent conceptual framework. In fact the axiomatic sciences were engaged in this kind of intellectualisation of values, and as ideal types, not reality, they could be employed by empirical social scientists.

In the value freedom essay, *Steigerung* is used on three occasions with different nuances, to refer to the greater 'wealth' of an art which has undergone technical progress and also to subjective rationality, to a greater consciousness of the meaning of one's own actions. Weber was never in any doubt that technical developments, namely advances in the practical implementation of specified ends, could be objectively identified; more ambiguity remains with the inner logic of a value.

It is here that the notion of *Eigengesetzlichkeit* plays a strategic role within his whole account of the rationalisation process. As we examined in our account of rationality, all action for Weber stems from irrational roots in the human being. Rationality always has an irrational base. In talking about action, this did not pose any great problem for Weber. Motives were either rational or irrational, and in the case of rational ones they invariably depended ultimately either on needs (by definition irrational) which were consciously pursued, or on values (which could not be proven).

Action was the focus of Weber's sociology, and so in a sense he could be content with this specification because it stayed within the realm of experience. But, as we have seen, values entered essentially into the sphere of action as points of orientation, as ideas. Then what is their basis in experience? Two answers compete with each other in Weber's account, in a struggle never to be resolved. On the one hand, as with musical melody, values emerge out of the ultimate springs of human action, out of desire, pleasure and need, especially out of sexuality. The history of the arts is a story of the development of these basic needs, reaching ever greater sophistication, without ever necessarily providing greater satisfaction or worth.

On the other hand, values could also be traced back to ultimate axioms, propositions which could not be imagined away and which served as the premises for any logical argument. Here Weber was convinced that the value spheres were inevitably based upon conflicting premises, and that the development of any one value was bound to generate conflict with another. Each value had its own autonomy and the pursuit of this necessarily involved individuals in bitter choices and conflicts within themselves and with others.

Those fields of tension he examined in detail in his *Zwischenbetrachtung*, the essay which in 1915 examined the tensions between the pursuit of salvation and other spheres of value, including politics, economics, aesthetic values, the erotic and the intellectual spheres. The very tensions between those spheres for Weber generated a derived need, the metaphysical need to resolve those conflicts and to find a common meaning to them all and to life.

Here we are close to the premises of Weber's account of rationalisation. It would be wrong, however, to suggest that he had worked out their relationship in any formal way. It would be all too easy at this point to lapse into a formula. The rationalisation process might be seen as the product of a Western psychological type, or of a Western mentality if one were to emphasise Weber's concern for 'basic directions of behaviour'. At the other extreme it would be possible to see Weber as another idealist historian who had discovered the force of Western history in the operation of key irreducible axioms inhabiting an ideal realm. Both would do complete injustice to Weber's intellectual thrust.

He could not produce a formula for Western rationalisation precisely because it emerged out of the *interplay* of these factors. Ideas, values, were themselves latecomers in human development, but at the same time were distinct from an ephemeral material world; basic human needs existed in people from time immemorial but science was only beginning to grasp them. Weber could not fix the relationship between values and needs, if only because he was so sensitive to the nuances of the change in that relationship over time. Committed to empirical science, he knew he was fated to record the passing of things even as he sought to grasp the process as a whole.

While never reduced to a formula, all these ideas about the connections between values and the rationalisation process are on one occasion at least summoned up in a single context in one of the most explosive passages in Weber's work. In no more than one page he alludes to rationalisation from without and revolutionary belief from within, to the growth of (*Steigerung*) adaptive possibilities, of 'ideas' arising in differing spheres, be they religious, artistic, scientific or social, which convinced those inspired with them of their value. Those ideas inspire the originator. They become, however, the framework to which the broad mass of the people normally merely adapts and which is usually meant when we refer to rationalism. But, in the first place, it is the power from within an idea which takes possession of the creator, which overturns the existing order. 'It is', Weber concludes, 'in this purely empirical and value-free sense to be sure the specifically "creative" revolutionary force of history' (WG II: 666).

In this passage, which seeks to define the nature of charisma, we are as close as we can get to the underlying structure of Weber's thinking about values which moves between the poles of inspiration and logic, between a sense of being possessed by the demon, on the one hand, and the routine performance of rules, on the other. It is related to a question Weber asked in his analysis of law: just how does innovation occur when the majority of people are content to work on well-established assumptions? He answered that by suggesting that the most important source was the often abnormal experience of particular individuals which carried with it a compelling obligating force for them and others (ibid.: 1188–9). In this respect he was quite prepared to acknowledge the importance of psychological considerations.

If we turn to Windelband, whose *History of Philosophy* was cited by Weber in his value-freedom essay, we will find in him too a concern for the psychological origins of values in the emotional experience of the individual. Valuation was a 'proper study for psychologists' (Windelband, 1921: 209). But Windelband, like Rickert and later Scheler, argued that the psychological experience was of a reality beyond, it was an experience of a realm of timeless values. It was against this kind of leap into the unknown that Weber set his empirical social science. It accounts for what at second inspection can only seem like outrageous temerity: namely, the assertion that a creative and revolutionary force in history was to be found in the irrational inspirations of individuals and this was in a *'purely empirical and value-free sense'*.

A truly empirical analysis of values could not make them into ideal anchorage points for those adrift in a meaningless chaos of events. Rather than identifying a timeless rank order of values which was the aspiration of the axiology of the neo-Kantians, Weber, in contrast, could only see temporary and shifting rationalisation of values in differing directions in opposition and conflict with each other, a world of God and demons. On several occasions he cited James Mill as his authority for asserting that, 'If one proceeds from pure experience one arrives at polytheism' (Essays: 147). The telling word here is 'experience': for Weber, the basis of empirical science.

For this reason nothing could be further from the spirit of Weber's account of the rationalisation process than to see it as the predictable outcome of the interaction of a set of metaphysical timeless elements. On the contrary, values as logically constructed ideas only result from the agonising labours of intellectuals, priests and others working on inspirations which appear as novelties and

revolutionary surprises to old established orders. A truly historical, and that means empirical, appreciation of the rationalisation
process can only see it as a contingent and unique process,
undirected even if moving overall in a direction.

Gouldner (1955) and others who have emphasised the remarks
which Weber made about the inevitability of rationalisation have
overlooked the fact that it was precisely the problematical basis of
the direction of the process which Weber regarded as the focus of
his work. He was researching into rationalisation, and that for him
precisely precluded any reliance on non-human forces. That in
turn did not mean to say that the roots of human action were not in
themselves mysterious enough on any account, from whatever
base in actual experience or however probed by empirical
research.

5   Values and the scientist

The essay on value freedom was a critical engagement not only
with the dogmatists of various political persuasions – conservative,
nationalist, socialist – who sought to use their science as a medium
for preaching, but also with the neo-Kantians, in whose ranks
Weber has often been numbered but from whom he was deeply
divided on one fundamental point. The citing of James Mill was a
marker for his disagreement with them. For Mill spoke from the
tradition of Anglo-Saxon empiricism, and it was above all as an
empirical scientist that Weber saw his own role in life. A genuine
philosophy of value could not in Weber's view ignore the fact that
values came into irreconcilable conflict with each other in the
world.

Windelband and Rickert sought to overcome the conflicts of the
real world by constructing a completely ordered and harmonious
system of values. For Weber that came into conflict with the
psychological origins of values, but it was also internally inconsistent. In other words, although Weber here was uncharacteristically polite (Rickert was a friend) and did not say so in so many
words, it was also bad philosophy, since every genuinely logical
and consistent analysis would show that there was no rational way
in which conflicts between certain ultimate value positions could
be resolved: questions about the ends justifying the means, or

whether beauty was to be preferred to truth, were unanswerable by scientific means. Neither empirical research nor logic could provide the answer. Only the dogmas of the churches could succeed in doing so, and that by fiat.

Decisions on value questions were made by individuals in their daily lives and they involved making choices and compromises between values not on the basis of science, but on the basis of their own convictions. In this way individuals gave meaning to their own lives. That was not relativism, said Weber. On the contrary it gave individuals the greate responsibility of all, the choice of their own fate (Meth: 18; WL: 470). Nothing could be further then from an advocacy of a value-neutral position. On the contrary, everything Weber says on this point conforms to the passionate devotion to the task, the sense of duty and the desire to listen to the deepest personal strivings, the demon, which we saw in the early chapters amounted to his own world-view.

It is therefore one of the paradoxes about Weber's famous doctrine of value-freedom that it outlines the affiliations and mutual relationships between science and values in multiple and sophisticated ways. The field of objectivity can only be kept free *from* value-judgements by the most intense concern *for* values. A glance at the certainly incomplete set of propositions which follows will be a sufficient indication of this necessity:

1. Science is guided by values, such as integrity, rigour, clarity, truth.
2. Human beings are valuing beings. They live lives through and for values.
3. History only makes sense if it is considered from the standpoint of values.
4. Social scientists choose their lines and objects of inquiry by reference to values.
5. Scientists can show people how to obtain the ends they set for themselves.
6. Scientists can show people the consequences of following certain ends.
7. Philosophers can show people what basic principles are implied by their acting in a certain way and indicate where inconsistencies are involved.

8. Empirical sociologists can show how people's value ideas have guided their behaviour and had consequences for them and others.
9. Interpretative psychologists can investigate the underlying sources of value ideas in the needs and basic drives of individuals.
10. Intellectuals take values and rationalise them in all kinds of directions in accord with their interests.

This simplified list of ideas, which run through Weber's thinking on values, show the breadth of considerations which were involved. It is true that his direct concern in the last ten years of his life as a scientist was mainly with proposition 8, but it was impossible to treat this in isolation from the others for they defined the activity of a scientist, and because the sociologist was bound to take account of their orientations even as an empirical fact. Hence the sociologist *as* intellectual had also to consider the sociology *of* intellectuals even while, as a human being, acknowledging his own 'standpoint that hates intellectuals as the worst devil' (Essays: 152).

It is no wonder that in dealing with this complex set of feedbacks the subsequent commentators have often found apparent contradictions and inconsistencies in Weber's account. The most powerful criticism has come from those who adopt either a modified natural law position or a cultural relativist view. Leo Strauss argued from the former position that it was not possible to write an empirical sociology which did not involve value judgements, since values constituted the social world of human beings and an account of it was a series of judgements on whether they did or did not follow values. In that sense value-judgements were objective (Strauss, 1950).

Peter Winch (1958) advanced a similar argument, but this time emphasised the cultural specifics of particular societies which did not permit an observer a detached position from the values under consideration. For Strauss, then, Weber was a relativist because he was unwilling to allow value standards to pervade his analysis; for Winch he was not relativist enough because he imagined there was an objective way in which social life might be explored and explained.

The diversity of critical standpoints from which the doctrine of value-freedom has been challenged is even more dramatically exemplified by attacks on him from the far right and far left. Strikingly, Weber's greatness is acknowledged from both directions, and yet each sees him as limited by his bourgeois class position. A talented Nazi theorist, Christoph Steding, wrote in 1932 that Weber was an outstanding bourgeois representative of the declining bourgeois class and that his liberal individualism was the basis of a relativism which prevented him from taking any kind of effective political action (1932: 1–29).

A British communist, John Lewis, has equally seen him as a representative of the bourgeoisie. He holds his sociology to comprise 'the outlook, the prejudices, the values, of a typical member of the German business community' (1975: 52). But even acknowledging his subjective bias, Weber considers he can be ruthlessly objective about the inner working of society, which Lewis presents as an improbable posture.

All this talk about Weber's class position ignores the fact that he acknowledged it himself and yet was scathing about the German bourgeoisie. At the same time it fails to come to terms with the intellectual content of the propositions Weber was advancing. For the theoretical edifice of Weber's work depended upon both recognising the place of values and such influences as class position on one's work, and at the same time identifying just in what precise way anything like objectivity could be obtained.

Clearly, if our proposition 8 is limited by the other 9, it is a highly qualified position which Weber adopts. For this very reason it deserves a detailed and serious treatment. Weber was asserting that it was possible to reach out beyond the confines of one's values to truths which did hold for those holding different values. That is not an easy position to sustain; but it does at least contain its own justification for seeking to persuade others of its validity. The opposite view denies itself any grounds for being advocated at all.

Weber never pretended to have solved all the problems raised by the idea of an empirical science of values and it would be foolish for us to imagine he did. But it would be even more foolish to disregard the genuine advance in sophistication which his arguments represent. His understanding of science meant that there could be no going back along the road towards simpler faith.

But he clearly left behind a set of genuine intellectual problems which subsequent generations, by addressing rather than ignoring or worse treating as solved, can use as points for further development. He clearly leaves tasks for the social scientist. Indeed he provides the most convincing testimony of all to the independent intellectual worth of intelligence applied to human society. His work is the most powerful of all justifications for a science of the social.

The kind of value-free work which that involves will include attempting to answer the following kinds of problems which are raised, but not answered by Weber's own treatment of the issues and which equally have become salient as a result of subsequent social development:

Are there limits to the degree of value conflict, which it is possible to accommodate, within a given set of social relationships?

Does the medium of expression of values place limits on their content?

Are some values more effective than others in providing a basis for social interaction?

Must values become more abstract if they are to appeal across cultures?

How is value change induced in individuals and in society?

What is the 'shape' of values, what sort of ideas are they, how are they identified, classified, where are their boundaries?

What is the effect on political and social systems of the rise of value discourse? What does it mean that everybody is talking about 'values' now?

Is Weber right in arguing that there are inherent logical limits to value positions, or ultimate value axioms?

These are serious questions which anyone working from Weberian foundations will find important, difficult and worth attempting to answer. Whether there is any interest outside scientific circles in those questions and the answers to them depends on the extent to which the values of the scientific community have become so specialised that they are beyond the comprehension of the wider community. On Weber's analysis, if that has happened the dangers for both sides are great.

13
Society and the Market

Weber's account of understanding and his empirical analysis of values require us to ground each in processes happening between people in definite relationships with one another. Both understanding and values are generated in the course of social life and are themselves only to be understood through that reference.

This perception led Weber through the writing of history to social research, the empirical study of values and eventually to sociology. For social relationships are neither fixed realities nor transcendental necessities. They are facticities, highly variable products of human action. They are thus *sui generis*, not equatable with any other phenomenon.

Weber's justification for sociology was at bottom the need to depict and account for a particular kind of reality. For him existence *was* a predicate. It does actually matter for his science whether a marriage or a bureaucracy of a certain kind exists or not. Sociology's concern is first to establish the facts. That is a very different task from refining a concept of marriage or bureaucracy. For this reason he insisted on the distinction between ideal type and reality.

Unlike almost any other major sociologist, Weber's conception of the subject does not depend on a prior assumption about the nature of society. That comes at the end of the exploration, not the beginning. It does not mean society does not exist, merely that issues of whether, in what way, where and when are open for an empirical discipline.

In this sense sociology is an ontological science. It seeks to discover in just what ways people make a reality of their relationships with each other. It seeks to penetrate what is there, recognising always that it is probing into something often elusive, ephemeral and fragile.

I conclude these explorations in Weberian social theory with an examination of his views on the market and society, where he made it clear that neither could be considered without reference to the other and both depended on the actions of people, rational or irrational.

1 A vocabulary for groups

Only those who do not read beyond Weber's definitions of action, that is beyond Section 2 of Chapter I of *Economy and Society*, could possibly imagine that he was not concerned with the structure of groups. Throughout his texts human groups appear as key points of orientation for actors and scientist alike. A dominant purpose in outlining the basic concepts as he did was to provide clarity and precision in the language employed to describe groups.

The definitions of the basic terms are designed to lead us step by step to talk clearly about groups. Extraordinarily, to this day no better architectonic for sociology, in terms of precision, conciseness and operational utility, has been produced. Sections 9 and 10 provide us with the guidelines for a vocabulary for group analysis. Sections 11–17 provide bases for the classification of groups and the analysis of group structure.

Two premises underpin the whole operation. The first is that it is impossible to refer to groups without referring to what people do. The second is that groups are constituted by meaningful social action. The first premise avoids idealism by grounding the reality of groups in people. The second avoids materialism by insisting that groups arise out of needs, feelings, beliefs and ideas.

Both premises imply history. Social action under the conditions of the life cycle, a changing environment and the contingencies of other people's actions, is always in flux. The fundamental problem for any sociological vocabulary is how to create a stable set of meanings for scientific purposes without at the same time implying a false stability in the real world (Albrow, 1974).

In one sense there was a built-in safeguard in Weber's approach to social scientific concept formation against imputing false stability. His concepts were ideal types, not reflections of reality.

However, that is only a minimal precaution because the types themselves may be constructed to emphasise or minimise process and change. Weber supplied additional emphasis on process and change in the following ways:

1. All groups, from the married couple to the state, are seen as types of social relationship, and therefore, like them, depend on the likelihood of action taking place which is orientated to other people on the basis of a meaning. In other words, without actions, no group exists.

2. Weber's most inclusive classification of groups was adapted from Tönnies' distinction between *Gemeinschaft*, community, and *Gesellschaft*, association, social structures characterised respectively by informality, spontaneity and traditional bonds between people, on the one hand, and calculative, formally rule-bound relationships, on the other. Weber sought to dispel any rigid dichotomy between these two concepts and emphasised process by adding the prefix *Ver-* to create *Vergemeinschaftung* and *Vergesellschaftung* in each case. Both are difficult to render into English; Parsons chose communal and associative relationship respectively. Both terms reflect something which has happened to a relationship. With *Vergemeinschaftung* the parties have come to feel that they belong to it. With *Vergesellschaftung* the parties expect in some way that their own interests will be satisfied. On this basis, a kinship group does not have to operate as a *Gemeinschaft* for all its members. Some may be motivated by self-interest.

3. Social relationships may involve procedures which regulate the entry of people to the interactions which take place within them. Closure to outsiders as a process is intimately related to the satisfaction of the interests of the participants. Moreover, within a social relationship, participation may be regulated to give differential rights to the members. As far as Weber is concerned, in a sociological sense, rights are simply the entitlements members of a group acquire and are assigned which give them the chance to secure advantages. Processes of closure and allocation of rights do not happen without action dedicated to their maintenance.

4. It is when an order regulating relationships, which are closed to outsiders, is maintained by a leader and an administrative staff that Weber begins to speak of the organised group (*Verband*) and identifies sub-types according to the claims which

are made on members. This analysis culminates in the state which can claim a monopoly of the means of physical coercion in a territorial area and over its members.

The dominant impression which is left by a careful reading of his analysis of social relationships, and the groups which are formed out of them, is that he was concerned above all to document in precise detail the interpretative steps the analyst had to take in order to assert the existence of a group, or alternatively to construe the action of an individual as being orientated towards a group. He was emphatic that his concepts were themselves points of orientation for empirical research and in reality would combine and cross each other in innumerable variations as well as being nuanced by all kinds of intermediate types. In social research the first question about a group related to the nature of its existence.

A fragment of Weber's writing on the nation provides a vivid illustration of the fruits of this approach when applied to a topic which in his own time, as now, aroused enormous emotion. His method automatically ensures that the analysis stands outside feelings and treats them as facts. 'Nation' is a concept, he says, which is used in everyday speech without any common empirical features, but it does impute a common feeling of solidarity to certain groups of people. The problem is that the criteria for delimiting those groups are not agreed (E&S II: 922).

The 'nation' is not identical with a language community, with the members of a political community, with historical experience, with common descent or ethnic solidarity. At the same time it appears that groups may actually win the right to be called a nation, while other groups explicitly deny its applicability to themselves, as with the international proletarian movement. Apart from this, those groups which regard themselves and are regarded as nations may interpret that concept in very different ways. In general, however, the idea appears to be promoted especially by the intellectuals who live in the shadow of political power structures and seek to derive prestige from that proximity to political power for their own interpretation of culture. It is an idea which enhances the esteem of power-holders and is developed by intellectuals to justify a cultural mission.

Here Weber has no difficulty in identifying groups, in particular political and language communities, power structures and bodies with like interests. But the 'nation' itself cannot be attributed with anything other than an existence simply and solely in ideas and feelings. It has no genuine objective correlates. It appears to exist as a call to come together. Weber's method then permits us to distinguish groups which have as real an existence in the activities of individuals as does the modern state, from groups which are largely imaginary bearing some possible relationships to real groups but basically being evoked by particular interested parties to promote a cause.

The fact that Weber himself was a committed nationalist adds an ironic spice to his analysis, especially as he expressed considerable disdain for 'intellectuals'. But his form of asceticism required self-denial and a shedding of illusion. Weber was acutely sensitive to the association of power and ideas, and was ever anxious to avoid the self-gratification and intoxication which always attended the intellectual putting ideas at the service of power.

2 Collective concepts

Shedding illusions underlies Weber's consistent critique of all collective concepts. The use of such concepts in everyday contexts was unavoidable. They were the meaning content of human groups of all kinds and in the modern world were an indispensable part of the rationalised structure of the state and the business organisation. This was mirrored and constructed in the legal doctrines of collective personality. They are part of social reality in the sense of thoughts existing in the minds of particular people and as elements of the doctrines of dogmatic disciplines, like law.

But the empirical social researcher was not a dogmatic scientist. The purpose of social research was to establish facts and seek explanations for them, not to promote collective concepts which would inevitably mean serving particular groups of people rather than one's own idea of scientific integrity. Weber reserved some of his most scathing comments for academic colleagues who sought to evoke collective pathos in the lecture theatre.

He was at his acerbic best in the first congress of German sociologists held in Frankfurt in 1910 when engaging with a presentation by Alfred Plötz on the concepts of race and society. Plötz had asserted that the flourishing of society depended on the flourishing of the race. Weber asked what that could possibly mean. Could he really be arguing that some unity of blood relationship was responsible for definite cultural traits? Plötz edited a journal full of imaginative hypotheses about the possible relationships of race and society. But as yet, Weber said, he could not find a single fact relating to a sociological process which could be derived from inborn or inherited characteristics which one race possessed and another did not. From his own visit to the United States he knew that an unwashed black man and an unwashed white man had exactly the same smell and the white 'lady' sits holding the reins of the horses shoulder to shoulder with the black man and manifestly does not suffer from it (SSP: 460).

'If', Weber added, 'one were to replace the purely conventional concept "society" (*Gesellschaft*) with social relations and social institutions, then one can say: it is the feature of social institutions that they are to some degree the rules of the game, whereby, through their factual validity, certain human inherited characteristics have an increased chance of "winning" selection *or*, which is not the same because it proceeds in part by quite different laws, propagating themselves (ibid.: 459). Moreover, these differential chances would operate in any future socialist society as well as in the present day.

It was not only Plötz's invocation of 'race' as a unitary collective concept for explanatory purposes to which Weber objected. He objected equally to his thinking of 'society' as a living organism. 'But sociological inquiry never gains by the attempt to combine a number of relatively precise concepts into a single vague one.' 'We have', said Weber, 'the chance to relive in our minds the rational actions of individual human beings which gives us a great advantage over our understanding of animal societies. Why should we relinquish this in favour of an analogy with the bee-hive?' (SSP: 461; Selections: 389).

We find in Weber's disagreement with Plötz three distinct objections to the use of the concept of society by social scientists. They are:

1. That the idea is part of everyday conventional thinking
2. that it is vague
3. that the analogy with animal societies deflects the scientist from utilising the far better sources available for understanding human association.

The last of the objections Weber softened in his final version of the sociological concepts, allowing a functionalist approach to have a vital preliminary place in thinking about social relations. It is necessary to know what a king or entrepreneur or magician does, that is, what their typical actions are, before going on to analyse motives. Even that process, however, Weber says, is achieved through Rickert's 'value-relevance' (*Wertbeziehung*). In other words, if we can interpret that, it is only through understanding values that we can judge what counts as appropriate action for the king, etc. Even here Weber is allowing less scope for the analogy with animal societies than might at first sight appear to be the case (E&S I: 18).

The other two objections were open to no such equivocation. If the scientist could do no better than the ordinary person in terms of concept formation, then there was no point to science. For Weber rigour and precision, ascetic and painful qualities, were the hallmarks of science and the duty of the scientist to represent.

Mommsen has found a late expression of this in an unpublished letter written three months before his death: in the previous year he had been appointed to a chair in Munich where he had managed to negotiate with the authorities that he should teach sociology rather than political economy and finance, 'two subjects which he had outgrown' (Marianne Weber, 1975: 646). Weber wrote to an economist he respected highly, Robert Liefmann: 'If I have just now become a sociologist (according to my contract of employment), it is essentially to put an end to that everlasting spooky business of working with collective concepts. In other words, sociology too can only be conducted with a strictly "individualistic" method, beginning with the action of one or more, few or many, individual people (Mommsen, 1974: 256).

By 1920 Weber had had ample experience through the First World War and German pre- and post-war politics to confirm his deep suspicion of collective concepts in the social sciences. For it was not just ordinary people who conducted their daily lives through them and went peacefully about their business. Those concepts were the rallying calls for demagogues. 'Race' and 'nation' were invoked precisely to arouse the feelings associated with them and to mobilise people for causes.

From that point of view, however, 'society' was equally suspect. It had become the focal concept for all those who wished to see the overthrow of the capitalist institutions of the time. If there was to be a science of society, as was persistently advocated and, even more, if social reorganisation was to take place on its basis, then it would be a science which would have to find alternatives to such an emotive, all-embracing and imprecise term. If that were the case, however, this would bring the Weberian science of society, his interpretative sociology, into direct confrontation with Marxism.

3   Marx's idea of the social

Weber's work is frequently interpreted as the bourgeois answer to Marx. His own acknowledgement of his class background, his scepticism about the technical possibility of a socialist organisation of production under modern conditions and his emphasis on the importance of ideas as elements in explaining the course of history, may be cited to support this view.

This is, however, to overemphasise the importance of Marx for the agenda of Weber's work. On the other side, Roth and Wittich argue that the critique of historical materialism does not override Weber's other polemical and positive interests in *Economy and Society* (E&S I: LXIX). I in turn have shown that the inner dynamic for Weber's own intellectual production was derived from his resolution of the conflict between Kant and Nietzsche, or, in other words, the contradictions within bourgeois culture. It was this which enabled him to treat Marx as a talented author with popular appeal.

The problem, then, that Marx presented was analogous and indeed related to the problem posed by the working class for Bismarck. Certainly the 'social question' was a major issue for the rulers of the German Empire, but it was resolved by and absorbed into the processes of economic and military expansion, which were not a mere response to that question but had their own dynamic in tensions between landed, military and industrial interests in the conflict between nation-states.

There was never a head-on clash between Weber and the Marxists. He derived his intellectual strength from pre-Marxist sources and used that, as did Bismarck with the proletariat, to deflect the attack and to draw benefit from the undoubted intellectual achievements of Marx, Engels and their followers.

Early Marxist responses to Weber often sought to reject him

outright, but certainly from Gramsci onwards the approach has
been more like Weber's own to Marx, namely to seek to assimilate
(see Weiss, 1981). The strategy of intellectual assimilation is, of
course, premised on having a stronger foundation and greater
capacity to begin with. Generosity to the opponent is the
condescension of an assumed superiority. In Weber's case it was
condescension of an assumed superiority. In Weber's case it was
expressed most succinctly in the famous dictum which concludes
The Protestant Ethic and the Spirit of Capitalism, namely that
materialistic and spiritualistic approaches were equally 'one-sided'
if they were thought to be the results of research.

his side. The first we have explored at length, namely the
specification of the variety of ways in which ideas had to be
included in any causal explanation of the course of human action.
This does not, however, exhaust Weber's sense of the many-
sidedness of historical truth. There were not simply two spheres to
bring together. There were many and they were represented by all
the value positions which human beings could adopt, that is the
economic, the religious, the political, the aesthetic, the legal and
so on. Weber never sought to complete the list. He regarded it as a
potentially limitless. One of those spheres could be, however, the
social.

Now 'the social' was precisely the sphere which the historical
materialists claimed as their own and as only properly interpreted
in a materialist sense. Weber addressed this problem directly in his
editorial for the *Archiv* in 1904, the 'Objectivity' essay. The
problem with the materialist conception of history was that it was
taking one set of factors, the economic, to be the only true or real
one, and was seeking a comprehensive explanation for the whole
of history. This was what was happening when the claim was made
to explain the social through the economic because 'social' was
construed so widely that it comprised the whole of historical reality
(Meth: 68).

As we shall see, Weber had an answer to this problem of the all-
embracing nature of the concept of the social which he developed
in his technical conceptual papers. But the purpose behind that
exercise was more far-reaching than it appears when presented as
a technical solution to a problem in everyday language. For Weber
was well aware of the fact that Marx and his followers sought to
evoke a total response to a life situation by using 'social' and its

cognate term 'society' in the broadest possible sense. The maximum degree of scope was required for those two terms to underpin and justify a revolution which would change every aspect of life. Revolution was the overturning of a complete social system. The idea of the social provided Marx with the necessary sense of totality and completeness.

That totality was secured by associating the bonding which occurred between human beings with cooperation, on the one hand, and a rootedness in human nature, on the other: 'The production of life, both of one's own in labour and of fresh life in procreation, now appears as a two-fold relation: on the one hand as a natural, on the other as a social relation – social in the sense that it denotes the co-operation of several individuals' (Marx and Engels, 1976: 43). The idea of the social was then attached to all that human beings might produce, but of course it was the process of production which had led ultimately to the alienated form of social relations in societies based on the division of labour (Albrow, 1987). It was the all-embracing nature of this idea and its implicit presumption that cooperation was the true nature of human relations against which Weber reacted.

4   Weber's analysis of the social

Ironically it was a radical assault on Marxist views of the social which prompted Weber to take up the issue. The neo-Kantian philosopher of law, Rudolf Stammler (1856–1938), had sought to refute the materialist conception of history by demonstrating from first principles that it was not economic production but law which was the foundation of society. His *Wirtschaft und Recht nach der materialistischen Geschichtsauffassung* (*Economy and Law according to the Materialist Conception of History*) (1896) actually did Marxism the service of announcing serious academic concern with its doctrines. Stammler's fear was that they could serve to undermine the bases of social order.

Weber attacked Stammler in terms far more savage than any he ever addressed to the Marxists. He had already, in the editorial he wrote when he assumed the editorship of the *Archiv*, distanced himself from any attempt to offer a single factor theory of the social and had explicitly accused the historical materialists of doing just that. For this reason he could feel free to accuse Stammler of perpetrating the same error from the opposite direction.

In fact, Weber's hostility to idealist interpretations of social life was more intense than his rejection of materialism, if only because he did at least share with the latter the aspiration to develop empirical science. Stammler sought, in Weber's view, to exclude the possibility that human beings might relate to each other on a natural basis.

This led to absurdities like regarding breast-feeding in Prussia as social but not among Australian aborigines because, in the former case, the Prussian legal code required it, but in the latter there were no externally imposed rules (WL: 574). For Weber both natural regularities and explicit norms could equally define human relationships and he goes on to suggest that 'social life' might be defined thus: 'all those empirical processes the external regulation of which by human rules is "in principle", i.e. without actual nonsense, conceivable' (WL: 579).

The importance of this formulation is considerable in that it is a clear indication of Weber's determination to retain the Kantian notion of personality as central without falling into neo-Kantian idealism. The regulation of human behaviour involved taking possession by self or others of these features which might otherwise be conceived of as simply natural. But it was still a shaping of facticity, the creation of personality from urges, needs and spontaneous reactions. Culture was grounded in, even if not determined by, nature and to take the social out of the realm of natural causality altogether was to confuse the ideal and dogmatic formulations of jurists with empirical reality. Legal ideas could not create social reality out of nothing.

There was no question then in Weber's critique of Stammler of the social being removed into the sphere of ideas. On the contrary, his idea of the social makes its extent dependent upon what is discovered about the regularities which are identified in the behaviour of human beings which could potentially be controlled. But at the same time Weber is centring the idea of social life on the human will.

In doing so Weber was equally distancing himself from historical materialism, as he made clear in a section of a chapter entitled, 'The Economic Relationships of Organized Groups', written some time between 1910 and 1914. It was very rare, he wrote, to find groups which were not in some way or other economically determined. But the degree of this influence varied enormously and, as opposed to the assumptions of historical materialism, economic constants were often associated with very variable social structures (E&S I: 340–1). It was not even possible to assume a functional relationship between economy and social structures if by this was meant a clear-cut reciprocal determination: 'For the structural forms of social action (*Strukturformen des Gemeinschaftshandelns*) have, as we will see time and again, their "autonomy" (*Eigengesetzlichkeit*) and can also, irrespective of that, be shaped by other than economic causes' (WG I: 201; cf. E&S I: 341).

As Roth and Wittich say, 'A work on economy and society must sooner or later take a stand on historical materialism – Weber took his stand at the first appropriate moment' (E&S I: LXIX). But they also point out that Weber had other concerns than simply rebutting historical materialism. We may add that for Weber any kind of single factor theory was erroneous and that his prime interest was weaving together considerations from a variety of polemical contexts which enabled him to do justice to the complexity of causation and to identify some at least of the variety of irreducible spheres of life.

This is where Weber's allusion to the 'autonomy' (*Eigengesetzlichkeit*) of the 'structural forms of social action' is of critical significance. For this was the term he always employed when seeking to disentangle crucial factors in the complexity of cultural phenomena. It identified key sectors of social life which could not be reduced one to another and which contained at their core a basic element or principle which acted as a kind of anchorage point for the other elements in the sector. Autonomy meant having its own laws.

'Structural forms of social action' is equally significant. Debate about the concepts of social and society was not confined to the discussion of the materialist conception of history. They were also being worked out in the context of the expansion of German universities and competing bids for establishing sociology as an academically acceptable subject. A convergence around the idea of the social as a basis for disciplinary specialisation and professional status underpinned the move to establish the German

Sociological Society in 1909. Weber was an active participator in that move along with Tönnies and Simmel.

The view brilliantly expounded by Simmel (1908) was that the interaction of individuals created forms of social life, social relations, which were the framework within which human beings could pursue their concrete purposes, ideals, and interests. It was those forms sociology was to study. Weber respected Simmel highly but was not fully satisfied with his grounding of sociology. He did not find the idea of interaction specific enough, he felt Simmel confused ideal and actual meaning, and he considered the form-content distinction to be very relative to context.

Even so, Weber incorporated some of the vital elements of Simmel's approach into his own work. He acknowledged the importance of taking up a position in relation to the ideas of the social and society, and it was this which, together with his insistence on value-free scientific rigour, was behind his enthusiastic advocacy of the new Sociology Society. He was also prepared to employ a formulation, 'the structural forms of social action', which allowed for the importance of 'formal' features in social life.

Nevertheless, these strong resemblances between Simmel's and Weber's formulations should not lead us to underestimate the determination the latter had to ground his version of sociology in empirical social research and his equal resolve to detach the subject from any unwarranted imputation of superior reality to collective ideas. He was moving towards a formulation which would make the reciprocal determination of individual action and social structure, and indeed the very framework of human groups, much looser and more open to strictly empirical research than was permitted by the highly imaginative, but nonetheless at the end ultimately ideal typical schemes of Simmel.

We find therefore that, when Weber crystallizes his idea of the social in the categories essay, it is based on the orientations of individuals. Social action is the primary object for interpretative sociology (WL: 417), and that is action with a subjectively-intended meaning orientated to other people. Individuals and their actions are the 'atoms' for sociology (WL: 415). This concept is refined further for the final version of *Economy and Society*.

It would be a mistake to assume that Weber's refinement of the idea of the social for scientific purposes, and with a view to narrowing the field of sociology, meant that he was only interested in the inner logic of the social. He could not be so confined in his interests since his empirical preoccupations were towards explaining the relations *between* the social and other spheres of life, how in reality ideas were worked through in action. The extent to which the inner logic of the social placed limits on the dreams of human beings was precisely the kind of issue which Weber felt had to be addressed head-on if one was not to fall into utopian ideas about the perfect society. His fundamental objections to state socialism were to its impracticality, rather than at the level of values which might direct individual lives and consciences.

As opposed to Simmel, Weber felt that an explanatory science of social action was bound to take account of the actual purposes of human beings which went far beyond mere orientation to other people and which could indeed even lead them to withdraw from 'society' altogether, as in religious contemplation. The social was bounded not only by the natural but also by meaningful action which sought other goals and adhered to different logics. In consequence, explanation of the course of social action necessarily had to take account of the other life spheres – the political, religious, artistic – even, and above all, the economic.

5   The market

Weber was a trained lawyer. For brief periods he held university chairs in economics. He was not prepared to relinquish the rigour and precision of those disciplines when he came to examine the social. If there was to be a discipline called sociology it had to establish itself in the intellectual space defined initially by those older established subjects.

This requirement was made even more pressing by the ideological use of the idea of society. The intellectual thrust of Weber's last ten years of work was always in the direction of finding a concept of the social which could be used by an empirical, research-based science with claims to objectivity. It was a search which took him to the boundaries of the intellectual understanding of his time without, however, tempting him ever to cross them.

We have seen how one part of Weber's refinement of the social was accomplished through a delimitation of the idea of a rule and an insistence on the difference between the ideal formulation of a rule and action which was orientated to rules. We may say that the dust unto dust principle holds as much for rules as for human life. They arise out of the uncogitated necessities and regularities of social life, and they are interpreted and applied through the facts of power and understanding for practical purposes.

In this sense Weber rescued the idea of the social from the lawyers (and Stammler in particular). His relation to the economists was rather different. Partly the difference is due to the real circumstances. He interpreted the rationality of the legal system as being guaranteed by the professional activities of lawyers and legal experts. It was therefore not a mere crystallisation of everyday activities, but a regulation of them backed by state power. Encroachment on the social was an ever-present possibility.

By comparison, the rationality of economic activity was rooted in the self-interest of the individual, and economists had to fight off the claims of socialists and others who sought to assert the primacy of the social over the economic. In consequence, Weber was happy to assert that the mundane roots of law resided in the primacy of everyday social life, but he resisted the view that the everyday nature of economic activity automatically reflected its intrinsically social nature.

Weber's concern for the complexity of this relationship has given us *Economy and Society*, which was originally intended to be one contribution to a series he was to edit, called 'Outline to Social Economics', to which Michels, Sombart, Schumpeter and others were to contribute. His own volume was to have been called 'The Economy and the Normative and de facto Powers' and this has been retained as the title for the second and older part in the Roth and Wittich edition.

The second and longest chapter of the first part of *Economy and Society* was devoted to 'basic sociological categories of economic action'. It was not, Weber stressed, economic theory, but an outline of the most important economic concepts and of the simplest sociological relationships within the economy. In style it resembles the first chapter of sociological concepts and the two are intimately interrelated. It has been relatively neglected by sociologists but it is an essential elaboration of Weber's ideas of action and structure.

He defines economically orientated action as that which in its meaning is directed towards the provision of satisfaction of a demand for utilities. Economic action is the peaceful use of control over resources for that end and is primarily rational and planned. An economy can be spoken of when the economic action is independent, and an economic enterprise when it is organised on a continuous basis.

The terms of these definitions are then defined in turn. For instance, 'utilities' are the estimated chances of future possibilities of use as means for the agent's purposes. Utilities might reside in 'goods' or 'services' or 'economic chances'. The latter term covered all those social relationships, customs, positions or legal and conventional orders which could be a source of resource control. Introduced as an incidental qualification to the idea of utilities, it reflects the way in which Weber sought to bind economic and sociological viewpoints in one framework of concepts. It is a key facet of his analysis of social stratification since the economic utilisation of social position was fundamental for understanding class and status group formation.

But this intricate intermeshing of concepts was achieved by an initial separation, by definitions which distinguish the social from the economic (and both from the exercise of power). Not all social acts were economic; not all economic acts were social. Some acts were both social and economic. The case of the non-social economic act was a limiting case, but nonetheless important for establishing the purity of the concept. An economic act which took no account of third parties was not social (WG I: 11). This was what Weber called the 'robinsonade', after Robinson Crusoe, an unrealistic but imaginable case which clarified the meaning of the idea of the 'economic'.

Economic action was primarily rational, but not all rational action was economic. Quite aside from value-rational action, purposively rational action might be simply technically rational, that is concerned only with the scientifically best established means for achieving an end. There could be all kinds of technical action, even ascetic and religious techniques. That did not make it economic. Only when the scarcity of means in relation to a set of ends was taken into account did economic considerations enter.

Weber's treatment of economic concepts is typical of his approach to concept formation in general, namely he makes precise distinctions in order to prepare for the empirical examination of the relationship between the elements which have been distinguished. In order to examine the relationship of the economic and the social, the two ideas have to be presented in their purity. At the heart of the economic is the utter impersonality of the idea. But a sociological approach to the economic will show how that idea is pursued in and through social action, that is action orientated to other people.

Here, had Weber followed Marx's example, he would have stressed the cooperative nature of work, the origins of the division of labour in the family and the power of collective labour. Weber's starting point, on the contrary, was the purely rational, self-interested agent, because the development of the economy made it clear that this was a meaningful component of human action and as such a determinant of, and determined by, a whole set of other social actions. It was a clearly distinguishable sphere of life.

Weber was fascinated by the market as a social phenomenon precisely because it represented the polar opposite to bonding on the basis of love, fraternity or purely personal attraction. Here social relations were based upon the economic principle, each person or agent seeking to maximise their advantages through exchange with others: 'the market community as such is the most impersonal relationship of practical life into which humans can enter with one another' (E&S II: 636). But, we should note, Weber still calls the market a 'community'. For he was equally concerned to identify the general presuppositions for markets to work and it was in this context that he worked out some of his most important ideas on the bases of social relationships.

In the 1913 categories essay the market was the prime example of *Einverständnis* (common understanding). The parties to a deal might well engage in rational association (*Vergesellschaftung*), but this was premised on the belief that not only would the parties respect the exchange agreement, but that other people would too, even though they were not present, nor indeed knew anything about the agreement at the time. The expectation was that other people would respect that expectation, even though there were no formal agreement. Indeed it was wrong to think of it as a tacit agreement because the others who shared this understanding were unknown, at least in the case of a money economy. Such common understandings too did not have to carry moral or normative weight, although this was often the case. Basically, the common understanding was a point of orientation which it was in the interests of all parties to uphold as being valid (WL: 432).

In a brief, incomplete essay on the market, Weber stresses this foundation to the point of calling it a *Vergemeinschaftung* which, we will recall, represented the bringing of people together on the basis of a feeling of belonging. In the same essay he pointed out that the origins of free exchange are always outside primary relationships. The market exists at the boundaries between localities, tribes and descent groups, and is originally the only peaceful form of interaction between them.

If we put these two ideas together, we can see that Weber is approaching the point of identifying the minimal condition for talking of a human community, namely a shared assumption that other people are like oneself. In the case of the market this assumption is that people in general have interests, will seek to realise them in exchange, will wish to maintain the means of exchange and will respect the outcome of an exchange. Out of such assumptions will arise maxims like 'honesty is the best policy', not out of exalted values or out of brotherly love (E&S II: 637).

In these respects Weber argued that it was wrong to consider the market as the major locus of conflict in society. The most intimate human relationships were pervaded by conflict also. What distinguished market relations was their impersonality, their exclusive concern with the maximising economic interests. In this respect markets were associated with peace rather than with war. Here he cited the economist Oppenheimer approvingly who had said that rational exchange was the conceptual opposite of the appropriation of goods by coercion of any kind (ibid.: 640).

If the categories essay and the fragment on the market emphasised the peaceful side of the market, it is nonetheless the case that Weber fully recognised another side in his later chapter on the sociological categories of economic action. Here he moves from the presuppositions of the market to the motives of the participants and is quite explicit, at this level, that prices are the outcome of market struggle, the products of power constellations. They arise not simply out of demand, but out of effective demand, that is the outcome of unequal distribution of goods and incomes. The formal equality of people in the market says nothing about the actual bargaining power they may possess.

There was no intrinsic reason why markets should operate to ensure the greatest welfare or social justice. Participants would use every opportunity to enhance their own advantages, aim to acquire a monopoly position and generally exploit those over whom they possessed power. Socialist ideas were bred on the basis of this material irrationality of markets, which permitted precise calculation but could not guarantee the achievement of all the material needs of participants, let alone spiritual values.

Such defects were not, however, easily rectified. Weber contrasted the planned economy with the free market economy, and indeed this is an important subsidiary theme in his analysis of the relationship of the economic and the social, for the planned economy seeks to produce and distribute goods according to material criteria of welfare. It seeks to subordinate self-interest to higher values. Weber doubted that the technical means for securing this were available.

He had, however, an additional reason for being sceptical about such planned economies, namely that economic action was not eliminated in such an economy, if by economic action one simply meant the pursuit of one's own interests. What happened was that the situation changed and that interests were sought in other ways, namely through seeking privileges and concessions. Appropriation processes and interest struggles would remain a fact of daily life (E&S I: 203).

In this respect we can see that Weber's concept of economic action carried with it always the potential for the disruption of established social relationships. It was the antithesis of solidarity, of collective action for a common cause or of altruistic self-sacrifice. In this respect it shared a quality with religious contemplation; its core idea was beyond society. And yet it implied a common humanity.

However, importantly, it was also the source of another perspective on social structure, distinct from conceptions of legal order or primordial community. It drew attention to the fact that individuals were placed in situations of control over resources, of chances to take advantage of that control. In capitalist society it was the basis of class position. Markets gave rise to factual distribution of chances for income and people could make use of those chances. The impersonality of the market superimposed upon the social order, the distribution of prestige, another kind of organisation, the chance to secure income on the basis of one's control of utilities.

Any kind of social order, in the sense of a distribution of prestige and honour, patrimonial, feudal, socialist, could of course serve as the basis for the pursuit of economic interest, but in essence limits were always placed on the extent to which it could be pursued. It was where free exchange in the market developed that class position became the most important structuring principle for social relationships. But identity of position based on self-interest was no guarantee at all that association between occupants of those positions would develop.

In these dry formulations, and much abbreviated because they exist only in note form, Weber both defined the basis of class, in essence all those people in a similar market position, and then challenged the Marxist assumption that concerted class action would necessarily result. In fact the conditions for class action were most propitious under rather special circumstances, namely where classes were in direct contact, where masses shared the same class position, where they could gather together, e.g. in work-places, and where clear goals were established, normally by intellectuals from outside the class.

We can see that these special requirements were defined by Weber in such a way that he was clearly sceptical about the chances of successful class action. We should probably seek the deeper reason for this in his definition of economic action. As he said at one point, apart from the propertyless, completely unskilled worker, you could say that everyone had a different class position, since each person would have different amounts of property, skills, assets, which would be used in the market.

Ultimately, we can conclude, it is the non-social core of the economic idea which, once grasped, permits the individual to transcend the social order, to orientate to a world of facts and to calculate a purely personal gain. It is this which in part precludes the positing of 'society' as the determinant of individual action. But it is equally this which implies a common humanity beyond the varieties of culture and social structure. Kant's transcendental subject finds a partner not by gazing into the eyes of the loved one, but by changing currency in a foreign hotel.

6 The place of society

Johannes Winckelmann, who devoted his career to the care of the Weber texts, pointed out that for Weber there was no more point in expecting explanations to come from invoking 'society' than there was for the natural scientist in having such expectations of the concept of 'nature' (1966: 202). It was only by pursuing special points of view and having a particular intellectual or practical purpose that explanatory understanding was gained.

We may recall Weber's 'Objectivity' essay here, where he insisted that the idea of the 'social' had to be given some content. That view, coupled with his scepticism about the collective concept of society in particular and about collective concepts in general, was established for him some time before he set himself the task of laying the foundations for an empirical sociology. But he did not depart from those convictions and they provide the distinctive presuppositions for his sociology.

Weber's definition of the social makes it possible to use that idea at a series of stages or levels, from the unconscious through to the most rarefied formulations of state ideology or social theory. At the most basic level of all, orientation to the other, there is no difference between human beings and other animals. In this respect there is no conflict between Weber's approach and that of the inspirer of symbolic interactionism, G.H. Mead, who insisted on what he called the conversation of gestures in which animals engaged as the primary ground for all communication.

But there is a world of difference between the mother breast-feeding a baby and the interaction of stock exchange dealers, and little to be gained from seeing them as equally 'social'. The world of difference has been produced by cultural development and an understanding of that means understanding the transformations which the social has undergone in the process. The most useful key to understanding that is through the idea of rationality and an appreciation of the rationalisation process. To take the 'social' as an undifferentiated notion is to be unable to appreciate historical change, and to stay with a static concept of society, which will almost certainly carry normative implications.

And so Weber's idea of the social is one in which it is necessary to grasp the different levels of meaning which emerge historically, but which can coincide at any one time too in an individual's action. The desire for another person, the enjoyment of someone's company, the provision for future family needs, the fulfilment of a work instruction, the meeting of an obligation imposed by the state, the maintenance of one's social esteem, the following of the dictates of one's own conscience, represent different levels of the social which the individual in the modern world may orientate to almost simultaneously in closely related acts. Differing values and social structures compete with each other for the priority place in the individual's concerns.

With these considerations in mind Weber saw no harm in talking of the relation of cultural contents, literature, art, science, etc. to the general structural forms of human groups, or 'society'. He did so in these terms at the beginning of Chapter 3 of Part 2 of *Economy and Society* (WG I: 212). But the content did affect the form: the family was not like the work group and not like a friendship group. In every case the typical motives of the parties would affect the structure, and when one reached the level of the structured group (*Gebilde*), there the purposes embodied in the rules would affect its organisation.

Most important of all, the ideas which the separate life spheres contained were brought down to earth in the daily conduct of human beings. In this sense the social was inherently the sphere in which conflicts between ideas were worked out, and decisions were made because they had to be made. Often those conflicts of ideas were equally conflicts between people resolved by superior power. In both cases we are involved in facticity, not in ideas. Weber's insistence that it was possible for human beings to have an orientation to ideas, and even to escape social determination in some respects, was only a way of identifying the marginal importance these forms of action had in relation to the immense scope and power of the facticity of the social. The category of value-rationality only applied to a 'fairly modest' proportion of social action (WG I: 13), and most action was conducted in only dim awareness of its meaning.

The conflict of the life spheres and the strategic position of the individual in negotiating between them was for Weber a primary life experience. It was therefore no mere transcendental argument which made him place the human being at the centre of his sociology. It was the sheer empirical fact that social life was organised in such a way that every individual was forced to construct and reconstruct social relations on a day-to-day basis through his or her own actions. The concept of society could give virtually no purchase on that experience. To that extent only, Weber might have concurred with Margaret Thatcher's denial of the existence of society.

He would have resisted her rejection of sociology for the same reason. Precisely because human beings have to struggle to establish and maintain meaning in their lives, and this is done in contact with each other, the analysis of how that is done can provide a fundamental extension of human understanding of our own fate. An empirical sociology is there to serve enlightenment of the masses or the leaders. It is the extension to human understanding which is made necessary by the separation of the life spheres, by the rationalisation of technique and values. We learn by experience, and sociology is a necessary extension to that experience in a world of conflicting cultures and values.

Weber's sociology is not led by the idea of society. On the contrary, our understanding of society arises *out* of his sociology. He operated on the basis of a world/spirit distinction, rather than heaven and hell. But if he could not have subscribed to Sartre's dictum, 'hell is other people', he would have agreed that 'the world is other people'. Weber's empirical thrust took him to the social because it was there that the idea came down to earth. Respect for facts and respect for people were intimately connected and his appeals to objectivity were equally invocations of a common humanity. From this point of view on Weber's analysis, the market was more important in the manufacture of what could sensibly be called society than any number of appeals to a common value of cooperation.

Conclusion: From Social Theory to Sociology

1 Collapse of consensus

Like any other cultural product, whether it be ballet or bee-keeping, poetry or prisons, social theory is made by people at certain times and under certain circumstances. If we use the term 'social theory' to refer to any connected series of propositions which represent reflection upon the relations of individuals to society or upon the nature of the social, then it can be applied to doctrines which have arisen in different millennia in widely separated parts of the globe.

The fourth century BC was a golden age for social theory. Mencius advised the Chinese Emperor; Kautilya sought through his own advice to secure the power of the first ruler of a unified Indian state; while Aristotle was tutor to Alexander the Great and wrote the first comparative study of government, which served as the basis for Western theory until the nineteenth century. In the sense employed here all wrote social theory. With varying emphases they were all concerned with social relations; in their case with the maintenance and decay of power structures and the varying responses which were to be elicited from rulers and people alike.

The rulers of the great pre-industrial Empires had certain problems in common. Other types of structure have generated and been interpreted by theory characteristic to them. The mediaeval Roman Catholic church produced St Thomas Aquinas, the Renaissance Italian city prince found a mentor in Machiavelli and the twentieth-century industrial firm was served by F.W. Taylor. Karl Marx appointed himself to be the theorist for the internatio-

271

nal working-class movement. Manifestly social theory is not necessarily cumulative, nor does it move in one direction.

It is only in the twentieth century that these highly diversified intellectual products have been grouped together under the name 'social theory'. Only in this century has there arisen a group of employees, normally in higher education institutions, who work full-time on the interpretation, production and dissemination of these ideas. In state socialist societies these people have had normally to work within one broad theory, historical materialism or Marxist-Leninism. In Western societies a host of competing orientations has arisen.

If social theory is defined as we have done here, this is scarcely surprising. There will be as many types of theory as there are varieties of social structure and kinds of intellectual interest there are in reflecting on them. 'Social theory', then, has the same kind of scope and possibility for precise demarcation as 'natural science'. We can hardly expect one overarching theory to take in war, child-rearing, strategic management and social mobility, any more than we would expect the natural scientist to bring microbiology, lasers, semi-conductors and ozone depletion within one framework.

Social theory is embedded within the whole range of what have come to be known as social sciences, business administration to communication studies, human geography to applied psychology, sociology to international relations. Where it is singled out as a distinct field of study, then necessarily this overwhelming diversity becomes an immediate issue. Is there a common unifying feature, a thread to guide us through the maze, or a set of principles common to all?

In this sense social theory becomes philosophy of social science. Just as with the natural sciences, considerations of the unity of science become remote from the day-to-day work of the natural scientist and are only targeted by philosophers, so the unity of the social sciences and reflection on the nature of the social becomes a philosophical subject. From time to time a unifying principle may be proclaimed, say structure, or meaning, or rationality, or a system produced as by Talcott Parsons, but such enterprises are passing events, the very quest for unity will be challenged and the special social sciences proceed in their own way with gathering pace.

As a statement of the current situation, it is not possible to better the remarks by Anthony Giddens and Jonathan H. Turner in their introduction to a volume of essays, *Social Theory Today* (1987):

> Of course such a bold delineation conceals a host of more specific problems and topics; any definition of social theory is bound to be controversial. The reader looking for consensus over the nature and goals of social theory will thus be disappointed. Indeed this lack of consensus, as several contributions to this book imply, may be endemic to the nature of social science. At the very least, whether there can be a unified framework of social theory or even agreement over its basic preoccupations, is itself a contested issue (1987: 1).

Yet this very emphasis on a variety of approaches is, as they suggest, a fairly recent phenomenon. They link it to new developments within the philosophy of science and point out that the idea of science as a body of deductively linked laws has lost prestige. They highlight the passing away of what they call the logical empiricism associated with the idea of 'unified' science which dominated the social sciences for a period after the Second World War.

The earlier period to which Giddens and Turner refer may be exemplified from a prominent text published in 1957, Howard Becker's and Alvin Boskoff's *Modern Sociological Theory in Continuity and Change*. Boskoff's introduction to this volume of essays sees social theory as emerging from a diffuse set of generalised statements and judgements about a wide range of social phenomena which could be characterised simply as 'social thought'. So much of that was related to evaluative concerns that it was to be regarded as 'social philosophy'. Social theory emerges as an auxiliary compartment of social thought when social phenomena are viewed with some measure of objectivity and when thinkers and philosophers become devoted to generalised descriptions and explanations of social affairs *as they actually occurred* rather than as they 'ought to be' (1957: 5).

Within social theory, according to Boskoff, a more specialised set of concerns centred around an analytically separable realm of empirical phenomena, the social and the societal. From Comte to Cooley there developed a new and adventurous field within the scientific division of labour. 'Following the revolutionary transformations in social theory, sociology has become a special science' (ibid.: 31).

There is no doubting the gulf which separates the two texts we have cited, each reflecting very well the period in which they are written. Becker and Boskoff identify an implicit and emerging consensus, Giddens and Turner later find that even the possibility of a consensus in social theory is a disputed idea. In the thirty-year period between them the social sciences in the West underwent massive expansion, new requirements were made of them and new sub-disciplines arose. Marxist theory came to provide the most popular accounts of global developments and macro-social structure, while relations between individual and society were the focus for substantial schools of theory and research inspired by the phenomenological critique of Max Weber by Alfred Schutz and the social psychology of G.H. Mead which was the seedbed of symbolic interactionism. Critiques of orthodox theory from the Frankfurt School, most prominently Marcuse and later Habermas, completed the process of dispelling even the quest for consensus, let alone the reality. Theory came to be seen as a matter of perspectives on society, or principled reflections on those perspectives, while sociology became a disaggregated congeries of special fields of research.

The story does not, however, end here. Before it can be taken further, some recapitulation is necessary. For a start we should note that Becker and Boskoff were writing at a time when the influence of Weber was at a high point – 'the most discussed sociologist of the past fifty years' was their judgement (1957: 26). Moreover, their emphasis on empirical and unified science was not remote from Weber's interests.

There is no doubt that in the last three decades respect for and divergence from Weber have progressed at an equal rate. He has become the benchmark against which advance is measured. In important respects he is therefore the prime representative of the theoretical world we have lost. Yet his work as a whole, the quest for salvation, the foundations of social order, the working of markets, the search for mutual understanding, speak to present-day readers with the same freshness and immediacy as they did seventy years ago. The question arises, how has this disjunction between the wider reception of Weber, and the denial of his version of social theory arisen? Might there be more than a suspicion that the maze, which is called social theory today, arises out of that denial and that Weber might offer a way through it?

2 Weber's empirical project

In an attempt to answer the questions we have just raised we should turn again to Weber's intellectual task as he saw it. He was dedicated to 'science', the production of knowledge by systematic and critical enquiry. This process involved both the humanities and the natural sciences. Generalisation, causal explanation and the development of explanatory theories were the goals of the natural sciences. The humanities operated within the field of human culture and as such were concerned with spheres of meaning.

However, it was also possible to approach the spheres which the humanities studied with the same goals as the natural scientists shared, searching for generalisations and explanations. Empirical science of this kind could either look for explanations of unique sequences of events, in which case they were historical, or they could concentrate on the general. In both cases, however, they were bound to consider the human being as agent, in other words to search for the real basis of all meaning in people and their actions. A generalising empirical science of those spheres where human beings generated meanings, or in other words, an empirical science of culture, could not see those meanings as any other than human products, and human action as their basis.

As we have seen, Weber's sociology arose out of a concern to develop an empirical science of culture. The reason he did this after a period of initial scepticism about the claims of sociology, was not because he held to some such empty formula as 'society determines culture' but because the very process of generating meanings involved the orientation of people one to another. Social structures, patterns of social relations, became the bearers of ideas in the sense that they were communicated and refined in the day-to-day interactions in which people engaged in those structures. Ideas also took on a real meaning as they were embodied in actions, which almost always (though not invariably) involved orientation to other people.

In Weber's sociology the 'social' becomes the *medium* for culture, not its determinant as in versions of materialism, nor its expression as in versions of idealism. But since the social itself could only be seen as the product of human action, of thinking, feeling and willing people, the empirical study of social life had to be seen as a description and explanation of the way human beings create both society and culture.

Weber did not speak of 'social theory'. But it would be a dire mistake to imagine that he did not therefore address the questions which in the last thirty years have been subsumed under that heading. Indeed, a richly complex analysis of the sciences and philosophy underpins the considerations he made on his way to sociology. He either addressed explicitly or by implication all the objections to an empirical science of the social which have so often been made in the name of social theory. Moreover, he sustained the view that there were levels of reality, properly qualified as social, which were proper objects for empirical study, and to which his sociology was dedicated.

He had no wish to impose his definition of the subject on anyone. It was a question of convenience what label was used to designate the intellectual field he had distinguished. But it was particularly convenient too to use that name, because what hitherto passed as sociology was to him so often speculation, appeals to mysterious entities, ideology or simply nonsense, all surrounding ideas of society and the social which had become, for reasons which themselves needed investigation, the subjects of popular and state concern. Sociology was to be his counterweight to that kind of social thought.

Equally, in his consideration of materialist and idealist versions of social theory, in his emphatic affirmation of the individual as agent, in asserting the nature and limits of objectivity, in defining culture as the sphere of meaning and values as the focus for human endeavours, in asserting the importance of interests, and above all in seeing rationality as the principle which linked science, understanding and human action, Weber was identifying the range and scope of issues which have preoccupied social theory ever since, and, *at the same time*, declaring that his empirical sociology was both independent of and a contributor to the answers to the problems of social theory. Weber's sociology was designed to take us *out of* the maze of social theory:

3 Social facts

An interest in facts and the pursuit of social theory are not necessarily combined by one and the same individual, or indeed even by the same professional group. Aristotle collected facts, Mencius was largely unconcerned. Marx brought theory and facts together, Marcuse found facts rather uninteresting. Weber's work began with facts and proceeded to develop a certain kind of theory which he called sociology and which represents a distinctive intellectual response to the world.

Let us make abundantly clear what Weber's position on facts was. They were the outcome of human deeds, or existed in relation to human activity if one thinks of the natural world. They were constructed through accounts of the world and could be both interpreted and treated as objects in the course of human action. They were a shared human resource, essential to the constitution of social life, and could be the subject of scientific activity. The modern world was a world of facts in a way the world had never been before. Making sense of the facts meant making sense of the world. With an appreciation of the significance of facts, or more generally facticity (see above), we are finally in a position to state the nature of Weber's achievement in his intellectual work in general and his grounding of sociology in particular.

Weber's science of the social operates through the interrelationship of three phases of the world we inhabit: facts, understanding and the social. Neither one of these can be defined or grasped in isolation from the other two. Facts are points for common orientation by people in interaction, understanding is of people and what they produce and itself creates facts, the social both depends upon and is a basis for understanding.

The term 'social fact' is then almost pleonastic. But Weber's great contemporary, Durkheim, recognised equally that facticity was centrally important to the very existence of those wider social structures which were normally called societies. Social facts had to be treated as things by the sociologist. He too was as determined as Weber to rescue them from speculative philosophy, but he was less concerned than Weber to point out that the facticity of everyday life was ultimately the foundation for facts at any level. They both considered the relation of ideas to the real world to be the testing ground for their scientific approach.

For, if Weber's science of the social moves through the phases of facts, understanding and the social, where, might we ask, is the place of ideas? It was of the essence of Weber's approach that ideas had to be assimilated to the world of facts. The justification for that goes to the heart of his intellectual response to the world. It is the distinctive feature of his sociology and sets it off from all other kinds of social theory.

The full appreciation of this belongs to his theory of value and the key points of difference between himself and the neo-Kantians. Ideas are part of everyday reality not as pure intellectual constructions, but as thoughts which spring from circumstances, in exchanges between people, as reflections on practice, or as institutionalised in structures of meaning which transcend individual lives. As such they can be facts, events or conditions of action. As values, ideas can become a potent point of orientation, sources of common inspiration, but only intellectuals could delude themselves into thinking they determine the course of events. They are one factor among many.

Weber was not interested in ideas for the sake of ideas – almost a definition of the group he affected to spurn, the intellectuals. At the same time, not only did he allow for the fact that ideas could change the course of events, he regarded it as a prime responsibility of the scientist not to allow enthusiasm for ideas, in particular values, to distort accounts of the facts or to incite others to act in one way or another. The doctrine of freedom from value judgements was a doctrine of respect for the facts, which meant as much as anything a respect for other people's values, and people themselves. And, since those values were an intrinsic part of the world around us, it was necessary to devise accounts which would do justice to them.

In this way Weber came to the doctrine of ideal types which has so often mistakenly been seen as the beginning and end of his scientific method. It was certainly vital, for it gave him the means of representing structures of ideas without imputing reality to them and at the same time without committing him to any view about their rightness, apart from their degree of rationality. Much of Weber's specification of ideal types does amount to a non-empirical social theory of a very high order. We only have to think of his theory of legitimation to recognise this, but it was never pursued except in so far as he could provide points of orientation for his empirical work.

The construction of ideal types on a systematic basis was one way in which sociology differed from the writing of history and in this sense it was more theoretical. The other difference was that it sought to produce general statements of fact which crossed times and cultures. In this sense Weber's science of the social took him beyond the interests of the state in social facts. He sought to discover facts of universal significance.

In this respect Weber's sociology was a genuine successor to Hegel's philosophy. But instead of seeking a universal reality in the human mind, Weber sought to identify the processes which were creating a world of universal facts out of one in which there appeared at first to be irreducible variety. The world order to which his sociology could apply was one of power, markets, technical and formal rationality, and where conflicting ultimate values battled for the human soul.

Weber's insistence that ideal types are only aids to an empirical sociology meant that he set up a barrier against two kinds of fallacy which he combatted throughout his career. The first was the belief that the perfection of ideas would produce the perfect society. He had no time for utopian speculation. Ideas had always to return to reality which gave them meaning in the first place. He would have regarded the kind of social theory which Gouldner at one time advocated, the establishment of theoretical communities, as a bizarre self-deception.

The second fallacy was that society was an integrated whole, organised around certain principles and embracing every aspect of the individual's life. The whole point of Weber's insistence on the central place of facts was that the degree to which people did or did not work together or understand each other was a matter of fact, both for them and for the sociologist. There could be no *a priori* assumption that the facts of social life corresponded to an ideal type of any group or society. Although, of course, merely establishing the facts of the case could contribute to the kind of common understanding which would be conducive to the formation of relationships and groups.

4 Reflexivity

This is the principle of reflexivity, or what Giddens has called the double hermeneutic, which arises because not only do sociologists seek to penetrate and understand the features of everyday life, but their concepts are in turn reinterpreted and incorporated into everyday life.

It is a process of which Weber was acutely aware. A science, such as economics, could easily be a vital element in transforming the world because by basing itself in rationality it could take hold of everyday action, and at the same time become a point of reference for actors in the real world.

Weber sought to reduce that kind of intervention to an absolute minimum as far as his sociology was concerned. This was not because he underestimated the potentiality for influencing and reshaping values. On the contrary, the history of intellectuals in society was that they had devoted their lives precisely to this. He aspired above all to a science which was beyond prophecy. Nothing was easier than for intellectuals to attach themselves to this or that movement and refine its ideas but they should never deceive themselves or others into thinking that their commitment was anything other than faith. Weber stated his position at the end of his 'Objectivity' essay:

> Now all this should not be misunderstood to mean that the proper task of the social sciences should be the continual chase for new viewpoints and new analytical constructs. *On the contrary*: nothing should be more sharply emphasized than the proposition that the knowledge of the *cultural significance of concrete historical events and patterns* is exclusively and solely the final end which, among other means, concept construction and the criticism of constructs also seek to serve (Meth: 111).

The problem with conceptualising the relations of actors' and sociologists' concepts in terms of the double hermeneutic is that it does tend to emphasise the dynamic interplay of ideas to the exclusion of the double reinforcement of facticity. In his *The Constitution of Society*, Giddens accords key significance in the structuration of social systems to 'Acceptance-as-real' embodied in concrete modes of procedure and declares that 'The reflexive monitoring of social conduct is intrinsic to the "facticity" which the structural properties of social systems display' (1984: 322). It is this facticity which Weber's empirical sociology was designed to describe and account for, because it was this which counted as the real world.

The reason Weber emphasised the empirical nature of his sociology was because the social itself was grounded in facticity, not in ideas, and sociology itself was the extension of the quest for common understanding and the constitution of facts without which modern social life cannot be sustained. In this sense there is a unity of theory and method in Weber's intellectual enterprise, for the approach to facts which he adopts, describing, interpreting, explaining and generalising, generates the wider understanding which can be the same basis for social interaction on the most general levels of meaning as is implicit in the routine daily interactions which people accomplish in their day-to-day exist-ence. The methods by which the sociologist finds out the facts in people's everyday activities are generalised to work in relation to the most all-embracing systems of action, but ultimately draw only on the same resources as people have to make sense of their own lives.

The significance of this in relation to social theory is far-reaching. Since social life is grounded in facts, purely conceptual explorations run many dangers. The most obvious is that they may be remote from reality, or simply irrelevant to most people's concerns. They may reflect the imaginative capabilities of the author, but little more. They may seek to persuade or to excite feelings, while masquerading as something else. They may generate interminable argument which is of interest to the participants only and marginalises them from the rest of society. Most dangerous of all, the authors may persuade themselves that this is the only route to truth.

Weber's work, implicitly or explicitly, acknowledges that a wide variety of intellectual responses to the world is possible. He dismissed none of them out of hand, except in so far as deceit was involved. Even the prophet had a place, just not in the lecture theatre of the university. But in the modern world sociology had to be the base to which any possible social theory would have to return. We have to ask whether Weber's sociology lived up to those requirements.

5 Voice of the twentieth century

What I will contend here is that Weber's sociology uniquely captured persisting and developing features of the twentieth century. For this reason his work gains ever increasing respect. But this has largely been unaccompanied by an understanding of the man and his programme. The lessons therefore for sociology and its relations with social theory have not yet been appreciated. To support this very large claim below is listed a set of eleven distinctive features of our own time which his work has highlighted. Taken together they amount to a comprehensive penetration of the reality of the present age.

1.   *Individualisation of the human being.* The uniqueness, separateness and particularity of each person has become the focus and legitimation for social institutions from bureaucracy to the household. The creation of the individual under modern conditions of group formation was anticipated by the Protestant Reformation and rationalised in Kant's ethics. It was explored in most depth by Simmel. It becomes the presupposition for Weber's method.

2.   *Contestability of social boundaries.* From nationality to credit-worthiness, from the family to class, from age to gender, membership of groups has contested meaning, and the existence and salience of boundaries between people categorised by such membership are problematical for themselves and observers. Weber's insistence on the need to assess group structure in terms of probabilities of action and the assertion that the existence of groups was never guaranteed in the abstract, but always an empirical issue, reflect this situation.

3.   *Management of the social.* Social arrangements are seen as a sector to be managed, calculated and restructured. A knowledge of them becomes a source of power and in the modern world management by this knowledge both shapes and is embodied in bureaucracy.

4.   *The separation of life spheres.* The political, economic, religious, erotic, intellectual and other activities of human beings are separated out into distinctly identifiable spheres, producing distinct structures of meaning and occupational specialisation to match.

5.   *The production of facts.* The facticity of all understanding and the dependence of the social on understanding mean that where flux and uncertainty pervade social relationships, facts are generated to provide ever renewable resources for stability. The

state, organisations and educational institutions as well as the mass media devote a major part of their activities to the production and dissemination of facts (and falsehoods, too, but there are limits to the amount of disinformation which is viable in this kind of society).

6. *The discovery of values.* Ideas are recognised not just as thoughts which individuals have, but as generalised forms of thought characterising whole groups and ultimately humanity as a whole. The judgements which people make between good and bad are conceptualised as the application of abstract standards open to inspection by others and at the same time commanding allegiance. Anticipated by the neo-Kantians, Weber finds that his real world cannot be understood without recognising that people orientate to values in their action.

7. *The stratification of meaning.* The operation of social structures of vastly differing scope simultaneously in the same population, from families to political parties, from schools to factories, from the individual to the state, is only possible through actions of one and the same individual taking on a multiplicity of meaning at one and the same time. Each act therefore carries a range of meanings open to a variety of interpretations by actor and observer alike. (This is a vital aspect of what Giddens calls structuration.)

8. *The generation of conflict.* Within and between individuals and within and between groups, and between the individual and the group, conflict is routinely and normally generated as spheres of meaning are separated, as contests arise over goals and resources. Both Weber and Simmel recognised conflict as inherent in modern social structure rather then essentially destructive to it, although a degree of destructiveness involved was always empirically possible.

9. *The intensification of rationality.* At every level of social action from the individual setting goals to policy of the state, from the pursuit of profit to the process of scientific research to the development of new means of communication, there is a growth of rationality which becomes identified as the universal principle for human action and the best criterion for common understanding. It is institutionalised in systems of action of an ever more embracing kind. Because of its twin features of universal intelligibility and capacity to provide technical mastery of the real world it has, as

the rationalisation process, become the driving force in human history. Anticipated by Hegel, Weber strove to demystify the idealist intuition of his predecessor and identify in precise respects how rationality informs and transforms human actions.

10.   *The magnification of irrationality.* The scope and cumulative effects of irrationality grow with the extension of rationality. More and more people are placed under the constraints of rationalised systems which they do not understand, while those systems produce larger, unmanageable, unwanted effects. The choices of managing or mobilising irrationality become more dangerous all the time to the extent of calling the survival of systems of meaning into question.

11.   *The creation of one world.* The universalisation of Western culture, and in particular the claims and successes of its version of rationality in penetrating and subordinating other cultures, as well as the resistance of those cultures in drawing on their own essential values, is a central experience colouring every aspect of social life in the twentieth century. Weber's comparative studies of religion and the social bases of nationalism as well as power and the market provide the basis for understanding the relationship between multi-culturalism and globalisation.

These eleven themes are not put in precisely the terms which Weber used. They are singled out and identified separately to varying degrees in his work. (4), (6), (8) and (9) are quite explicit. (5) and (11) are more implicit and the others lie between those extremes. But they do represent an astonishingly exact anticipation of the broad lines of development of the twentieth century.

They do not amount to prophecies, although in his more pessimistic moods Weber spoke of the unavoidable nature of the rationalisation process and his image of the iron cage recurs with a sense of foreboding. His idea of the charismatic leader has been held to anticipate Hitler, but I am not inclined to give him credit there, if only because Weber did not provide within his conceptual scheme sufficiently for terror as an instrument of power. The argument on this point could go on for a long time and does.

These are identifications of broad lines of development which result from an analytical method which is shown to have worth precisely because so much which has happened since can be seen to follow on those lines. They do not amount by any means to the sum total of Weber's contribution to our understanding for they only look to development. He was equally incisive on variable features of social systems, for instance what little he wrote on gender makes it quite apparent that he had a profound appreciation of the cultural determination of relations between the sexes and that he recognised the importance of power in the most intimate relationships.

His analysis of the potential problems of socialist states was remarkably prescient. He appreciated that socialist values, arising out of basic experiences of common life and sharing, especially from family relations, not primitively but in more modern times, would be subject to particular stresses in large organisations and above all in the state. Since he wrote his sentences only three years after the Russian Revolution, his analysis of planned economies and what he called the market for privileges can be seen in the light of the experience of seventy years to have identified the central problems of socialist states on the basis of purely theoretical analysis.

His sociology, then, has succeeded in grasping the spirit of the twentieth century in an extraordinary manner and I am going to suggest that this product of Protestant culture and the Prussian state was able to do so, not simply because of his talent and industry, necessary though these were, but because that particular background of his was an anticipation of so much which the rest of the world has subsequently had to experience.

The Protestant experience was the prototype of having to live at multiple levels of meaning: a rebellion against old authority, a dedication to daily routines, and a secret faith in a meaning hidden to others. The Protestants were the first people to experience acutely the modern problems of multiplicity and conflict of different levels of meaning in daily action, and in that sense anticipated a process which continues apace in the rest of the world to this day.

The Prussian experience of power imposed through rationality, the unification of social organisation around those twin principles in the modern state, has been equally paradigmatic for the twentieth century. The irony that the Prussian state has passed into history should not be lost on those who imagine that such structures are unshakable. The point is, however, that as a generic form of structuration process the twentieth century has seen the complexity of state/individual relations grow continuously.

If the assessment of Weber's work offered here is valid, the question then arises: why have his foundations for sociology been so persistently neglected, and could sociology even now build on them anew?

6   The retrieval of sociology

In one sense Weber's project was clearly ideological, that is if by ideology one means a set of ideas which claim to represent the world as it is rather than the possibilities of it being otherwise. It is a point made by critical theorists and radicals alike. In another sense the project was ordinary commonsense and superficial in its acceptance of social structure as a fact, a point made by phenomenological critics. There are many ways in which the world can be thought away, or reconstructed in the mind, or simply ignored. Many of those ways are ingenious, intellectually exciting, and sometimes even full of consequence for social theory. If we take just the case of economics, Weber was very ready to acknowledge that pure thought experiments provided the basis for the advance of that discipline.

I have examined at length the reason for Weber's insistence on developing an empirical sociology rather than other forms of social theory. It has never captured the theoretical allegiance of working sociologists in the way the ideas of Marx, Durkheim, Parsons, Mead or Schutz did. For a start the temptation to examine his ideal types and to remain at the level of logical critique of their construction has been overwhelmingly tempting. It takes less time and resources than replicating his studies of religion. Secondly, the articulation of his ideal types with his method generally and his substantive sociology is difficult to construe, concealed in part by the fragmentary form of publication in English – problems which this book seeks to rectify.

But there is another aspect to the reception of Weber's work in the West. It reached a high point in the 1950s and very early 1960s through the efforts of sociologists like C. Wright Mills and John Rex and many others. But if the medium was Max Weber, the message was often another, in Mills' case a brilliant radicalism.

In the late 1960s and the 1970s sociology was frequently submerged beneath a flood of perspectives on society, often imaginative and exciting for the student, but beneath which the idea of a discipline called sociology was often lost to sight. By and large Weber became the chopping block on which critical tools necessary for reorganising society were sharpened. In Britain the stereotype of the radical and destructive sociology lecturer was popularised in a successful novel and later television series, *The History Man*, by Malcolm Bradbury. It was an image evoked frequently in attacks on the discipline in the 1980s.

As that period of ferment in the universities and among younger people generally passes into history, it is easier to see that it was dependent on conditions of age structure and economic cycle more than upon any longer-term change. In many respects the world once again appears more to fit the Weberian mould than to hold out the hope for any early disappearance of bureaucracy and capitalism. The Weberian analysis of stratification and the operation of markets takes on a particular poignancy as the state socialist societies themselves strain under the pressures he identified.

But sociology itself still suffers from the identity crisis of the 1970s. Not only consensus, which was never achieved, but also the hope of commonly acknowledged intellectual advances appear to have passed away. The sociologically inspired reflections of Thomas Kuhn (1962) on revolution in science, with one paradigm collapsing in the face of another, has encouraged the quest for so many paradigms that sociology has become non-paradigmatic, a congeries of disparate considerations with some kind of concern for the social. The idea of the sociologist as someone with special skills and understanding of a field of study has declined even among sociologists themselves.

This is not the case everywhere, of course, and in societies which are seeking to reform and restructure, sociologists are enjoying more official recognition than has ever been the case. In the Soviet Union sociology has recently been established at degree level in Leningrad and Moscow, and the work of Tatiana Zaslavskaya in particular on the restructuring of industry has been influential at key policy levels. In China the astonishing work of Fei Hsaio Tung (1983) in Kaixian'gong village over a fifty-year period, from the time when he worked with Malinowski at the London School of Economics in 1936, has contributed to the introduction of the responsibility system for peasant agriculture.

In each case it is the disinterested pursuit of scientific work which has commanded attention, and requests for advance and guidance in relation to planned social change have subsequently resulted. It would not, however, be reasonable to expect that in Western societies, or in developing countries in the Third World, the same kind of restructuring should take place for the recognition of sociological work to arise. Indeed, sociologists in the West should ask themselves whether there is more than just a cyclical downturn in the demand for their work or whether a more fundamental change has taken place. It would be unreasonable to suppose that the conditions which generated sociology in the West at the beginning of the century will be sustained indefinitely.

Those who speculate on the passing of modern society and the arrival of the post-modern period could conceivably succeed in identifying features of contemporary culture which make the kind of science Weber envisaged, and which he practised so successfully, unmarketable under the new conditions.

Both the computerisation of data bases and the generation of privatised responses to video images probably reduce the necessity for the absorption of facts as a basis for social participation and at the same time reduce the requirement for shared understandings of social structure. The scope and penetration of state control may alter in such a way that it is less reliant on research findings.

Finally, there is a very general mood among sociologists that the relationship between culture and social structure has altered in a deep but as yet undefined way, so that cultural action with a very indeterminate meaning in social relationships becomes an autonomous sphere of experience, requiring little sociology for its explication. Weber's own hints about the non-social nature of religious contemplation suggest that his own way of thinking leaves open such a possibility.

Against the background of the search to identify the postmodern, it could be the case that the confusion of social theory in the last thirty years is genuinely the prelude to the disappearance of Western sociology. Under those circumstances a plea to reassess the Weberian achievement and to build on it would fall on deaf ears. The speculative style of these suggestions would themselves prefigure the kind of social theory which might be sufficient to evoke the mood of the times – imaginative scenarios half way between science fiction and advertising copy. A future society without sociology can be imagined.

For the present, my own proposal is to return to Weber and to build on his achievement. In this respect it might be most useful to re-erect some boundaries between sociology and social theory. We could take a cue from Ralf Dahrendorf and accept that: 'Sociology is theory, and no amount of "decided reason" will set it to dealing actively with the social and political problems of our time' (1968: 274). We could adopt too a distinction between sociological theory and social theory, such as Norbert Elias advocates, where we reserve the former term for empirically based interpretations and explanations of processes of social change at a relatively general level, and confine the latter to conceptual and normative explorations. Both those suggestions are entirely within the spirit of the Weberian project.

But this would not remove the moral basis which underpins Weberian sociology. The empirical science he envisaged sought always to bring the interpretation and explanation of the course of social action back to its meaning for the individual human being, in particular or in general.

The individual was the transcendental presupposition for his sociology. Weber was the first to acknowledge that the interest of the social scientist directed itself to a phenomenon which was constituted by its value to human beings, in this case the self-same human being. That choice represented a value commitment on his part to which he devoted the whole capacity of his intellect throughout his career.

That kind of humanism and the commitment to an objective sociology, interpreting and explaining the course of individual action into the as-yet unknown social order for the twenty-first century, may still prove to be the best resistance to the disaggregation of the human soul which post-modernism appears to threaten.

But in returning the focus always to the responsible agent, the sociologist can allow human beings glimpses of their own image and possibilities to control their own fate before it slips from their grasp.

References

I Max Weber's works

A full bibliography of Max Weber's works in German and in English translation is contained in Dirk Käsler's *Max Weber: An Introduction to his Life and Work* (Cambridge: Polity Press, 1988). Listed here are editions of those works to which reference is made in the text with the abbreviation which has been used for reference purposes.

Abbreviation	German title
RS I, II, III	*Gesammelte Aufsätze zur Religionssoziologie*, 3 vols (Tübingen: J.C.B. Mohr, 1920).
SSP	*Gesammelte Aufsätze zur Soziologie und Sozialpolitik* (Tübingen: J.C.B. Mohr, 1924).
WL	*Gesammelte Aufsätze zur Wissenschaftslehre* (Tübingen: J.C.B. Mohr, 1922).
PS	*Gesammelte Politische Schriften*, 2nd edn (Tübingen: J.C.B. Mohr, 1958).
WG I, II	*Wirtschaft und Gesellschaft*, 2 vols, 4th edn (Tübingen: J.C.B. Mohr, 1956).
GHM	*Zur Geschichte der Handelsgesellschaften im Mittelalter* (Amsterdam: E.J. Bonset, 1970).
	English title
Essays	Gerth, H.H. and Mills, C.W. (eds) *From Max Weber: Essays in Sociology* (London: Routledge and Kegan Paul, 1948).
PE	*The Protestant Ethic and the Spirit of Capitalism* (trans. Talcott Parsons) (London: Allen and Unwin, 2nd edn, 1976).
S of Rel	*The Sociology of Religion* (trans. Ephraim Fischoff) (London: Social Science Paperbacks and Methuen, 1966).

Meth   *The Methodology of the Social Sciences* (trans. Edward A. Shils and Henry A. Finch) (Glencoe, Ill.: The Free Press, 1949).

E&S I, II   *Economy and Society*, 2 vols (ed. Guenther Roth and Claus Wittich) (Berkeley: University of California Press, reissue 1978).

Stammler   'R. Stammler's "Surmounting" of the Materialist Conception of History' (trans. Martin Albrow) *British Journal of Law and Society* 2 (1975) 129–52; 3 (1976) 17–43.

GEH   *General Economic History*, trans. Frank H. Knight) (New York: Collier Books, 1961).

Selections   Runciman, W.G. (ed.) *Max Weber Selections in Translation* (Cambridge: Cambridge University Press, 1978).

II Books and articles cited

Albrow, M. (1970) *Bureaucracy* (London: Macmillan).

Albrow, M. (1972) 'Weber on Legitimate Norms and Authority: A Comment on Martin E. Spencer's Account', *British Journal of Sociology* XXIII: 483–7.

Albrow, M. (1974 'Dialectical and Categorical Paradigms of a Science of Society', *The Sociological Review* 22: 183–201.

Albrow, M. (1975) 'Legal Positivism and Bourgeois Materialism: Max Weber's View of the Sociology of Law', *British Journal of Law and Society* 2: 14–31.

Albrow, M. (1982) 'Beyond Naturalism: Values as a Topic for Interpretative Sociology', in H.J. Helle (ed.) *Kultur und Institution* (Berlin: Duncker and Humblot).

Albrow, M. (1987) 'The Application of the Weberian Concept of Rationalization to Contemporary Conditions', in S. Whimster and S. Lash (eds) *Max Weber, Rationality and Modernity* (London: Allen and Unwin) pp. 164–82.

Alexander, J.C. (1983) *Theoretical Logic in Sociology*, vol. 3: *The Classical Attempt at Theoretical Synthesis: Max Weber* (London: Routledge).

Aristotle (1946) *Politics* (trans. Ernest Barker) (Oxford: Clarendon).

Aristotle (1955) *Ethics* (trans. J.A.K. Thomson) (Harmondsworth: Penguin).

Aron, R. (1957) *German Sociology* (London: Heinemann; 1st French edn, 1936).

Aron, R. (1971) 'Max Weber and Power-Politics', in O. Stammer (ed.) op. cit.: 83–100.

Baumgarten, E. (1964) *Max Weber. Werk und Person, Dokumente* (Tübingen: J.C.B. Mohr).

Becker, H. and Boskoff, A. (1957) *Modern Sociological Theory in Continuity and Change* (New York: Dryden).

Beetham, D. (1987) 'Mosca, Pareto and Weber: a Historical Comparison', in W.J. Mommsen and J. Osterhammel (1987) op. cit.: 139–58.

Bell, D. (1976) *The Coming of Post-Industrial Society* (Harmondworth: Penguin).

Bendix, R. (1960) *Max Weber: An Intellectual Portrait* (Berkeley: University of California Press).

Bendix, R. and Roth, G. (1971) *Scholarship and Partisanship: Essays on Max Weber* (Berkeley: University of California Press).

Bradbury, M. (1975) *The History Man* (London: Secker and Warburg).

Broad, C.D. (1978) *Kant: an Introduction* (Cambridge: Cambridge University Press).

Brubacker, R. (1984) *The Limits of Rationality* (London: Allen and Unwin).

Burger, T. (1976) *Max Weber's Theory of Concept Formation: History Laws and Ideal Types* (Durham, N.C.: Duke University Press).

Channing, W.E. (1884) *Complete Works* (New York: Christian Life Publishing Co).

Cicourel, A.V. (1964) *Method and Measurement in Sociology* (New York: The Free Press).

Collins, R. (1986) *Weberian Sociological Theory* (Cambridge: Cambridge University Press).

Dahrendorf, R. (1968) *Essays in the Theory of Society* (London: Routledge).

Dahrendorf, R. (1987) 'Max Weber and Modern Social Science', in W.J. Mommsen and J. Osterhammel (1987) op. cit.: 574–80.

Darwin, C. (1859) *The Origin of Species* (London: John Murray).

Dilthey, W. (1973) *Gesammelte Schriften vol.7: Der Aufbau der geschichtlichen Welt in den Geisteswissenschaften* (Stuttgart: Teubner).

Eden, R. (1983) *Political Leadership and Nihilism: A Study of Weber and Nietzsche* (Tampa: University of Florida).

Elias, N. (1984) 'Notizen zum Lebenslauf', in *Macht und Zivilisation* (ed. P. Gleichmann, J. Goudsblom and H. Korte) (Frankfurt: Suhrkamp) pp. 9–82.

Fei, Hsiao Tung (1983) *Chinese Village Close-up* (Beijing: New World Press).

Fleischmann, E. (1964) 'De Weber à Nietzsche' *Archives Européennes Sociologiques* 5: 190–238.

Garfinkel, A. (1967) *Studies in Ethnomethodology* (Englewood Cliffs, N.J.: Prentice Hall).

Gerber, H.E. (1954) *Nietzsche and Goethe* (Berne/Stuttgart: Paul Haupt).

Gerth, H.H. and Mills, C.W. (eds) (1948) *From Max Weber: Essays in Sociology* (London: Routledge and Kegan Paul).

Giddens, A. (1984) *The Constitution of Society: Outline of the Theory of Structuration* (Cambridge: Blackwell/Polity Press).

Giddens, A. (1989) *Sociology* (Cambridge: Polity Press).

Giddens, A. and Turner, J.H. (1987) *Social Theory Today* (Cambridge: Polity Press).

Goethe, J.W. (1834) *Faust* (trans. A. Hayward) (London: Moxon).

Goethe, J.W. (1907) *Maximen und Reflexionen* (ed. Max Hecker) (Weimar: Goethe Gesellschaft).

Goethe, J.W. (1933) *The Practical Wisdom of Goethe* (ed. Emil Ludwig) (London: Allen and Unwin).

Goethe, J.W. (1978) *Werke*, vol. 1 (Munich: Bech; 11th rev. edn).

Goldman, L. (1971) *Immanuel Kant* (London: New Left Books).

Gottl, F. (1901) *Die Herrschaft des Wortes* (Jena: Fischer).

Gouldner, A. (1955) 'Metaphysical Pathos and the Theory of Bureaucracy', *American Political Science Review* 49: 496–507.

Green, M. (1974) *The von Richthofen Sisters* (London: Weidenfeld and Nicolson).

Habermas, J. (1971) 'Discussion on Value-Freedom and Objectivity', in O. Stammer (eds) op. cit.: 59–66.

Habermas, J. (1981) *Theorie des kommunikativen Handelns*, 2 vols (Frankfurt: Suhrkamp).

Hegel, G.W.F. (1942) *The Philosophy of Right* (trans. T.M. Knox). (Oxford: Clarendon; 1st German edn, 1821).

Hegel, G.W.F. (1956) *The Philosophy of History* (trans. J. Sibree) (New York: Dover; 1st German edn, 1837).

Hennis, W. (1987) 'A science of Man: Max Weber and the Political Economy of the German Historical School', in W.J. Mommsen and J. Osterhammel (eds) op. cit.: 25–58.

Henrich, D. (1952) *Die Einheit der Wissenschaftslehre Max Webers* (Tübingen: J.C.B. Mohr).

Heuss, T. (1958) 'Max Weber in seiner Gegenwart', in Max Weber, PS, VII–XXXI.

Hughes, H.S. (1958) *Consciousness and Society: The Reconstruction of European Social Thought* (New York: Alfred A. Knopf).

Hughes, H.S. (1959) *Consciousness and Society* (London: MacGibbon and Kee).

James, W. (1935) *The Varieties of Religious Experience* (London: Longmans; 1st edn, 1902).

Jaspers, K. (1913) *Allgemeine Psychopathologie* (Berlin).

Jaspers, K. (1932) *Max Weber – Deutsches Wesen im politischen Denken, im Forschen und Philosophieren* (Oldenbourg: G. Stelling).

Kalberg, S. (1980) 'Max Weber's Types of Rationality', *American Journal of Sociology* 85: 1145–79.

Kant, I. (1785) *The Foundations of the Metaphysics of Morals*, in Kant, I. (1949).

Kant, I. (1933) *Critique of Pure Reason* (trans. Norman Kemp Smith) (London: Macmillan; 2nd German edn, 1787).

Kant, I. (1949) *Critique of Practical Reason and Other Writings in Moral Philosophy* (trans. Lewis Beck) (Chicago: University of Chicago Press).

Käsler, D. (1988) *Max Weber: An Introduction to his Life and Work* (Cambridge: Polity Press).

König, R. and Winckelmann, J. (eds) (1963) *Max Weber zum Gedächtnis* (Cologne/Opladen: Westdeutscher Verlag).

Kuhn, T.S. (1962) *The Structure of Scientific Revolutions* (Chicago: Chicago University Press).

Lange, F.A. (1950) *History of Materialism* (trans. E.C. Thomas) (New York: The Humanities Press).

Lewis, J. (1975) *Max Weber and Value-Free Sociology: A Marxist Critique* (London: Lawrence and Wishart).

Locke, J. (1961) *An Essay Concerning Human Understanding*, 2 vols, (London: Dent; 4th edn, 1700).

Macintyre, A. (1985) *After Virtue* (London: Duckworth).

Marcuse, H. (1971) 'Industrialization and Capitalism', in O. Stammer (ed.), op. cit.: 133–151.

Marx, K. and Engels, F. (1976) *Collected Works* vol. 5: *The German Ideology* (London: Lawrence and Wishart).

Mitzman, A. (1970) *The Iron Cage: An Historical Interpretation of Max Weber* (New York: Alfred A. Knopf).

Mommsen, W.J. (1974) *Max Weber: Gesellschaft, Politik und Geschichte* (Frankfurt: Suhrkamp).

Mommsen, W.J. (1981) 'Die antinomische Struktur des politischen Denkens Max Webers', *Historische Zeitschrift* 233: 35–64.

Mommsen, W.J. (1984) *Max Weber and German Politics 1890–1920* (Chicago/London: Chicago University Press; 1st German edn, 1959).

Munsterberg, H. (1900) *Grundzüge der Psychologie* (Leipzig).

Nietzsche, F. (1909a) *The Birth of Tragedy* (trans. W.A. Haussmann) (Edinburgh: Foulis; 1st German edn, 1872).

Nietzsche, F. (1909b) (1st German edn, 1886) 'An Attempt at Self-Criticism', in 1909a.

Nietzsche, F. (1910a) *The Genealogy of Morals* (trans. Horace B. Samuel)   (Edinburgh: Foulis; 1st German edn, 1887).

Nietzsche, F. (1910b) *The Will to Power*, 2 vols (trans. A.M. Ludovici) (Edinburgh: Foulis).

Nietzsche, F. (1968a,b) *The Twilight of the Idols and the Anti Christ* (trans. R.J. Hollingsdale) (Harmondsworth: Penguin; 1st German edns 1889, 1895).

Oberschall, A. (1965) *Empirical Social Research in Germany* (Paris/The Hague: Mouton).

Outhwaite, W. (1975) *Understanding Social Life: The Method Called Verstehen* (London: Allen and Unwin).

Parsons, T. (1937) *The Structure of Social Action* (New York: Free Press).

Parsons, T. (1947) *Introduction to Weber's Theory of Social and Economic Organization* (Glencoe, Ill.: The Free Press).

Paulsen, F. (1902) *Immanuel Kant: His Life and Doctrine* (London: Nimmo).

Paulsen, F. (1906) *The German Universities and University Study* (London: Longmans).

Rickert, H. (1902) *Die Grenzen der Naturwissenschaftlichen Begriffsbildung* (Tübingen: J.C.B. Mohr).

Ringer, F. (1969) *The Decline of the German Mandarins: The German Academic Community 1890–1933* (Cambridge, Mass.: Harvard University Press).

Runciman, W.G. (1972) *A Critique of Max Weber's Philosophy of Social Science* (Cambridge: Cambridge University Press).

Schaaf, J.J. (1946) *Geschichte und Begriff* (Tübingen: J.C.B. Mohr).

Scheler, M. (1966) *Der Formalismus in der Ethik und die materiale Wertethik*, 5th edn (Berne/Munich: A. Francke).

Scheler, M. (1973) *Gesammelte Werke*, vol. 7: *Wesen und Formen der Sympathie, Die Deutsche Philosophie in der Gegenwart* (Berne/Munich: A. Francke).

Schelting, A. von (1934) *Max Webers Wissenschaftslehre* (Tübingen: J.C.B. Mohr).

Schluchter, W. (1981) *The Rise of Western Rationalism* (Berkeley: University of California Press).

Schopenhauer, A. (1883) *The World as Will and Idea* (trans. R.B. Haldane and J. Kemp) (London: Trübner; 1st German edn, 1818).

Schumpeter, J. (1954) *Economic Doctrine and Method: An Historical Sketch* (Oxford: Oxford University Press).

Schutz, A. (1960) *Der sinnhafte Aufbau der sozialen Welt* (Vienna: Springer; 1st German edn, 1932).

Silbermann, A. (1963) 'Max Webers musikalischer Exkurs', in König, R. and Winckelmann, J. (eds) op. cit.: 448–69.

Simmel, G. (1905) *Die Probleme der Geschichtsphilosophie* (Leipzig:

Duncker and Humblot; 2nd rev edn).

Simmel, G. (1908) *Soziologie: Untersuchungen über die Formen der Vergesellschaftung* (Leipzig: Duncker and Humblot).

Simmel, G. (1923) *Goethe* (Leipzig: Klinkhardt and Biermann; 1st edn, 1913).

Simmel, G (1968) *The Conflict in Modern Culture and Other Essays* (trans. K. Peter Etzhorn) (New York: Teachers College Press).

Small, A. (1909) 'The Vindication of Sociology', *American Journal of Sociology* XV: 1–15.

Sombart, W. (1915) *The Quintessence of Capitalism* (New York: Dutton).

Spengler, O. (1926) *The Decline of the West* (New York: Knopf).

Stammer, O. (ed.) (1971) *Max Weber and Sociology Today* (Oxford: Blackwell).

Stammler, R. (1896) *Wirtschaft und Recht nach der materialistischen Geschichtsauffassung* (Leipzig: Veit; 2nd edn, 1906).

Steding, C. (1932) *Politik und Wissenschaft bei Max Weber* (Breslau).

Strauss, D. (1835) *Life of Jesus* (trans. Marian Evans) (London).

Strauss, D. (1873) *The Old Faith and the New* (trans. M. Blind) (London; 1st German edn, 1872).

Strauss, L. (1950) *Natural Right and History* (Chicago: Chicago University Press).

Tawney, R.H. (1938) *Religion and the Rise of Capitalism* (West Drayton: Pelican; 1st edn, 1926).

Taylor, C. (1975) *Hegel* (Cambridge: Cambridge University Press).

Tenbruck, F.M. (1959) 'Die Genesis der Methodologie Max Webers', *Kölner Zeitschrift für Soziologie and Sozialpsychologie* 11: 573–630.

Tenbruck, F.M. (1987) 'Max Weber and Eduard Meyer', in Mommsen, W.J. and Osterhammel, J. (eds), op. cit.: 234–67.

Troeltsch, E. (1912) *Protestantism and Progress* (London: Williams and Norgate).

Vaihinger, H. (1935) *The Philosophy of 'As if'* (London: Routledge; 1st German edn, 1911).

Weber, A. (1950) *Kulturgeschichte als Kultursoziologie* (Munich: Piper; 1st edn, 1935).

Weber, Marianne (1975) *Max Weber: A Biography* (New York: Wiley).

Weiss, J. (1975) *Max Webers Grundlegung der Soziologie* (Munich: Verlag Dokumentation).

Weiss, J. (1981) *Das Werk Max Webers in der marxistischen Rezeption und Kritik* (Cologne/Opladen: Westdeutscher Verlag).

Whimster, S. (1987) 'Karl Lamprecht and Max Weber: Historical Sociology within the Confines of a Historian's Controversy', in Mommsen, W.J. and Osterhammel, J., op. cit.: 268–83.

Winch, P. (1958) *The Idea of a Social Science and its Relation to Philosophy* (London: Routledge and Kegan Paul).

Winckelmann, J. (1966) 'Max Weber's Verständnis von Mensch und Gesellschaft', in *Max Weber Gedächtnisschrift der Ludwig-Maximilians-Universität München* (ed. K. Engisch, B. Pfister and J. Winckelmann) (Berlin: Duncker and Humblot) pp. 195–243.

Windelband, W. (1907) *Lehrbuch der Geschichte der Philosophie* (Tübingen: J.C.B. Mohr; 1st edn, 1889).

Windelband, W. (1909) *Die Philosophie im deutschen Geistesleben des XIX. Jahrhunderts* (Tübingen: J.C.B. Mohr).

Windelband, W. (1921) *An Introduction to Philosophy* (trans. Joseph McCabe) (London: Fisher Unwin).

Wood, A.W. (1970) *Kant's Moral Religion* (Ithaca and London: Cornell University Press).

Zweig, S. (1925) *Der Kampf mit dem Dämon* (Leipzig: Insel).

Index of Names

Index of Subjects